New Longman Shakespeare

Henry V

William Shakespeare

edited by John O'Connor

LONGMAN

Pearson Education Limited
Edinburgh Gate
Harlow
Essex
CM20 2JE
England and Associated Companies throughout the World

ISBN: 0582 42711 8

First published 2000
Printed in Singapore

The Publisher's policy is to use paper manufactured from
sustainable forests.

Contents

Introduction

To the student

Shakespeare wrote *Henry V* so that it could be performed by actors and enjoyed by audiences. To help you get the most out of the play, this edition includes:
- a complete **script**
- **notes** printed next to the script which explain difficulties and point out important features
- **activities** on the same page which will help you to focus on the scene you are reading
- page-by-page **summaries** of the plot
- **exam questions** after each Act, which will give you practice at the right level
- **background information** about *Henry V*, Shakespeare's theatre and the verse he uses
- **advice** on how to set out titles and quotations in your essays.

To the teacher

New Longman Shakespeare has been designed to meet the varied and complex needs of students working throughout the 11–16 age-range.

The textual notes

These have been newly written to provide understandable explanations which are easily located on the page:
- notes are placed next to the text with clear line references
- explanations of more complex words are given in context and help is provided with key imagery and historical reference.

The activities

1 **Activities accompanying the text**
These are based on the premise that the text is best enjoyed and understood as a script for performance:

- In addition to a wide variety of reading, writing, listening and speaking activities, students are encouraged to: improvise, learn the script for performance, freeze-frame, rehearse, hot-seat, devise graphs and charts and create various forms of artwork, including storyboards, collages and cartoons.
- To provide a clear structure, activities are placed opposite the section of text to which they refer and come under five headings:
  - **i Character reviews** help students to think about the many different aspects of a given character which are presented in the course of the play. There might be as many as twenty of these activities on a single major character.
  - **ii Actors' interpretations** draw upon actual performances and ask students to consider comments from actors and directors in film and stage productions.
  - **iii Shakespeare's language** activities, focusing on everything from imagery to word-play, enable students to understand how the dramatist's language works to convey the central ideas of the play.
  - **iv Plot reviews** help students to keep in mind the essential details of what is happening in the story as well as asking them to consider how the plot is structured.
  - **v Themes** are explored according to their predominance in each play.
- 'Serial activities' (Henry 1, … 2, … 3, for example) enable students to focus in detail on a single key feature.

In addition, students who find extended tasks on Shakespeare a daunting prospect can combine several of these more focused activities – each in itself free-standing – to form the basis of a fuller piece of work.

2 **Exam-style activities**

At the end of each act – and also at the end of the book – there are activities which require SATs and GCSE style responses and offer opportunities for assessment.

3 **Summative activities**

Thinking about the play as a whole … is a section which offers a wide range of summative activities suitable for all levels.

Differentiation
Many students using this edition will be approaching Shakespeare for the first time; some might be studying the play for their Key Stage 3 SATs exam; others will be working towards GCSE.

Introduction

To answer their very different needs and interests, many of the activities have been differentiated to match the National Curriculum Level Descriptions and GCSE criteria. Activities of this kind are presented in three levels:

A Foundation level activities, which support an initial reading of the play and help students to build a solid basic knowledge and understanding

B Activities geared towards the needs of Year 9 Key Stage 3 students preparing for SATs

C More advanced activities in line with GCSE requirements.

Plot summaries

As students work through the play, their understanding of the play's plot is supported by:
• a brief headline summary at the top of each spread
• regular Plot Review activities
• a final detailed summary, scene by scene.

Background

Detailed fact-sheets are provided on:
• Shakespeare's England
• Plays and playhouses
• The Globe theatre
• The social and historical background (to each particular play)
• Shakespeare's life and his times.

Studying and writing about the play

To help students who are studying the play for examinations, there are sections on:
• Shakespeare's verse (with examples from the particular play)
• Study skills: titles and quotations.

Characters in the play

Introducing the play
The CHORUS

The English court
King HENRY V
Duke of GLOUCESTER } *Henry's*
Duke of BEDFORD } *brothers*
Duke of EXETER *Henry's uncle*
Duke of YORK *Henry's cousin*
Earl of WESTMORELAND
Earl of SALISBURY
Earl of WARWICK
Lord SCROOP of Masham } *traitors,*
Earl of CAMBRIDGE } *conspiring*
Sir Thomas GREY } *with the*
} *French*
Archbishop of CANTERBURY
Bishop of ELY

The French court
King CHARLES VI
Queen ISABEL
LEWIS, the DAUPHIN *their son*
Princess KATHARINE *their*
daughter
MONTJOY *the French herald*
The CONSTABLE *of France*
Duke of BERRI
Duke of BOURBON
Duke of BRETAGNE
Duke of ORLEANS *the King's*
nephew
Lord RAMBURES
Lord GRANDPRE
ALICE *lady-in-waiting to*
Princess Katharine
An Ambassador

Henry's former companions
PISTOL
BARDOLPH
NYM
Mistress NELL QUICKLY *hostess of a tavern*
The BOY *formerly Falstaff's page*

In Henry's army
FLUELLEN *a Welsh captain*
GOWER *an English captain*
JAMY *a Scots captain*
MACMORRIS *an Irish captain*
Sir Thomas ERPINGHAM
John BATES }
Alexander COURT } *soldiers*
Michael WILLIAMS }
A Herald

From other parts of France
The GOVERNOR of Harfleur
Monsieur LE FER *a soldier*
Duke of BURGUNDY

other Lords, Ladies, Officers, Soldiers, Citizens, Messengers and Attendants

1 Prologue

The Chorus apologises for the shortcomings of their theatre and asks the audience to assist the performers by using their imaginations.

1–2 **O for a Muse ... invention** *The Prologue wishes that his imagination and creativity (invention) had brilliant heavenly inspiration. In Greek mythology the nine Muses inspired creative people. Fire was considered to be the lightest and most brilliant of the four elements.*

4 **swelling** magnificent

5 **Harry** *the affectionate name for Henry V*

like himself presented in a way that would be worthy of his greatness

6 **assume ... Mars** take on the appearance and manner of the god of war

7 **Leashed ...** *a leash of hounds consisted of three on one lead*

should famine ... employment all the terrible aspects of war (personified) would wait (crouching at Henry's feet) to be used

8 **gentles** gentlefolk; ladies and gentlemen

9 **flat, unraiséd spirits** dull, uninspired performers

10 **scaffold** stage

11 **cockpit** arena where cock-fighting might take place

12 **vasty** wide, spacious

13 **wooden O** *the theatre, with its timber frame, was O-shaped (see pages 236–237). He is probably referring to the Curtain Theatre, rather than the famous Globe, which had not quite been built when Shakespeare was writing Henry V.*

the very casques even the helmets (let alone the men who wore them)

14 **affright** terrify

15–17 **Since a ... accompt** Since a curved figure (a zero) can turn 100,000 into 1,000,000, let us act ors, mere zeros in comparison with this great sum ...

accompt account (= (1) sum; (2) story)

18 **imaginary forces** powers of imagination

19 **girdle** surrounding 'belt'

21–22 **Whose high ...** whose high, raised up and protruding cliffs are separated by the dangerous English Channel

23 **Piece out ...** use your imaginations to make up for our defects

25 **puissance** power; armies

27 **proud** arrogant and high-spirited

28 **deck** dress up and equip

30 **Turning the ...** Making things which took many years to happen take place in a short time. (*The events of the play took place between 1414 and 1420.*)

31 **for the which supply** to aid you in this task (of using your imaginations)

Prologue

Enter CHORUS.

CHORUS   O for a Muse of fire, that would ascend
The brightest heaven of invention,
A kingdom for a stage, princes to act
And monarchs to behold the swelling scene!
Then should the warlike Harry, like himself,   5
Assume the port of Mars; and at his heels,
Leashed in like hounds, should famine, sword and
    fire
Crouch for employment. But pardon, gentles all,
The flat unraiséd spirits that have dared
On this unworthy scaffold to bring forth   10
So great an object. Can this cockpit hold
The vasty fields of France? Or may we cram
Within this wooden O the very casques
That did affright the air at Agincourt?
O, pardon! Since a crookéd figure may   15
Attest in little place a million –
And let us, ciphers to this great accompt,
On your imaginary forces work.
Suppose within the girdle of these walls
Are now confined two mighty monarchies,   20
Whose high uprearéd and abutting fronts
The perilous narrow ocean parts asunder.
Piece out our imperfections with your thoughts:
Into a thousand parts divide one man,
And make imaginary puissance;   25
Think, when we talk of horses, that you see them
Printing their proud hoofs i' the receiving earth;
For 't is your thoughts that now must deck our
    kings,
Carry them here and there; jumping o'er times,
Turning the accomplishment of many years   30
Into an hour-glass: for the which supply,
Admit me Chorus to this history;
Who prologue-like your humble patience pray,
Gently to hear, kindly to judge, our play.

Exit

1.1 London: an ante-chamber in the King's palace

The Archbishop of Canterbury and the Bishop of Ely are concerned about a Bill being discussed in parliament. If it goes through, the Church stands to lose a great deal of its land and wealth.

Activities

Plot review (1): the Bill

In this first scene we find out that two leading churchmen, the Archbishop of Canterbury and the Bishop of Ely, are extremely worried about a Bill which might pass through parliament. Write a brief article for *The Chronicle*, June 1414 (you can decide whether it is a broadsheet or tabloid newspaper), explaining the details of the Bill. Write about:

- the first time people tried to get it through parliament (lines 1–5)
- who stands to lose what if the Bill gets through (lines 7–11)
- who stands to gain what (lines 12–19)
- whether the King is likely to support it or not (lines 69–74)
- what offer the Church has made to the King (lines75–89).

Think up an appropriate headline and conclude your article by stating your opinion on whether the Bill ought to be supported or not.

1–5 **that self bill ...** *They are discussing a Bill which was likely to be passed through parliament in 1410, and was withdrawn only because of the civil disorder (scambling and unquiet time). The Bill, to deprive the church of a great deal of its wealth, now looks like being revived.*

self same

7 **If it pass ...** If it is approved and gets through parliament

9–10 **temporal lands ...** the land which has been left to the church in pious men's wills but which does not have religious uses (such as farms)

14 **esquires** candidates for knighthood

15–16 **to relief ...** to provide relief for lepers and old people, and the weak, past physical work

17 **almshouses** charitable homes for the poor

18 **coffers** chests (the treasury)

beside in addition to that

19 **drink deep** consume much of our resources

22 **... grace and fair regard** religious and of good reputation

26 **mortified** deadened

28 **Consideration** The process of examining your own spiritual life

29 **And whipped ...** drove his sins out of him *(like the angel expelling Adam from paradise)*

Act 1

Scene 1

London. An ante-chamber in the KING's palace.

Enter the ARCHBISHOP OF CANTERBURY *and the* BISHOP OF ELY.

CANTERBURY	My lord, I'll tell you; that self bill is urged,
	Which in the eleventh year of the last king's reign
	Was like, and had indeed against us passed,
	But that the scambling and unquiet time
	Did push it out of further question. 5
ELY	But how, my lord, shall we resist it now?
CANTERBURY	It must be thought on. If it pass against us,
	We lose the better half of our possession;
	For all the temporal lands which men devout
	By testament have given to the church 10
	Would they strip from us; being valued thus:
	As much as would maintain, to the king's honour,
	Full fifteen earls and fifteen hundred knights,
	Six thousand and two hundred good esquires;
	And, to relief of lazars and weak age, 15
	Of indigent faint souls past corporal toil,
	A hundred almshouses right well supplied;
	And to the coffers of the king beside,
	A thousand pounds by the year: thus runs the bill.
ELY	This would drink deep.
CANTERBURY	'T would drink the cup and all. 20
ELY	But what prevention?
CANTERBURY	The King is full of grace and fair regard.
ELY	And a true lover of the holy church.
CANTERBURY	The courses of his youth promised it not.
	The breath no sooner left his father's body, 25
	But that his wildness, mortified in him,
	Seemed to die too; yea, at that very moment
	Consideration, like an angel, came
	And whipped the offending Adam out of him,
	Leaving his body as a paradise, 30

1.1 London: an ante-chamber in the King's palace

The bishops then discuss the amazing changes that have been noted in the new King, Henry V: after a wild adolescence, he now shows himself to be a serious, well educated and talented ruler.

Activities

Character review: Henry (1): first impressions

Even before his first appearance in the play, we learn a great deal about Henry.

(A) Think about the main changes that were seen in Henry as soon as he became King. Write down two statements to show what he was like while he was still a prince (lines 54–59); and five statements to describe him now that he is King (lines 25–52).

(B) Imagine that you are a leading noble who is trying to encourage the people to support and admire their new King. Using the line references in A, draw a 'before and after' advertisement, featuring some of Canterbury's and Ely's comments and adding appropriate images (from magazines or your own artwork) to bring out the key points. Include the 'strawberry and nettle' image.

(C) Henry's reformation was spectacular: what impression of the new King do you receive from the final scene of *Henry IV, Part 2* (see pages 241–4)?

34 **heady currance** powerful current

scouring cleansing

35 **Hydra-headed** *like the monster with many heads*

36 **lose his seat** lose its 'throne' (its power over him)

38 **Hear him but ...** Just hear him

40 **prelate** senior churchman

41 **commonwealth** state

42 **all in all** exclusively

45 **cause of policy** complex political question

46 **Gordian knot** *Alexander the Great famously cut through a knot which no one could untie.*

48 **a chartered libertine** officially allowed to be totally free

49 **And the mute ...** and people listen silently and in wonder

51–52 **So that the art ...** So that the practice and experience of living are more important than his theoretical knowledge

54 **courses vain** trivial activities

55 **His companies ...** his companions were uneducated, uncultured and superficial

58–59 **sequestration from ...** withdrawal from public places (**open haunts**) and keeping company with common people (**popularity**)

66 **crescive ...** increasing through its natural ability to grow

To envelop and contain celestial spirits.
Never was such a sudden scholar made.
Never came reformation in a flood,
With such a heady currance, scouring faults;
Nor never Hydra-headed wilfulness   35
So soon did lose his seat and all at once
As in this king.

ELY   We are blesséd in the change.

CANTERBURY Hear him but reason in divinity
And all-admiring, with an inward wish,
You would desire the king were made a prelate.   40
Hear him debate of commonwealth affairs,
You would say it hath been all in all his study.
List his discourse of war, and you shall hear
A fearful battle rendered you in music.
Turn him to any cause of policy,   45
The Gordian knot of it he will unloose,
Familiar as his garter; that, when he speaks,
The air, a chartered libertine, is still,
And the mute wonder lurketh in men's ears,
To steal his sweet and honeyed sentences;   50
So that the art and practice part of life
Must be the mistress to this theoric:
Which is a wonder how his grace should glean it,
Since his addiction was to courses vain,
His companies unlettered, rude and shallow,   55
His hours filled up with riots, banquets, sports,
And never noted in him any study,
Any retirement, any sequestration
From open haunts and popularity.

ELY   The strawberry groweth underneath the nettle 60
And wholesome berries thrive and ripen best
Neighboured by fruit of baser quality;
And so the prince obscured his contemplation
Under the veil of wildness; which, no doubt,
Grew like the summer grass, fastest by night,   65
Unseen, yet crescive in his faculty.

CANTERBURY It must be so; for miracles are ceased;
And therefore we must needs admit the means
How things are perfected.

7

1.1 London: an ante-chamber in the King's palace

The bishops have made an offer to Henry: if he will oppose the Bill, they will give him a great sum of money to finance his proposed war with France. Henry claims that he is the rightful King of France and is about to hear the French Ambassador's reply to the claim.

Activities

Character review: The Archbishop of Canterbury (1)

A Henry has a decision to make: should he accept Canterbury's offer of money, and oppose the Bill? There are a number of question which might be going through his mind.

- Who will be happy if he opposes the Bill?
- Which people want the Bill to get through parliament?
- Why might he find Canterbury's offer useful?
- What problems does he have if he does not accept Canterbury's offer?

B In pairs, improvise the scene (which Shakespeare does not show) in which Canterbury discussed the Bill with Henry and made the offer (lines 73–91). Conclude the scene with someone announcing that the French Ambassador has arrived.

C 1.1 begins and ends with the prelates' (leading churchmen's) worries concerning the proposed Bill. What are the prelates' motives? Do you agree with those people who believe that Canterbury is urging the war with France purely in order to defeat the Bill? What advice would you give to the actors (a) to bring out this interpretation, or (b) to show that his motives were genuine?

70 **How now ...** How do we make this bill less severe?

71 **commons** House of Commons

71–72 **Doth ... incline ...** Does the King seem to favour it or not?

72 **indifferent** not taking sides

74 **cherishing the exhibiters** supporting the bill's proposers

76 **Upon our spiritual convocation** based upon the outcome of a formal meeting of the bishops

77 **causes** affairs

79 **As touching** to do with. *The Archbishop is offering Henry a greater sum of money than has ever before been given by the church to any previous kings (**predecessors**) to support his claim to France (which will involve an expensive military operation).*

84 **Save** except

85 **would fain** would like to

86 **The severals ...** the details and clear lines of descent

88 **seat** throne

89 **Derived from Edward ...** *See page 66.*

90 **What was the impediment ...?** What happened to interrupt you?

93 **Craved audience** Asked for a formal meeting with the King

95 **embassy** message from the ambassador

8

ELY
But, my good lord,
How now for mitigation of this bill   70
Urged by the commons? Doth his majesty
Incline to it, or no?

CANTERBURY
He seems indifferent,
Or rather swaying more upon our part
Than cherishing the exhibiters against us;
For I have made an offer to his majesty,   75
Upon our spiritual convocation
And in regard of causes now in hand,
Which I have opened to his grace at large,
As touching France, to give a greater sum
Than ever at one time the clergy yet   80
Did to his predecessors part withal.

ELY   How did this offer seem received, my lord?

CANTERBURY With good acceptance of his majesty;
Save that there was not time enough to hear,
As I perceived his grace would fain have done,   85
The severals and unhidden passages
Of his true titles to some certain dukedoms
And generally to the crown and seat of France,
Derived from Edward, his great-grandfather.

ELY   What was the impediment that broke this off?   90

CANTERBURY The French ambassador upon that instant
Craved audience; and the hour, I think, is come
To give him hearing. Is it four o'clock?

ELY   It is.

CANTERBURY Then go we in to know his embassy;   95
Which I could with a ready guess declare,
Before the Frenchman speak a word of it.

ELY   I'll wait upon you, and I long to hear it.

Exeunt

1.2 The council-chamber in the King's palace

Henry asks Canterbury to explain what the Salic Law is and why it might stand in the way of his claim to the French throne. Before hearing the Archbishop's arguments, he reminds him of the serious consequences of going to war.

Activities

Character review: Henry (2): his image

What impression do you gain of Henry from these production photographs?

Branagh, 1989

RSC, 1975

RSC, 1997

3 **liege** my lord

4 **cousin** *The word can mean any close relative, but in fact, Westmoreland had married Henry's aunt.*

4–5 **be resolved … of** come to a solution concerning

weight importance

6 **task** are a burden on

10 **unfold** explain

11 **the law Salic** *The law by which the crown of France could supposedly only be handed down through the male line.*

12 **Or … or** either … or

14 **fashion, wrest, or bow your reading** adapt, twist or bend your interpretation

15–17 **Or … truth** or, by arguing cunningly (**nicely**), burden (**charge**) your soul with guilt – which knows the truth – by inventing illegitimate and deceitful claims

19 **in approbation** in putting to the proof; acting in support of

20 **incite** encourage

21 **impawn** pledge

24 **contend** fight

25–28 **whose … mortality** Every innocent drop of blood would be a cause of misery, a bitter accusation against the person who unjustifiably starts a war and causes such violent destruction of men's brief lives.

Scene 2

London. The Presence chamber.

Enter KING HENRY, GLOUCESTER, BEDFORD, EXETER,
WARWICK, WESTMORELAND, *and* Attendants.

KING HENRY Where is my gracious Lord of Canterbury?

EXETER Not here in presence.

KING HENRY   Send for him, good uncle.

WEST- Shall we call in the ambassador, my liege?
MORELAND

KING HENRY Not yet, my cousin. We would be resolved,
Before we hear him, of some things of weight   5
That task our thoughts, concerning us and France.

Enter the ARCHBISHOP OF CANTERBURY *and the* BISHOP OF ELY.

CANTERBURY God and his angels guard your sacred throne,
And make you long become it!

KING HENRY   Sure, we thank you.
My learnéd lord, we pray you to proceed
And justly and religiously unfold   10
Why the law Salic that they have in France
Or should, or should not, bar us in our claim.
And God forbid, my dear and faithful lord,
That you should fashion, wrest, or bow your
    reading,
Or nicely charge your understanding soul   15
With opening titles miscreate, whose right
Suits not in native colours with the truth;
For God doth know how many now in health
Shall drop their blood in approbation
Of what your reverence shall incite us to.   20
Therefore take heed how you impawn our person,
How you awake our sleeping sword of war.
We charge you, in the name of God, take heed;
For never two such kingdoms did contend
Without much fall of blood; whose guiltless drops   25
Are every one a woe, a sore complaint

1.2 The council-chamber in the King's palace

The Archbishop explains that the Salic Law states that no one in Salic land can claim the throne through the female line, but that this law does not apply to France, as Salic land is in Germany.

Plot review (2): the Salic Law and Henry's claim

Henry's claim to the throne of France and the French arguments about the Salic Law are explained on page 244. Read the information carefully, and re-read 1.2.9–100. Then improvise an interview with Canterbury for a television current affairs programme, asking him the following questions:

1. What exactly is the basis of Henry's claim to the throne of France? How solid would you say that claim was?
2. What is this Salic Law that the French have presented in answer to Henry's claim? (lines 35–39)
3. Why was the Salic Law passed in the first place? (lines 46–51)
4. And it applies to France, does it? (lines 40–45 and 52–55)
5. Have the French always ruled over this territory they call Salic land? (lines 56–64)
6. I am told that the French themselves have broken the Salic Law. In what ways? One or two examples will do. (lines 64–95)
7. So you are saying that it has always been legal for someone to claim the French throne through the female line? (lines 98–100)

29 **conjuration** summons; official warning

30–32 *Henry demands assurance that Canterbury's conscience is clear and that he sincerely believes what he is about to tell the King about his claim to the French throne.*

35–64 *The Archbishop explains the origin of the Salic Law and claims that it was never intended to apply to France.*

40 **gloze** interpret

48 **holding in disdain** having no respect for

49 **dishonest manners** sexually immoral behaviour

50 **to wit** that is to say

51 **inheritrix** female inheritor

54 **doth it well appear** it is easy to see that

55 **deviséd** invented

58 **defunction** death

59 **Idly** mistakenly

60 **within ... Four hundred twenty-six** in 426 AD

64–90 *Continuing his explanation of the Salic Law, the Archbishop claims that the French have themselves broken the law, since several of their kings have inherited the crown through the female line.*

66 **heir general** someone who inherits, whether through the male or female line

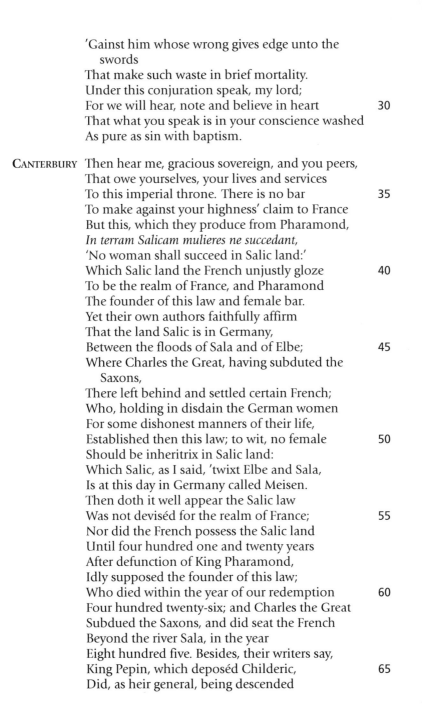

'Gainst him whose wrong gives edge unto the
    swords
That make such waste in brief mortality.
Under this conjuration speak, my lord;
For we will hear, note and believe in heart   30
That what you speak is in your conscience washed
As pure as sin with baptism.

CANTERBURY Then hear me, gracious sovereign, and you peers,
That owe yourselves, your lives and services
To this imperial throne. There is no bar   35
To make against your highness' claim to France
But this, which they produce from Pharamond,
In terram Salicam mulieres ne succedant,
'No woman shall succeed in Salic land:'
Which Salic land the French unjustly gloze   40
To be the realm of France, and Pharamond
The founder of this law and female bar.
Yet their own authors faithfully affirm
That the land Salic is in Germany,
Between the floods of Sala and of Elbe;   45
Where Charles the Great, having subduted the
    Saxons,
There left behind and settled certain French;
Who, holding in disdain the German women
For some dishonest manners of their life,
Established then this law; to wit, no female   50
Should be inheritrix in Salic land:
Which Salic, as I said, 'twixt Elbe and Sala,
Is at this day in Germany called Meisen.
Then doth it well appear the Salic law
Was not devmiséd for the realm of France;   55
Nor did the French possess the Salic land
Until four hundred one and twenty years
After defunction of King Pharamond,
Idly supposed the founder of this law;
Who died within the year of our redemption   60
Four hundred twenty-six; and Charles the Great
Subdued the Saxons, and did seat the French
Beyond the river Sala, in the year
Eight hundred five. Besides, their writers say,
King Pepin, which deposéd Childeric,   65
Did, as heir general, being descended

1.2 The council-chamber in the King's palace

The Archbishop adds that the law does not seem to have been observed by the French themselves – several of their kings have inherited the throne through the female line. He adds that the Bible supports the right of women to inherit. He encourages Henry to declare war.

Activities

Actors' interpretations: the churchmen

After such a long and involved explanation, Canterbury's conclusion – 'So that, as clear as is the summer's sun' (line 86) – often causes a laugh among the assembled nobles.

Do you think Canterbury and Ely should be played humorously throughout the scene, as they were in Olivier's 1944 film, or seriously, as in Branagh's 1989 version? In pairs, find evidence to support each of the following arguments and then decide which one convinces you.

1. Playing Canterbury and Ely for laughs helps the audience to get through some very long and otherwise tedious speeches.
2. You must not play them for laughs: it is important to show how serious Henry's questions are and how seriously he listens to Canterbury's advice.

69 **usurped the crown** became king by force

72 **to find ...** to make it look as though his title was valid

73 **corrupt and naught** fraudulent and worthless

74 **Conveyed himself** passed himself off as; pretended to be

79 **Could not keep ...** Lewis' (Louis') conscience would not let him rest easy until he was satisfied that his grandmother was directly descended from Ermengare, daughter of Charles of Lorraine. (*Louis' claim to the throne was therefore through two women.*)

88 **his satisfaction** *see lines 77–83*

all appear all are plainly seen

91 **Howbeit** however much

93–95 **And rather ...** The French prefer to hide in a tangled web of excuses, rather than openly reveal (**imbar**) that their titles, stolen from you and your ancestors (**progenitors**), are illegitimate (**crookéd**); (*or possibly*: obviously bar their own claims to the illegitimate titles stolen from you and your ancestors).

98 **book of Numbers** *the fourth book of Moses in the Old Testament of the Christian Bible (Numbers, chapter 27, verse 8)*

103 **great-grandsire** *Edward III*

104 **invoke** call up

Of Blithild, which was daughter to King Clothair,
Make claim and title to the crown of France.
Hugh Capet also, who usurped the crown
Of Charles the duke of Lorraine, sole heir male   70
Of the true line and stock of Charles the Great,
To find his title with some shows of truth,
Though, in pure truth, it was corrupt and naught,
Conveyed himself as heir to the Lady Lingare,
Daughter to Charlemain, who was the son   75
To Lewis the emperor, and Lewis the son
Of Charles the Great. Also King Lewis the tenth,
Who was sole heir to the usurper Capet,
Could not keep quiet in his conscience,
Wearing the crown of France, till satisfied   80
That fair Queen Isabel, his grandmother,
Was lineal of the Lady Ermengare,
Daughter to Charles the foresaid duke of Lorraine:
By the which marriage the line of Charles the Great
Was re-united to the crown of France.   85
So that, as clear as is the summer's sun,
King Pepin's title and Hugh Capet's claim,
King Lewis his satisfaction, all appear
To hold in right and title of the female:
So do the kings of France unto this day;   90
Howbeit they would hold up this Salic law
To bar your highness claiming from the female,
And rather choose to hide them in a net
Than amply to imbar their crookéd titles
Usurped from you and your progenitors.   95

KING HENRY   May I with right and conscience make this claim?

CANTERBURY   The sin upon my head, dread sovereign!
For in the book of Numbers is it writ:
'When the man dies, let the inheritance
Descend unto the daughter.' Gracious lord,   100
Stand for your own! Unwind your bloody flag!
Look back into your mighty ancestors!
Go, my dread lord, to your great-grandsire's tomb,
From whom you claim; invoke his warlike spirit,
And your great-uncle's, Edward the Black Prince,   105
Who on the French ground played a tragedy,
Making defeat on the full power of France,

1.2 The council-chamber in the King's palace

Canterbury reminds Henry that his great-grandfather, Edward III, and great uncle, Edward the Black Prince, enjoyed famous victories over the French. Ely and the nobles join Canterbury in encouraging Henry to go to war in pursuit of his claim to the throne of France.

Activities

Plot review (3): Henry's ancestors

Two of Henry's ancestors are referred to several times in the play: his great-grandfather Edward III and his great-uncle, Edward the Black Prince. Look at page 66 and lines 102–114 and 161–162. Then begin to design a poster which will show the family tree and also include references to the exploits of these famous ancestors. Keep your early designs to be added to later.

106 **played a tragedy** *Canterbury is talking about the battle of Crécy in 1346, in which the English defeated the French. Edward III (the Black Prince's* **most mighty father** *– line 108) watched his son (***his lion's whelp***) from a hill (lines 108–110) and used only a fraction of the English forces in the battle (lines 111–114).*

110 **Forage** prey

114 **for action** for lack of activity

116 **puissant** powerful

118 **that renownéd them** which made them famous

119 **thrice-puissant** *Henry is trebly powerful for the three reasons Ely has listed in lines 117–119.*

120 **May-morn of his youth** *Henry was actually 27.*

121 **Ripe** ready

124 **lions** *possibly a reference to the lions on the English shield.*

125 **cause and means and might** a just reason, enough wealth and a powerful army

126 **So hath ...** And so you have.

129 **pavilioned** encamped in army tents

132 **spiritualty** church

137 **lay down our proportions** estimate the troops required

138 **road** inroads; raids

140 **They of those marches** The English living on the borders

	Whiles his most mighty father on a hill	
	Stood smiling to behold his lion's whelp	
	Forage in blood of French nobility.	110
	O noble English, that could entertain	
	With half their forces the full pride of France	
	And let another half stand laughing by,	
	All out of work and cold for action!	
ELY	Awake remembrance of these valiant dead	115
	And with your puissant arm renew their feats!	
	You are their heir; you sit upon their throne;	
	The blood and courage that renownéd them	
	Runs in your veins; and my thrice-puissant liege	
	Is in the very May-morn of his youth,	120
	Ripe for exploits and mighty enterprises.	
EXETER	Your brother kings and monarchs of the earth	
	Do all expect that you should rouse yourself,	
	As did the former lions of your blood.	
WEST-MORELAND	They know your grace hath cause and means and might;	125
	So hath your highness; never king of England	
	Had nobles richer and more loyal subjects,	
	Whose hearts have left their bodies here in England	
	And lie pavilioned in the fields of France.	
CANTERBURY	O, let their bodies follow, my dear liege,	130
	With blood and sword and fire to win your right;	
	In aid whereof we of the spiritualty	
	Will raise your highness such a mighty sum	
	As never did the clergy at one time	
	Bring in to any of your ancestors.	135
KING HENRY	We must not only arm to invade the French,	
	But lay down our proportions to defend	
	Against the Scot, who will make road upon us	
	With all advantages.	
CANTERBURY	They of those marches, gracious sovereign,	140
	Shall be a wall sufficient to defend	
	Our inland from the pilfering borderers.	

1.2 The council-chamber in the King's palace

Henry and his nobles discuss what to do about the Scots, who might take the opportunity to attack, if the English army is abroad fighting the French.

Activities

Shakespeare's language: emotive language

The language used to describe the Scots and the English is extremely emotive (it plays on your feelings). Look at lines 142–177 and pick out the phrases which help to create a picture of bold, heroic England being sneakily attacked by cowardly and treacherous Scotland. Then use the language to write two brief entries for an English medieval travel book on 'The English' and 'The Scots'. Then write two other entries, from the Scots' point of view.

You might find the following words and phrases useful:

143 **coursing snatcher** lightning raiders

145 **giddy** unreliable

151 **Galling the gleanéd land with hot assays** injuring the land, stripped of its defenders, with violent raids

154 **ill neighbourhood** bad neighbourliness

173 **tame and havoc** break into and destroy

144 **main intendment** general hostile intentions

145 **still** always; constantly

148 **unfurnished** undefended

149 **breach** a hole made in defences

152 **Girdling** surrounding

155 **feared** frightened

156 **... exampled ...** For, if you listen to the examples, England can give of its own history ...

157 **chivalry** knights and nobles

158 **a mourning widow** *The widow England is grieving for her 'husband' (the soldiers fighting abroad).*

160 **impounded** imprisoned like a stray dog

161 **King of Scots** *David II, captured in 1346 while King Edward III was in France*

163 **chronicle** history

165 **wrack** shipwreck

sumless incalculable

169 **in prey** out searching for prey, out hunting

175 **crushed necessity** a false conclusion to your argument (*or possibly*: something we are forced to do, against our will)

177 **pretty** cunning, ingenious

179 **adv6séd** wise, prudent

180 **though high ...** of whatever rank

181 **parts** musical harmonies

KING HENRY   We do not mean the coursing snatchers only,
But fear the main intendment of the Scot,
Who hath been still a giddy neighbour to us;   145
For you shall read that my great-grandfather
Never went with his forces into France
But that the Scot on his unfurnished kingdom
Came pouring, like the tide into a breach,
With ample and brim fulness of his force,   150
Galling the gleanéd land with hot assays,
Girdling with grievous siege castles and towns;
That England, being empty of defence,
Hath shook and trembled at the ill neighbourhood.

CANTERBURY   She hath been then more feared than harmed, my
     liege;   155
For hear her but exampled by herself –
When all her chivalry hath been in France
And she a mourning widow of her nobles,
She hath herself not only well defended
But taken and impounded as a stray   160
The King of Scots; whom she did send to France,
To fill King Edward's fame with prisoner kings
And make her chronicle as rich with praise
As is the ooze and bottom of the sea
With sunken wrack and sumless treasuries.   165

WEST-   But there's a saying very old and true,
MORELAND   'If that you will France win,
     Then with Scotland first begin'
For once the eagle England being in prey,
To her unguarded nest the weasel Scot   170
Comes sneaking and so sucks her princely eggs,
Playing the mouse in absence of the cat,
To tame and havoc more than she can eat.

EXETER   If follows then the cat must stay at home:
Yet that is but a crushed necessity,   175
Since we have locks to safeguard necessaries,
And pretty traps to catch the petty thieves.
While that the arméd hand doth fight abroad,
The advivéd head defends itself at home;
For government, though high and low and lower,   180
Put into parts, doth keep in one consent,

1.2 The council-chamber in the King's palace

Drawing a parallel with a hive, in which the bees all have their own functions and roles, Canterbury advises that the English army should be divided, so that only a quarter of it is fighting in France and the remaining three-quarters is left to defend the country against the Scots.

Activities

Themes: order (1)

Canterbury's speech about the honey-bees is an important statement on the theme of order: the idea that everyone has their place and function in an ordered society.

A Go through the speech and pick out the main parallels (beehive – kingdom, etc.).

B 1. Think of reasons why this idea of an ordered society might have appealed to people like Canterbury but might not have appealed to his servant.
2. Where are the weaknesses in Canterbury's parallels between bees and working people?

C Debate the possible purposes of Canterbury's speech. For example, is it an important statement about the national unity and sense of order which existed in Henry V's time? Or is it nothing more than Elizabethan propaganda aimed to keep the working people in their place and maintain power for the ruling class?

182 **Congreeing** co-operating, working together

natural close concluding musical phrase (*or*: cadence

185 **divers** various

186 **Setting endeavour ...** keeping hard work going

187 **butt** target in archery

189 **rule in nature** instinct

191 **of sorts** of different ranks

192 **correct** hand out sentences

195 **Make boot upon** plunder

196 **pillage** plundered goods

198 **busied in ...** performing his function as king

200 **kneading** wax-moulding

201 **mechanic** manual workers

203 **surly** severe

204 **executors** executioners

205 **I this infer** this is my conclusion

206–207 **having ... consent** all sharing the same agreed purpose

contrariously in different ways

208 **loosèd several ways** fired from different directions

211 **dial's** sundial's

213 **borne** carried through

217 **Gallia** France (*ancient Gaul*)

219 **dog** Scotland

220 **worried** shaken (*as a dog 'worries' a bone*)

221 **hardiness and policy** courage and statesmanship

Congreeing in a full and natural close,
Like music.

CANTERBURY Therefore doth heaven divide
The state of man in divers functions,   185
Setting endeavour in continual motion;
To which is fixéd, as an aim or butt,
Obedience: for so work the honey-bees,
Creatures that by a rule in nature teach
The act of order to a peopled kingdom.   190
They have a king and officers of sorts;
Where some, like magistrates, correct at home,
Others, like merchants, venture trade abroad;
Others, like soldiers, arméd in their stings,
Make boot upon the summer's velvet buds,   195
Which pillage they with merry march bring home
To the tent-royal of their emperor;
Who, busied in his majesty, surveys
The singing masons building roofs of gold,
The civil citizens kneading up the honey,   200
The poor mechanic porters crowding in
Their heavy burdens at his narrow gate,
The sad-eyed justice, with his surly hum,
Delivering o'er to executors pale
The lazy yawning drone. I this infer,   205
That many things, having full reference
To one consent, may work contrariously:
As many arrows, looséd several ways,
Come to one mark; as ways meet in one town;
As many fresh streams meet in one salt sea;   210
As many lines close in the dial's centre;
So may a thousand actions, once afoot,
End in one purpose, and be all well borne
Without defeat. Therefore to France, my liege!
Divide your happy England into four,   215
Whereof take you one quarter into France,
And you withal shall make all Gallia shake.
If we, with thrice such powers left at home,
Cannot defend our own doors from the dog,
Let us be worried and our nation lose   220
The name of hardiness and policy.

KING HENRY Call in the messengers sent from the Dauphin.

1.2 The council-chamber in the King's palace

Henry has made up his mind and expresses his determination to declare war on France. The French Ambassador enters. Rejecting Henry's claim to the French throne, he presents him with a gift sent by the King's son, the Dauphin.

Activities

Character review: The Dauphin (1)

At this point in the play, the French do not know that Henry is about to claim the throne of France. This visit by the Ambassador is in answer to Henry's claim on 'certain dukedoms' (line 248) and the French Ambassador is actually delivering a reply from the Dauphin, son of the French King.

A Why has the Dauphin sent a gift of tennis balls (line 259)?

B Pick out all the insults aimed at Henry by the Dauphin in this short speech and explain the particular point of each one.

C Improvise the scene which might have taken place between the Dauphin and the Ambassador, in which the Dauphin explains (a) what he wants the Ambassador to say; (b) what tone he wants him to use (insulting? cool?); and (c) why the gift is appropriate. What private thoughts might the Ambassador have about these instructions?

224 **sinews** muscles

225 **France being ours ...** As France is rightfully mine, I will force it to accept my authority

226–229 **Or ... Or ...** Either ... or ...

227 **large and ample empery** free and unrestricted sovereignty

229 **urn** grave

230 **remembrance** inscription

231–234 **Either our history ... epitaph.** Either people in the future will speak enthusiastically and in praise of my actions, or my tomb will have no inscription – not even one in wax – let alone brass or stone.

233 **Turkish mute** *Slaves in Turkey had their tongues cut out to ensure secrecy.*

239 **Freely to render ...** to deliver our assigned message openly

240 **sparingly show you far off** tactfully give you the message in general terms

243–244 **Unto whose ...** *Henry's emotions are controlled by his virtue as a Christian king* (**grace**) *as securely as his prisoners are.*

249 **predecessor** ancestor

251 **you savour ...** you are behaving like an adolescent

253 **galliard** lively dance

254 **revel ...** you can't party your way into ...

255 **meeter** more fitting

256 **tun** barrel

Exeunt some Attendants

Now are we well resolved; and by God's help
And yours, the noble sinews of our power,
France being ours, we 'll bend it to our awe,   225
Or break it all to pieces. Or there we 'll sit,
Ruling in large and ample empery
O'er France and all her almost kingly dukedoms,
Or lay these bones in an unworthy urn,
Tombless, with no remembrance over them.   230
Either our history shall with full mouth
Speak freely of our acts, or else our grave,
Like Turkish mute, shall have a tongueless mouth,
Not worshipped with a waxen epitaph.

Enter Ambassadors *of France, followed by* Attendants *carrying a barrel.*

Now are we well prepared to know the pleasure   235
Of our fair cousin Dauphin; for we hear
Your greeting is from him, not from the king.

FIRST   May 't please your majesty to give us leave
AMBASSADOR Freely to render what we have in charge;
                Or shall we sparingly show you far off   240
                The Dauphin's meaning and our embassy?

KING HENRY We are no tyrant, but a Christian king;
                Unto whose grace our passion is as subject
                As are our wretches fettered in our prisons:
                Therefore with frank and with uncurbéd plainness   245
                Tell us the Dauphin's mind.

FIRST   Thus then, in few.
AMBASSADOR Your highness, lately sending into France,
                Did claim some certain dukedoms, in the right
                Of your great predecessor, King Edward the Third.
                In answer of which claim, the prince our master   250
                Says that you savour too much of your youth,
                And bids you be advised there's nought in France
                That can be with a nimble galliard won.
                You cannot revel into dukedoms there.
                He therefore sends you, meeter for your spirit,   255
                This tun of treasure; and, in lieu of this,
                Desires you let the dukedoms that you claim
                Hear no more of you. This the Dauphin speaks.

23

1.2 The council-chamber in the King's palace

The gift is a barrel of tennis-balls, a mocking reference to Henry's youth. Henry sends back a threatening message: he will attack France in pursuit of his lawful claim to the throne and the French people will come to regret the Dauphin's insults.

Activities

Character review: Henry (3): his response to the tennis balls

Annotate Henry's reply to the Ambassador (lines 260–299) to provide director's advice on how it should be delivered. Include advice on:
- general mood
- tone of voice at particular moments
- facial expressions
- movements.

Shakespeare's language: tennis word-play

What main points do you think he is trying to make in lines 262–267? Do the references to tennis help to get his points across, in your opinion? It will help to understand the different meanings that some of his words have: **rackets** (1) tennis rackets; (2) cannon noise; **strike** (1) play a winning shot; (2) hit; **crown** (1) the money placed as a bet; (2) the royal crown; **into the hazard** (1) into the holes in the far end of the court; (2) into danger; **wrangler** (1) opponent; (2) enemy; **courts** (1) tennis courts; (2) royal courts; (3) law courts; **chases** (1) points lost; (2) pursuing armies.

260 **is so pleasant with us** likes to have a joke at my expense

261 **your pains** the trouble you have taken

268 **comes o'er us** brings up, throws in our face

269 **Not measuring** not taking into account

270 **seat** throne

271 **living hence** spending time away from the court

272 **barbarous licence** disgraceful unrestrained behaviour

274 **keep my state** live in a way befitting my royal dignity

275 **show my sail ...** show my greatness like a ship in full sail

276 **rouse me** raise myself up

277–278 **For that ...** For that reason I set aside my majesty and behaved like a common man on working days

279 **rise there ...** appear as glorious as the rising sun

282 **pleasant** joking

283 **gun-stones** cannon-balls

283–285 **and his soul ...** the Dauphin's soul will be heavily burdened with the responsibility of the bloodshed and destruction which will arise in revenge for his mocking gift

289 **scorn** mockery

290 **lies all within** depends upon

294 **well-hallowed** righteous

KING HENRY What treasure, uncle?

EXETER (*Opening the barrel*) Tennis-balls, my liege.

KING HENRY We are glad the Dauphin is so pleasant with us.   260
His present and your pains we thank you for.
When we have matched our rackets to these balls,
We will, in France, by God's grace, play a set
Shall strike his father's crown into the hazard.
Tell him he hath made a match with such a
          wrangler   265
That all the courts of France will be disturbed
With chases. And we understand him well,
How he comes o'er us with our wilder days,
Not measuring what use we made of them.
We never valued this poor seat of England,   270
And therefore, living hence, did give ourself
To barbarous licence; as 't is ever common
That men are merriest when they are from home.
But tell the Dauphin I will keep my state,
Be like a king, and show my sail of greatness   275
When I do rouse me in my throne of France.
For that I have laid by my majesty
And plodded like a man for working-days,
But I will rise there with so full a glory
That I will dazzle all the eyes of France,   280
Yea, strike the Dauphin blind to look on us.
And tell the pleasant prince this mock of his
Hath turned his balls to gun-stones; and his soul
Shall stand sore chargéd for the wasteful
          vengeance
That fly with them: for many a thousand widows   285
Shall this his mock mock out of their dear husbands;
Mock mothers from their sons, mock castles down;
And some are yet ungotten and unborn
That shall have cause to curse the Dauphin's scorn.
But this lies all within the will of God,   290
To whom I do appeal; and in whose name
Tell you the Dauphin I am coming on
To venge me as I may, and to put forth
My rightful hand in a well-hallowed cause.
So get you hence in peace; and tell the Dauphin   295
His jest will savour but of shallow wit,

1.2 The council-chamber in the King's palace

The French Ambassador leaves and Henry concludes the meeting by telling his nobles to prepare for war.

Activities

Shakespeare's language: the royal plural

It is common for kings in Shakespeare's plays to use the 'royal plural' ('**We** are glad the Dauphin is so pleasant with **us**', etc.). Look back through Henry's reply to the Ambassador (lines 260–299) and pick out all the examples of the royal plural in lines 260–273.

From line 274 onwards, Henry uses the singular ('But tell the Dauphin **I** will keep **my** state', etc.). Why do you think this happens? What effect does it have?

Character review: Henry (4): Henry and God

Kenneth Branagh felt that Shakespeare's Henry is 'a genuinely holy man', but others have taken the view that Henry is a cunning politician who tries to make himself look religious, when in fact he has less praiseworthy motives for his actions, such as a lust for power.

Find (a) Canterbury's references to Henry's religious faith (in 1.1) and (b) Henry's own references in 1.2 (lines 13–32, 96, 223, 242–244, 263, 290–294 and 303–309). Discuss which view you find more convincing, and why.

301–302 **omit no happy hour ...** do not miss any favourable occasion which might help our venture

304 **Save those to God ...** except the prayers which must be said before preparing for war

305 **proportions** forces

308 **God before** with God leading us

309 **chide** rebuke and beat

311 **may on foot ...** may be got under way

26

When thousands weep more than did laugh at it.
(*To attendants*) Convey them with safe-conduct.
   (*To the ambassadors*) Fare you well.

Exeunt Ambassadors

EXETER   This was a merry message.

KING HENRY We hope to make the sender blush at it.   300
           Therefore, my lords, omit no happy hour
           That may give furtherance to our expedition;
           For we have now no thought in us but France,
           Save those to God, that run before our business.
           Therefore let our proportions for these wars   305
           Be soon collected, and all things thought upon
           That may with reasonable swiftness add
           More feathers to our wings; for, God before,
           We 'll chide this Dauphin at his father's door.
           Therefore let every man now task his thought,   310
           That this fair action may on foot be brought.

Exeunt. Flourish

Exam practice

Character review: Henry (5): his private thoughts

Imagine you are Henry. Write down and explain your thoughts and feelings as you leave your council-chamber after meeting the French Ambassador. You could begin: *This is going to be a real test of what kind of King I am ...*

Before you begin to write, you should decide what Henry thought and felt about:
- the Archbishop's explanation of the Salic Law
- your claim to the French throne
- the Dauphin's gift of tennis balls
- your reply to the French Ambassador.

Themes: theatre and the imagination (1)

Shakespeare begins *Henry V* with a figure called the Chorus. He is not a character in the usual sense (he does not have a name and does not take part in the action) but is someone who talks directly to the audience and performs a number of important functions.

1. Which features of Shakespeare's theatre building does the Chorus refer to? Look at the photographs on pages 236 and 237, and pick out the scaffold (line 10), cockpit (line 11) and wooden O (line 13).
2. What apologies does the Chorus make about the actors and the theatre (lines 9–15)?
3. In particular, what does the Chorus ask us the audience to do, to help make the play work? What do all the following requests have in common: 'Suppose...' (lines 19–22); 'Piece out...' (lines 23–25); 'Think...' (lines 26–27); 'For 'tis your thoughts...' (lines 28–31)?
4. The success of the play depends on a collaboration between actors and audience. In what ways might the actors be compared to the figure nought (lines 15–18)?

Themes: war (1)

What early idea of war do we receive from lines 5–8? Heroic? Frightening? Impressive? Think about: 'warlike Harry... port of Mars... Leashed in like hounds... famine, sword and fire...'.

Plot review (4): a time-chart

Start a time-chart which will record the events of the play in order. Include what we know has already happened before the play starts and set out the facts in a clear table which can be added to. It might begin like this:

	Time and place	Event
Before the play starts	1410, London	Commons try to get a Bill through parliament; deferred because of civil unrest
	1413, London	Henry V comes to the throne and rejects Falstaff and his other followers

Character review: Henry (6): differing opinions on the King

Throughout the play, the Duke of Exeter seems to be a staunch supporter of his nephew, Henry. Presumably, however, there were some lords who privately questioned the King's actions.

Write two diary entries for the day on which Henry met the lords and prelates and received the gift of the tennis balls. One entry is written by Exeter and expresses admiration for the way in which Henry led the meeting, dealt with Canterbury and responded to the French Ambassador. The other entry is written by a nobleman who is totally patriotic but has a habit of questioning people's motives and behaviour. He takes the view, for example, that, before beginning the meeting, Henry had already been persuaded to invade France with money from the Church, and simply wanted to get everyone's approval. He is also worried about Henry's extreme reaction to the Ambassador and wonders whether the King is totally in control of events.

Plot review (5): the events of Act 1

Working in a small group, create the front page for *The Chronicle* (see the activity on page 4) for the day after war is declared. In addition to a dramatic headline and a main article about the Dauphin's message and the declaration of war itself, include smaller articles on:
• the changes in Henry since he became King
• Henry's claim to France
• how to deal with the Scots
• the Church's financial support (and the rejection of the Bill)
• Henry following in the footsteps of his famous ancestors

2 Prologue

The Chorus describes the war-fever gripping the country, but reports that three English traitors, Cambridge, Scroop and Grey, have been paid by the anxious French to kill Henry before the fleet sails from Southampton.

Activities

Actors' interpretations: filming the Chorus

In the Baz Luhrmann film of *Romeo and Juliet*, the opening and closing Chorus speeches are delivered by a television newsreader. Act out this Chorus speech in a similar way, with the story set in the twentieth century:

- Shot 1: an urgent and excited newsreader tells the audience about the preparations for war (lines 1–11).
- Cut to shot 2: while the newsreader is still heard in 'voice-over', we see the traitor Scroop reading a letter – or receiving a phone call – from a contact in France (lines 12–19).
- Cambridge and Grey enter furtively and mime a discussion with Scroop while the newsreader continues with the story (lines 20–30). The camera picks out each man when the Chorus refers to him.

Themes: theatre and the imagination (2)

What does the final section of this speech (lines 31–42) add to the theme of theatre and the imagination?

1 **on fire** fired up, ready for action

2 **And silken dalliance ...** young men have put away all their fashionable party clothes

4 **Reigns solely** are the only things which exist

6 **mirror** model

7 **Mercuries** *Mercury, the Roman messenger god, wore winged shoes and hat.*

12 **advised by ...** informed by accurate secret information

14 **pale policy** conspiracy dictated by fear

19 **were ... kind and natural** if only all your children behaved like loving sons

21 **hollow** (1) empty, (2) deceitful
   bosoms hearts

22 **crowns** coins (*worth 25 pence*)

26 **gilt** gold coins (*with a pun on guilt*)

27 **fearful** frightened

28 **this grace of kings** this king who does most honour to the title

30 **Ere** before

31–32 **digest The abuse ... play** We will have to put up with the fact that the stage represents England one moment, France the next; we will squeeze all these different places and times into our play.

38 **charming** casting a spell on

30

Act 2

2

Prologue

Enter CHORUS.

CHORUS   Now all the youth of England are on fire,
And silken dalliance in the wardrobe lies.
Now thrive the armourers, and honour's thought
Reigns solely in the breast of every man.
They sell the pasture now to buy the horse,   5
Following the mirror of all Christian kings,
With wingéd heels, as English Mercuries.
For now sits Expectation in the air,
And hides a sword from hilts unto the point
With crowns imperial, crowns and coronets,   10
Promised to Harry and his followers.
The French, advised by good intelligence
Of this most dreadful preparation,
Shake in their fear, and with pale policy
Seek to divert the English purposes.   15
O England, model to thy inward greatness,
Like little body with a mighty heart,
What might'st thou do, that honour would thee do,
Were all thy children kind and natural!
But see, thy fault France hath in thee found out,   20
A nest of hollow bosoms, which he fills
With treacherous crowns; and three corrupted men,
One Richard Earl of Cambridge, and the second,
Henry Lord Scroop of Masham, and the third,
Sir Thomas Grey, knight, of Northumberland,   25
Have, for the gilt of France – O guilt indeed! –
Confirmed conspiracy with fearful France;
And by their hands this grace of kings must die,
If hell and treason hold their promises,
Ere he take ship for France, and in Southampton.   30
Linger your patience on; and we'll digest
The abuse of distance; force a play.
The sum is paid, the traitors are agreed,
The king is set from London, and the scene
Is now transported, gentles, to Southampton.   35
There is the playhouse now, there must you sit:
And thence to France shall we convey you safe,
And bring you back, charming the narrow seas

2.1 Eastcheap, London: the Boar's Head Tavern

In London, Henry's old companions prepare to join the army bound for France. Nym, who was expecting to marry Mistress Quickly, hostess of the inn, is aggrieved that she has married Pistol and hints that he will take his revenge.

Activities

Character review: Henry's former companions (1)

The characters we meet in 2.1 are all Henry's old friends, rejected when he became King.

Read lines 1–26 and draw a diagram which will show the current relationships between:

(a) Bardolph and Nym

(b) Nym and Pistol

(c) Pistol and Mistress Quickly (the hostess of the inn).

Add a note to explain Nym's feelings about Pistol.

Character review: Nym

One of Nym's first statements is 'I say little' (line 4). Draw a line down the centre of a sheet of paper. On the left write down some of Nym's more mysterious comments (such as 'there shall be smiles') and on the right, write what you think he is suggesting or implying.

39 **pass** passage

40 **We'll not offend ...** we won't (1) give anyone sea-sickness; (2) cause offence to anyone

Bardolph, Pistol and Mistress Quickly, hostess of the Boar's Head tavern, have all appeared in one or both of the earlier plays (Henry IV, Parts 1 and 2) as the young Henry's drinking companions. Nym (whose name can mean 'thief') is a new character.

3 **Ancient** ensign, standard-bearer

4–5 **when time shall serve** when the occasion arises

6 **wink** close my eyes

7 **iron** sword

8–9 **endure cold** tolerate being drawn from its sheath (*and used for fighting – rather than for toasting cheese*)

11 **bestow** provide

16 **That is my rest** that's what I will stake everything on

17 **rendezvous** last resort

20 **troth-plight** promised in marriage (*involving a much stronger agreement than the modern 'engagement'*)

24–25 **Though patience ...** It's tiring to be patient, but it achieves its purpose in the end

To give you gentle pass; for, if we may,
We 'll not offend one stomach with our play.　　40
But, till the king come forth, and not till then,
Unto Southampton do we shift our scene.

Exit

Scene 1

London. A Street.

Enter CORPORAL NYM *and* LIEUTENANT BARDOLPH.

BARDOLPH　Well met, Corporal Nym.

NYM　Good morrow, Lieutenant Bardolph.

BARDOLPH　What, are Ancient Pistol and you friends yet?

NYM　For my part, I care not: I say little; but when time
shall serve, there shall be smiles; but that shall be　　5
as it may. I dare not fight; but I will wink and
hold out mine iron. It is a simple one; but what
though? It will toast cheese, and it will endure
cold as another man's sword will: and there 's an
end.　　10

BARDOLPH　I will bestow a breakfast to make you friends, and
we'll be all three sworn brothers to France. Let it
be so, good Corporal Nym.

NYM　Faith, I will live so long as I may, that's the
certain of it; and when I cannot live any longer, I　　15
will do as I may. That is my rest, that is the
rendezvous of it.

BARDOLPH　It is certain, corporal, that he is married to Nell
Quickly, and, certainly, she did you wrong, for
you were troth-plight to her.　　20

NYM　I cannot tell. Things must be as they may. Men
may sleep, and they may have their throats about
them at the time; and some say knives have edges.
It must be as it may. Though patience be a tired
mare, yet she will plod. There must be　　25

2.1 Eastcheap, London: the Boar's Head Tavern

Bardolph tries to make peace, but Nym continues to be angry and Pistol displays his fiery character as they threaten each other with violence.

Activities

Character review: Mistress Quickly (1)

Like several other characters in Shakespeare's plays, Mistress Quickly's speech is sprinkled with malapropisms* and remarks which seem to contradict themselves.

1. Her claim to be running an honest establishment (lines 32–35) contains a sexual (or 'bawdy') pun which might cause us to doubt what she says. Find it, explain it, and discuss whether you think she intends the pun or not. What does the pun suggest about the kind of establishment that she actually does run?

2. Does she mean 'adultery' (line 37)? If not, what does she mean?

3. Look at her request to Nym (lines 44–45). (a) What does she actually mean instead of 'valour'? (b) In what way might 'valour' actually be an appropriate word?

*A malapropism is a mistake in which somebody substitutes a similar sounding word for the one they actually mean; the name comes from a Mrs Malaprop in a play by an eighteenth-century dramatist, Sheridan. Use the notes to help you find them in this speech.

30 **Base tike** low dog
33 **by my troth** on my honour
35 **honestly** not immorally
   prick *There is a bawdy play on words here: the hostess is accused of keeping a brothel (line 36:* **bawdy house**).
37 **well a day** my goodness!
40 **Offer nothing** don't provoke a fight
42 **Pish!** Rubbish!
43 **Iceland dog** *Nym presumably has long, shaggy hair*
45 **valour** courage
   put up sheath
47 **shog off** go away
   solus *Latin for alone*
48 **egregious** outstanding
51 **maw** stomach
   perdy by God (*par dieu*)
52 **nasty** foul
54 **take** (1) catch fire; (2) strike
   Pistol's cock *as a pistol, he is ready to fire; but there is also a bawdy meaning here*
56 **Barbason** *a name of a devil*
   conjure exorcise: 'you can't get rid of me with your threats'
57 **humour** mood *The humours were originally the four fluids which determined a person's character, but the word had become fashionable and over-used*

conclusions. Well, I cannot tell.

Enter PISTOL *and* HOSTESS.

BARDOLPH	Here comes Ancient Pistol and his wife. Good corporal, be patient here. How now, mine host Pistol!

PISTOL	Base tike, call'st thou me host?	30
	Now, by this hand I swear, I scorn the term;	
	Nor shall my Nell keep lodgers.	

HOSTESS	No, by my troth, not long; for we cannot lodge	
	and board a dozen or fourteen gentlewomen that	
	live honestly by the prick of their needles, but it	35
	will be thought we keep a bawdy house straight.	
	(NYM *and* PISTOL *draw*) O well a day, Lady, if he be	
	not drawn now! We shall see wilful adultery and	
	murder committed.	

BARDOLPH	Good lieutenant! Good corporal! Offer nothing	40
	here.	

NYM	Pish!

PISTOL	Pish for thee, Iceland dog! Thou prick-eared cur of Iceland!

HOSTESS	Good corporal Nym, show thy valour, and put up	45
	your sword.	

NYM	Will you shog off? I would have you solus.

PISTOL	'Solus', egregious dog? O viper vile!	
	The 'solus' in thy most marvailous face;	
	The 'solus' in thy teeth, and in thy throat,	50
	And in thy hateful lungs, yea, in thy maw, perdy,	
	And, which is worse, within thy nasty mouth!	
	I do retort the 'solus' in thy bowels;	
	For I can take, and Pistol's cock is up,	
	An flashing fire will follow.	55

NYM	I am not Barbason; you cannot conjure me. I have a humour to knock you indifferently well. If you grow foul with me, Pistol, I will scour you with

2.1 Eastcheap, London: the Boar's Head Tavern

In the middle of a further exchange of threats between Nym and Pistol, Falstaff's page enters to report that his old master is very ill and Mistress Quickly goes to see him.

Activities

Character review: Pistol (1)

Pistol's language is a marvellous mixture of bits and pieces picked up from different sources.

1. Use the explanatory notes to find examples of words and phrases which he seems to have borrowed from:
   (a) Latin
   (b) other languages.

2. It seems likely that Pistol's completely over-the-top manner of speaking is his attempt to sound like some of the spectacular and boastful heroes that he had seen portrayed on the stage in rather badly written plays. As well as speaking in verse (where the other characters in this scene use prose), his language includes:
   - unusual, extravagant words
   - odd pronunciations
   - outdated oaths
   - word-play
   - 'archaic' words usually heard only in old-fashioned plays
   - whole lines which sound as though they are taken from badly written plays
   - alliteration
   - classical references.
   (a) Match up each of these features with the following examples (it might be possible to put the examples in more than one category):

continued on page 38

58 **foul ... scour** *if the barrel becomes clogged up (***foul***), the user has to clean (***scour***) it*

61 **that's the humour of it** that's the way it is

62 **braggart** boaster

   wight man

64 **exhale** (1) draw your sword, or (2) breathe your last

66 **run ... hilts** plunge the length of my sword blade into him

68 **mickle** great

   abate fade away

73 **'Couple a gorge!'** *from* couper la gorge – *to cut the throat*

76 **spital** hospital

77 **powdering-tub** *a heated tub to sweat out venereal disease*

78 **lazar kite** leprous whore

78–79 *Cressida was a Trojan woman whose name had become associated with whores (such as Doll Tearsheet, a prostitute in* Henry IV, Part 2*).*

79 **espouse** marry

80 **quondam** former (previously known as Quickly)

81 **the only she** the only woman for me

   pauca in short (*Latin*)

85 **put thy face** *There are many jokes at the expense of Bardolph's red face.*

89 **he'll yield** he will die and be food for crows

	my rapier, as I may, in fair terms. If you would walk off, I would prick your guts a little, in good terms, as I may, and that 's the humour of it.	60
PISTOL	O braggart vile and damnéd furious wight! The grave doth gape, and doting death is near, Therefore exhale!	
BARDOLPH	Hear me, hear me what I say! He that strikes the first stroke, I'll run him up to the hilts, as I am a soldier. (*Draws*)	65
PISTOL	An oath of mickle might, and fury shall abate!	

They sheathe their swords.

	Give me thy fist, thy fore-foot to me give! Thy spirits are most tall.	70
NYM	I will cut thy throat, one time or other, in fair terms: that is the humour of it.	
PISTOL	'Couple a gorge!' That is the word. I thee defy again. O hound of Crete, think'st thou my spouse to get? No; to the spital go, And from the powdering-tub of infamy Fetch forth the lazar kite of Cressid's kind, Doll Tearsheet she by name, and her espouse. I have, and I will hold, the quondam Quickly For the only she; and – pauca, there's enough. Go to!	75

Enter the BOY.

		80
BOY	Mine host Pistol, you must come to my master, and your hostess. He is very sick, and would to bed. Good Bardolph, put thy face between his sheets, and do the office of a warming-pan. Faith, he's very ill.	85
BARDOLPH	Away, you rogue!	
HOSTESS	By my troth, he'll yield the crow a pudding one	

2.1 Eastcheap, London: the Boar's Head Tavern

Bardolph's peace-making activities finally bear fruit and Nym agrees to be friends with Pistol so long as he settles a gambling debt of eight shillings. Pistol offers a down-payment of a noble – most of the sum he owes.

90 **the king has killed** *Falstaff is dying of a broken heart after being rejected by Henry (see pages 241–244)*

95 **Let floods ...** *More overdone theatrical language*

98 **Base is the slave ...** (1) It's always the poor who pay; or (2) only the lowest people pay up

100 **As manhood ...** we'll settle this like real men

105 **an thou wilt** if you want to be

106 **Prithee, put up** I'm asking you, put your sword away

109 **noble** *coin worth 33 pence*

present pay cash down; immediate payment

110 **liquor likewise** alcohol as well

112 **live by Nym** (1) live alongside Nym, (2) live by stealing *(see note to the opening stage directions)*

113 **sutler** someone who sells provisions to the army

114 **accrue** build up

of these days. The king has killed his heart. Good   90
husband, come home presently.

Exeunt HOSTESS *and* BOY

BARDOLPH   Come, shall I make you two friends? We must to
France together. Why the devil should we keep
knives to cut one another's throats?

PISTOL   Let floods o'erswell, and fiends for food howl on!   95

NYM   You'll pay me the eight shillings I won of you at
betting?

PISTOL   Base is the slave that pays.

NYM   That now I will have: that's the humour of it.

PISTOL   As manhood shall compound! Push home!   100

They draw.

BARDOLPH   By this sword, he that makes the first thrust, I'll
kill him! By this sword, I will.

PISTOL   Sword is an oath, and oaths must have their course.

BARDOLPH   Corporal Nym, an thou wilt be friends, be
friends; an thou wilt not, why, then, be enemies   105
with me too. Prithee, put up.

NYM   I shall have my eight shillings I won of you at
betting?

PISTOL   A noble shalt thou have, and present pay;
And liquor likewise will I give to thee,   110
And friendship shall combine, and brotherhood.
I'll live by Nym, and Nym shall live by me.
Is not this just? for I shall sutler be
Unto the camp, and profits will accrue.
Give me thy hand.   115

They sheathe again.

NYM   I shall have my noble?

2.2 Southampton: the harbour

Mistress Quickly re-enters to report that Falstaff is seriously ill with a fever and they go off to visit the dying man. In Southampton, Bedford reassures Westmoreland and Exeter that Henry knows all about the planned assassination.

118 **that's the humour of it** if that's the way it is

121 **quotidian tertian** fever *(she is mixed up again: a quotidian fever had daily symptoms, a tertian every three days)*

123 **run bad humours** (1) vented his bad mood on; or (2) caused him to become melancholy

124 **even** plain truth

126 **fracted** broken

corroborate *this usually means strengthened; here possibly: corrupted*

128 **passes some humours and careers** has strange moods and behaves wildly

1 **traitors** *the traitors referred to by the Act 2 Chorus*

2 **apprehended** arrested

by and by soon

3 **how smooth and even ...** how calm and unflustered they are behaving

4–5 **As if allegiance ...** as if their hearts were ruled by faithfulness and constant loyalty

6 **note** knowledge

8 **bedfellow** *This refers to Scroop, Henry's close friend; it was common for people of the same sex to share beds.*

9 **dulled ...** *Henry had more than satisfied Scroop's appetite (now* **cloyed***), in the favours that he had done him*

PISTOL	In cash, most justly paid.
NYM	Well, then, that's the humour of 't.

Re-enter HOSTESS.

HOSTESS	As ever you came of women, come in quickly to Sir John. Ah, poor heart! He is so shaked of a burning quotidian tertian that it is most lamentable to behold. Sweet men, come to him.	120
NYM	The king hath run bad humours on the knight; that's the even of it.	
PISTOL	Nym, thou hast spoke the right; His heart is fracted and corroborate.	125
NYM	The king is a good king, but it must be as it may; he passes some humours and careers.	
PISTOL	Let us condole the knight; for, lambkins, we will live.	130

Exeunt

Scene 2

Southampton. A council-chamber.

Enter EXETER, BEDFORD *and* WESTMORELAND.

BEDFORD	'Fore God, his grace is bold to trust these traitors.	
EXETER	They shall be apprehended by and by.	
WEST-MORELAND	How smooth and even they do bear themselves, As if allegiance in their bosoms sat, Crownéd with faith and constant loyalty.	5
BEDFORD	The king hath note of all that they intend, By interception which they dream not of.	
EXETER	Nay, but the man that was his bedfellow, Whom he hath dulled and cloyed with gracious favours,	

2.2 Southampton: the harbour

The traitors, Scroop, Cambridge and Grey, all express their confidence in the whole country's loyalty. Aware of their deceit, Henry instructs Exeter to free a drunk who had been imprisoned for shouting insults at the King the day before.

Activities

Character review: the traitors

A What is a traitor? What have Scroop, Cambridge and Grey done which makes them guilty of treason? (Look back at the Chorus's speech on page 31, lines 12–35.)

B Act out 2.2.1–51 (a) as though the traitors were totally honest, loyal and genuine; (b) to show the audience that they are having trouble keeping up the pretence of being loyal; (c) to suggest that they are evil – perhaps by emphasising the snake-like s-sounds (sibilance) in Scroop's speeches (lines 19, 36–38 and 44–46). Which interpretation do you prefer?

C Shakespeare used two historians for his story about Henry V's reign: Raphael Holinshed and Edward Hall. (See question 18 on page 230.) Both of them say that, as well as accepting money from the French, the traitors were plotting to put the Earl of March on the throne in Henry's place (one of Richard II's descendants – see the family tree on page 66). Why do you think Shakespeare might have decided not to include this as a motivation for the traitors (except by hinting at it in Cambridge's explanation, lines 156–158)?

10 **for a foreign purse** in return for money from France

13 **of Masham** Scroop's title

15 **the powers we bear** the army we are taking

17 **Doing the execution ...** fulfilling the function

18 **in head** as an armed force

22 **That grows not ...** who is not in agreement with our aims (*to defeat the French and claim the throne*)

27 **sits in heart-grief** is unhappy

28 **shade** protection

30 **Have steeped their galls in honey** have given up their bitter feelings

31 **With hearts create ...** with emotions made up of duty and enthusiasm (**zeal**)

33–35 **And shall forget ...** I will sooner forget to do my duty than to reward deserving people according to their merits

38 **incessant** never-ending

40 **Enlarge** set free

41 **railed ... person** spoke insultingly about me

| | That he should, for a foreign purse, so sell | 10 |
| | His sovereign's life to death and treachery. | |

Trumpets sound, Enter KING HENRY, SCROOP, CAMBRIDGE, GREY, *and*
Attendants.

KING HENRY Now sits the wind fair, and we will aboard.
My Lord of Cambridge, and my kind Lord of
    Masham,
And you, my gentle knight, give my your thoughts.
Think you not that the powers we bear with us   15
Will cut their passage through the force of France,
Doing the execution and the act
For which we have in head assembled them?

SCROOP No doubt, my liege, if each man do his best.

KING HENRY I doubt not that; since we are well persuaded   20
We carry not a heart with us from hence
That grows not in a fair consent with ours,
Nor leave not one behind that doth not wish
Success and conquest to attend on us.

CAMBRIDGE Never was monarch better feared and loved   25
Than is your majesty: there's not, I think, a subject
That sits in heart-grief and uneasiness
Under the sweet shade of your government.

GREY True: those that were your father's enemies
Have steeped their galls in honey and do serve you   30
With hearts create of duty and of zeal.

KING HENRY We therefore have great cause of thankfulness,
And shall forget the office of our hand
Sooner than quittance of desert and merit,
According to the weight and worthiness.   35

SCROOP So service shall with steeléd sinews toil,
And labour shall refresh itself with hope,
To do your grace incessant services.

KING HENRY We judge no less. Uncle of Exeter,
Enlarge the man committed yesterday,   40
That railed against our person. We consider
It was excess of wine that set him on;

2.2 Southampton: the harbour

The three traitors advise Henry not to show mercy to the drunk. Henry gently overrules them and hands them letters which they expect to contain instructions about what to do in his absence.

Activities

Shakespeare's language: dramatic irony

Re-read lines 1–11, which show that Henry knows that these three lords have plotted to kill him. Because we know that Henry is aware of their treachery, some of his comments then take on a meaning that we understand but the traitors do not. When this kind of thing happens we call it dramatic irony.

A Find examples of dramatic irony in lines 1–69.

B 1. How would you advise the actor playing Henry to deliver line 69? Should he emphasise the dramatic irony or let the audience register it for themselves?

2. How does the dramatic irony help to:
   - involve the audience more?
   - show Henry's mastery of the situation?
   - make the conspirators look powerless?
   - add to the suspense?

C Annotate lines 1–69 to show (a) what Henry is thinking; (b) what Scroop is thinking; (c) how you, as a member of the audience, are reacting, especially to the dramatic irony. Then use your annotations to perform the scene in small groups.

43 **on his more advice** now that he has time to think better of his actions

44 **security** lack of caution; over-confidence

45–46 **lest example ...** if you let him go unpunished, other people might follow his example

50–51 **if you ... correction** if you spare his life after you have punished him severely

53 **heavy orisons** serious prayers, carrying much weight

54–57 **If little ... before us?** If we cannot turn a blind eye to minor misdemeanours, committed while drunk, how can we be lenient when we are faced with premeditated capital crimes?

distemper bodily disorder

60 **causes** affairs

61 **late commissioners** *people who have most recently been commissioned to act for the King in his absence*

63 **bade** asked

it *the written authority to act on behalf of the King*

71 **We will aboard** we will board ship for France

And on his more advice we pardon him.

SCROOP That's mercy, but too much security.
Let him be punished, sovereign, lest example   45
Breed, by his sufferance, more of such a kind.

KING HENRY O, let us yet be merciful.

CAMBRIDGE So may your highness, and yet punish too.

GREY Sir,
You show great mercy, if you give him life,   50
After the taste of much correction.

KING HENRY Alas, your too much love and care of me
Are heavy orisons 'gainst this poor wretch!
If little faults, proceeding on distemper,
Shall not be winked at, how shall we stretch our
    eye   55
When capital crimes, chewed, swallowed and
    digested,
Appear before us? We'll yet enlarge that man,
Though Cambridge, Scroop and Grey, in their dear
    care
And tender preservation of our person,
Would have him punished. And now to our French
    causes: 60
Who are the late commissioners?

CAMBRIDGE I one, my lord:
Your highness bade me ask for it to-day.

SCROOP So did you me, my liege.

GREY And I, my royal sovereign.   65

KING HENRY (*Giving papers*) Then, Richard Earl of Cambridge,
    there is yours.
There yours, Lord Scroop of Masham, and, sir
    knight,
Grey of Northumberland, this same is yours.
Read them, and know, I know your worthiness.
My Lord of Westmoreland, and uncle Exeter,   70
We will aboard to-night. Why, how now, gentlemen!
What see you in those papers that you lose

2.2 Southampton: the harbour

Reading the letters, the traitors realise that their planned crime has been discovered and they beg for mercy. Pointing out that they had themselves just been counselling against mercy, Henry reminds Cambridge and Grey of the many gifts he had bestowed upon them, but reserves particular comments for Scroop.

Activities

Actors' interpretations: the traitors are exposed

1. In groups of four, freeze-frame the moment when the traitors have read what is on the papers (lines 71–75).
2. Then rehearse the sequence from lines 61 to 79, trying to convey the shock and other emotions experienced by the traitors and by Henry himself. While that is going on, another group writes the letters which Henry hands to the traitors. Make them as frightening as you can.
3. Act out the rehearsed sequence – but don't let the actors playing the traitors see what is on the papers before they perform the scene.
4. Discuss what emotions the characters feel at different points in the sequence. Did it help not to show the actors beforehand what was written on the papers?
5. Use what you have learned about the traitors' feelings when you act out their responses to the charge of treason (lines 152–166). Should their repentance be sincere or not, in your opinion?

75 **cowarded** chased away out of sight (**appearance**)

80 **quick** alive

but late just a moment ago

81 **By your own counsel** following the advice that you have given

83 **into your bosoms** against you

86 **monsters** unnatural, deformed creatures

87–89 **how apt ... honour** how ready I always was to agree to give him everything in accordance with his position

90 **light crowns** worthless coins

lightly sinfully

91 **practices** plotting; treachery

92 **Hampton** Southampton

93 **This knight** *Sir Thomas Grey*

97 **counsels** secrets

99 **coined me** *Scroop was Henry's Treasurer until 1411.*

100 **Wouldst thou ...** if you had plotted against (**practised on**) me for financial gain (**use**)

103 **might annoy** could harm

104 **stands off as gross** is as glaringly obvious

105–109 **Treason ...** Treason and Murder (*personified*) have always (**ever**) worked as a team, like two devils, yoked together, helping each other, doing work which was so natural to them that its wickedness surprised no one.

So much complexion? Look ye, how they change!
Their cheeks are paper. Why, what read you there,
That hath so cowarded and chased your blood   75
Out of appearance?

They kneel.

CAMBRIDGE   I do confess my fault,
And do submit me to your highness' mercy.

GREY *and*   To which we all appeal.
  SCROOP

KING HENRY   The mercy that was quick in us but late,   80
By your own counsel is suppressed and killed.
You must not dare, for shame, to talk of mercy,
For your own reasons turn into your bosoms,
As dogs upon their masters, worrying you.
See you, my princes and my noble peers,   85
These English monsters! My Lord of Cambridge
    here,
You know how apt our love was to accord
To furnish him with all appertinents
Belonging to his honour; and this man
Hath, for a few light crowns, lightly conspired,   90
And sworn unto the practices of France,
To kill us here in Hampton: to the which
This knight, no less for bounty bound to us
Than Cambridge is, hath likewise sworn. But, O,
What shall I say to thee, Lord Scroop, thou cruel,   95
Ingrateful, savage and inhuman creature?
Thou that didst bear the key of all my counsels,
That knew'st the very bottom of my soul,
That almost might'st have coined me into gold,
Would'st thou have practised on me, for thy use?   100
May it be possible, that foreign hire
Could out of thee extract one spark of evil
That might annoy my finger? 'T is so strange,
That though the truth of it stands off as gross
As black and white, my eye will scarcely see it.   105
Treason and murder ever kept together,
As two yoke-devils sworn to either's purpose,
Working so grossly in a natural cause,

2.2 Southampton: the harbour

Henry is particularly hurt that Scroop should have betrayed him: he had known all his secrets and had appeared to be a loyal and honest personal friend.

Activities

Character review: Henry (7): the King and the man

When this play is performed, it is always interesting to see the tensions between Henry the King, with all his ceremonies, responsibilities and duties, and Henry the man, with all the emotions and needs experienced by ordinary people.

Look back through the earlier scenes and make a list of some of the things that Henry might have to do as part of his kingly duties, and some of the heavy responsibilities he carries.

1. In pairs, discuss which parts of Henry's speech to the traitors most obviously reflect the feelings of (a) Henry the King, and (b) Henry the man. Where are his duties as King obliging him to do things which he is finding terribly hard, given his feelings as a man?
2. Write Henry's journal for that day, in which he describes how he conducted the meeting with the traitors, what he considered his duties to be and what private emotions he felt.

Henry's language is clearly highly emotional here (lines 80–145 and 167–182). How can you tell from his:
• images (lines 83–84, 99, 106–109)?
• choice of nouns (lines 86)?

continued on page 50

110 **But thou …** But you, against the natural order of things (**gainst all proportion**), have added a sense of wonder to these acts of treason …

113 **wrought …** worked on you to make you behave unnaturally

115–118 **All other … piety** All other devils who clumsily tempt people try to hide the fact that treason will damn a man's soul, by lying, deceiving and pretending to appear religious

119 **tempered** influenced

122 **gulled** tricked; made a fool of

124 **vasty Tartar** deserts of hell

127–128 **O, how … ?** *Scroop has destroyed trust (**affiance**) by infecting it with suspicion*

128 **Show** appear

134 **not swerving …** not constantly changing their feelings

135 **garnished …** possessing all the qualities of the modest man

136–137 **Not working … neither?** not merely trusting the evidence of the eye or the ear alone, and, except where a clear judgement is possible, not trusting either

138 **finely bolted** refined

140–141 **To mark** to stain even the most virtuous man with suspicion

145 **God acquit** may God pardon them for their treachery

That admiration did not whoop at them.
But thou, 'gainst all proportion, didst bring in   110
Wonder to wait on treason and on murder:
And whatsoever cunning fiend it was
That wrought upon thee so preposterously,
Hath got the voice in hell for excellence.
All other devils that suggest by treasons   115
Do botch and bungle up damnation,
With patches, colours, and with forms being fetched
From glistering semblances of piety.
But he that tempered *thee*, bade thee stand up,
Gave thee no instance why thou shouldst do
          treason,   120
Unless to dub thee with the name of traitor.
If that same demon that hath gulled thee thus
Should with his lion gait walk the whole world,
He might return to vasty Tartar back,
And tell the legions 'I can never win   125
A soul so easy as that Englishman's.'
O, how hast thou with jealousy infected
The sweetness of affiance! Show men dutiful?
Why, so didst thou. Seem they grave and learnéd?
Why, so didst thou. Come they of noble family?   130
Why, so didst thou. Seem they religious?
Why, so didst thou. Or are they spare in diet,
Free from gross passion or of mirth or anger,
Constant in spirit, not swerving with the blood,
Garnished and decked in modest complement,   135
Not working with the eye without the ear,
And but in purgéd judgement trusting neither?
Such, and so finely bolted, didst thou seem.
And thus thy fall hath left a kind of blot,
To mark the full-fraught man, and best indued,   140
With some suspicion. I will weep for thee,
For this revolt of thine, methinks, is like,
Another fall of man. Their faults are open:
Arrest them to the answer of the law;
And God acquit them of their practices!   145

EXETER   I arrest thee of high treason, by the name of
          Richard Earl of Cambridge.
          I arrest thee of high treason, by the name of
          Henry Lord Scroop of Masham.

2.2 Southampton: the harbour

Scroop, Cambridge and Grey admit their guilt, are formally arrested and are taken off to execution.

Activities

- choice of adjectives (lines 95–96)?
- word-play (line 90)?
- rhetorical questions (lines 101–103, 128–132)?
- repetition (lines 128–132)?
- lists (lines 132–137)?
- balanced sentences (lines 168–174)?
- references to the breaking of the natural order (lines 86, 110)?
- references to damnation (lines 112–126)?
- references to Adam and Eve's expulsion from Paradise: the 'Fall of Man' (lines 141–143)?

Write about the ways in which Henry's language in this scene reflects his emotions.

Actors' interpretations: Henry and Scroop

In the Kenneth Branagh film, Exeter (played by Brian Blessed) rips the chains of office from around the necks of the three traitors and then slaps Scroop's face. Why does he single out Scroop for this special treatment? Is it the right thing to do, in your opinion? What might be in Exeter's mind at that moment?

152 **discovered** uncovered; revealed

154 **beseech** beg

156–158 **For me ... intended** *Cambridge was not won over by the attraction of the gold, but found it useful in helping him to achieve his aims more quickly (see page 42).*

160 **in sufferance** by suffering the punishment

166 **My fault ...** pardon what I have done, but punish me

167 **quit** pardon; absolve (**acquit**: *see line 145*)

169 **his coffers** the treasury of France

170 **golden earnest** advance payment in gold

175 **Touching our person** as far as the plot against me personally is concerned ...

176 **But we ... tender** But I have to look after the safety of the kingdom so carefully

180 **taste** experience (*of execution*)

182 **dear** grievous, most serious

| | I arrest thee of high treason, by the name of | 150 |
| | Thomas Grey, knight, of Northumberland. | |

SCROOP   Our purposes God justly hath discovered,
And I repent my fault more than my death,
Which I beseech your highness to forgive,
Although my body pay the price of it.   155

CAMBRIDGE   For me, the gold of France did not seduce,
Although I did admit it as a motive
The sooner to effect what I intended:
But God be thankéd for prevention;
Which I in sufferance heartily will rejoice,   160
Beseeching God and you to pardon me.

GREY   Never did faithful subject more rejoice
At the discovery of most dangerous treason
Than I do at this hour joy o'er myself,
Prevented from a damnéd enterprise.   165
My fault, but not my body, pardon, sovereign.

KING HENRY God quit you in his mercy! Hear your sentence.
You have conspired against our royal person,
Joined with an enemy proclaimed, and from his
    coffers
Received the golden earnest of our death;   170
Wherein you would have sold your king to
    slaughter,
His princes and his peers to servitude,
His subjects to oppression and contempt
And his whole kingdom into desolation.
Touching our person, seek we no revenge;   175
But we our kingdom's safety must so tender,
Whose ruin you have sought, that to her laws
We do deliver you. Get you therefore hence,
Poor miserable wretches, to your death:
The taste whereof, God of his mercy give   180
You patience to endure, and true repentance
Of all your dear offences! Bear them hence.

Exeunt CAMBRIDGE, SCROOP *and* GREY, *guarded*

Now, lords, for France; the enterprise whereof
Shall be to you, as us, like glorious.

2.3 Eastcheap, London: the Boar's Head Tavern

Henry lifts his men's spirits as they prepare to set sail for France. Meanwhile his former companions mourn the death of Falstaff and Mistress Quickly describes the old knight's dying moments.

Activities

Character review: Henry (9): dealing with the traitors

Look back to the activity on page 28 to remind yourself about Exeter and the invented cynical lord.
Continue both of their private journals with entries from each on the way Henry dealt with the traitors: Exeter is admiring of Henry's skill and the fact that he gave the men a chance to let him show mercy (in his reference to the drunk, lines 39–60); the cynical lord takes the view that Henry cruelly manipulated the traitors, playing cat-and-mouse with them, and ought to have simply had them arrested. Which view do you share?

Actors' interpretations: cutting or keeping a scene

In his 1944 film, Olivier cut the scene with the traitors. Why do you think he might have made such a decision? What is lost from the play if the scene is cut? Would you cut it or keep it?

184 **like** equally

185 **We doubt not …** I have no doubt that the war will be fair and profitable to us

189 **rub** problem; obstacle

191 **puissance** army

1 **Prithee** please (I pray thee)

3 **earn** grieve, mourn (yearn)

4 **vaunting veins** lively spirits

6 **earn therefore** mourn the fact

7 **Would** I wish

wheresome'er he is wherever he's gone

9–10 **Arthur's bosom** *She means Abraham's bosom.*

10–11 **'A made a finer end** he made a better end (*in not going to hell*)

11 **an** as if

12 **christom child** a baby just after baptism: totally innocent

'a parted he departed this world

13 **e'en at the turning of the tide** *It was an old belief that a person near death will die as the flood tide turns to the ebb.*

13–17 **I saw him fumble …** *In Shakespeare's time all these actions and conditions were associated with dying.*

17 **'a babbled …** he talked in a confused way

18 **quoth** said

We doubt not of a fair and lucky war,   185
Since God so graciously hath brought to light
This dangerous treason lurking in our way
To hinder our beginnings. We doubt not now
But every rub is smoothéd on our way.
Then forth, dear countrymen! Let us deliver   190
Our puissance into the hand of God,
Putting it straight in expedition.
Cheerly to sea! The signs of war advance:
No king of England, if not king of France.

Exeunt

Scene 3

London, Before a tavern.

Enter PISTOL, HOSTESS, NYM, BARDOLPH *and* BOY.

HOSTESS   Prithee, honey-sweet husband, let me bring thee to
Staines.

PISTOL   No, for my manly heart doth earn.
Bardolph, be blithe. Nym, rouse thy vaunting veins.
Boy, bristle thy courage up; for Falstaff he is dead,   5
And we must earn therefore.

BARDOLPH   Would I were with him wheresome'er he is, either
in heaven or in hell!

HOSTESS   Nay, sure, he's not in hell. He's in Arthur's bosom,
if ever man went to Arthur's bosom. 'A made a   10
finer end and went away an it had been any
christom child; 'a parted e'en just between twelve
and one, e'en at the turning o' the tide: for after I
saw him fumble with the sheets and play with
flowers and smile upon his fingers' ends, I knew   15
there was but one way; for his nose was as sharp
as a pen, and 'a babbled of green fields. 'How
now, Sir John!' quoth I. 'What, man! Be o' good
cheer.' So 'a cried out 'God, God, God!' three or
four times. Now I, to comfort him, bid him 'a   20
should not think of God; I hoped there was no
need to trouble himself with any such thoughts

2.3 Eastcheap, London: the Boar's Head Tavern

Pistol, Bardolph, Nym, Mistress Quickly and the Boy (Falstaff's page) reminisce about some of the things Falstaff used to say, and then they prepare to depart for Southampton.

Activities

Actors' interpretations: the death of Falstaff

In the Branagh film, all the characters sit silently on the stairs as Judi Dench's Mistress Quickly recounts the death of Falstaff.

1. Storyboard three or four frames of a film sequence which might be shown while the character is speaking.
2. Pick out some favourite phrases which (a) help us to visualise Falstaff's dying moments; and (b) are typical of Mistress Quickly's personality and the language she uses.
3. In threes, act out the episode, with one person reading the speech and two others taking the parts of Falstaff and Mistress Quickly.

---

23 **bade** asked

26 **up'ard** upwards

28 **cried out of** he spoke out against wine

33–34 **devils incarnate** devils in human form (made flesh); *Mistress Quickly confuses the word with 'carnation'*

36 **devil would have him** *Falstaff believed he would be sent to hell for his dealings with women.*

38 **handle** talk about

39 **rheumatic** a *'Quicklyism' for delirious*

39–40 **whore of Babylon** *insulting term used by Protestants for the Roman Catholic church*

44 **fuel** *the money to purchase the alcohol which gave Bardolph his red nose*

46 **shog** get going *(see 2.1.47)*

49 **chattels and ... movables** possessions

50 **Let senses rule** keep your wits about you

'Pitch and Pay' make sure everybody pays up: don't give anything on credit

52 **wafer-cakes** thin pastry *(men's promises are wafer-thin: frail and easily broken)*

53 **Holdfast** hold on to what you've got

54 **Caveto** Let 'Beware' be your watchword

yet. So 'a bade me lay more clothes on his feet. I
put my hand into the bed and felt them, and they
were as cold as any stone; then I felt to his knees,   25
and they were as cold as any stone, and so up'ard
and up'ard, and all was as cold as any stone.

NYM   They say he cried out of sack.

HOSTESS   Ay, that 'a did.

BARDOLPH   And of women.   30

HOSTESS   Nay, that 'a did not.

BOY   Yes, that 'a did; and said they were devils
           incarnate.

HOSTESS   'A could never abide carnation; 't was a colour he
           never liked.   35

BOY   'A said once, the devil would have him about
           women.

HOSTESS   'A did in some sort, indeed, handle women; but
           then he was rheumatic, and talked of the whore of
           Babylon.   40

BOY   Do you not remember, 'a saw a flea stick upon
           Bardolph's nose, and 'a said it was a black soul
           burning in hell-fire?

BARDOLPH   Well, the fuel is gone that maintained that fire.
           That's all the riches I got in his service.   45

NYM   Shall we shog? The king will be gone from
           Southampton.

PISTOL   Come, let's away. My love, give me thy lips.
           Look to my chattels and my movables.
           Let senses rule. The word is 'Pitch and Pay'.   50
           Trust none;
           For oaths are straws, men's faiths are wafer-cakes,
           And Hold-fast is the only dog, my duck.
           Therefore, Caveto be thy counsellor.
           Go, clear thy crystals. Yoke-fellows in arms,   55

2.4 France: the royal palace at Rouen

Mistress Quickly bids farewell to Pistol and his companions as they leave to join the fleet at Southampton. The French King, hearing of the English approach, instructs his nobles to ensure that their country is properly defended and fortified.

Activities

Actors' interpretations: comedy and pathos

This scene is usually played as a mixture of comedy and pathos (sadness). The comedy might come from Mistress Quickly's language (for example, her malapropisms, see page 34) and the joke about Bardolph's nose; the pathos can come from her simple, unaffected account of Falstaff's death.

Act the scene in two ways, firstly trying to make it as sad and serious as you can, then aiming to derive as much humour from it as possible. Finally, decide what you think the most effective mixture of comedy and pathos might be and try to perform it in that way. How will you perform Pistol's 'horse-leeches' line (55–57)? Is it light-hearted, or does it show that these men are nasty parasites?

55 **clear thy crystals** wipe your eyes

Yoke-fellows comrades

56 **horse-leeches** *parasitic worms that suck blood*

62 **let housewifery appear; keep close** spend your time as a housewife: stay indoors

64 **adieu** goodbye

2–3 **And more ... defences** and we need to be more careful than usual to see that our defences are equipped to protect the kingdom

7 **line** strengthen, reinforce

8 **with means defendant** with defences

10 **gulf** whirlpool *(see also 4.3.82)*

12 **late** recent *(these examples include the battles of Crécy in 1346 and Poitiers in 1352; see lines 50–62)*

13 **fatal and neglected** fatally underestimated; underrated, to our cost

14 **redoubted** feared, respected

15 **meet** fitting, appropriate

16–20 **For peace ... expectation** Peace should not be allowed to make a kingdom complacent, even if it is not expecting a conflict; instead, defences should be kept in order, troops assembled and preparations made, as though we were anticipating a war.

Let us to France, like horse-leeches, my boys,
To suck, to suck, the very blood to suck!

BOY   And that's but unwholesome food, they say.

PISTOL   Touch her soft mouth, and march.

BARDOLPH   Farewell, hostess. (*Kissing her*)   60

NYM   I cannot kiss, that is the humour of it; but, adieu.

PISTOL   Let housewifery appear: keep close, I thee
command.

HOSTEES   Farewell; adieu.

                                  Exeunt

Scene 4

France. The KING'S Palace.

Flourish. Enter the FRENCH KING, *the* DAUPHIN, *the* DUKES OF
BERRI *and* BRETAGNE, *the* CONSTABLE, *and others.*

FRENCH   Thus comes the English with full power upon us,
KING   And more than carefully it us concerns
          To answer royally in our defences.
          Therefore the Dukes of Berri and of Bretagne,
          Of Brabant and of Orleans, shall make forth,   5
          And you, Prince Dauphin, with all swift dispatch,
          To line and new repair our towns of war
          With men of courage and with means defendant;
          For England his approaches makes as fierce
          As waters to the sucking of a gulf.   10
          It fits us then to be as provident
          As fear may teach us, out of late examples
          Left by the fatal and neglected English
          Upon our fields.

DAUPHIN   My most redoubted father,
          It is most meet we arm us 'gainst the foe;   15
          For peace itself should not so dull a kingdom,
          Though war nor no known quarrel were in question,

2.4 France: the royal palace at Rouen

The Dauphin speaks insultingly about Henry's supposed immaturity, but the Constable and the King are both aware of how dangerous it would be to underestimate him.

Activities

Character review: the French king

According to many historians, the French King, Charles VI, suffered from mental illness, and several productions of this play, including Olivier's film, have shown him to be dithering and powerless – almost a comic figure, in fact.

Act his opening speech (lines 1–14) in two ways: first, as though not really in control of events; then as competent and decisive. Try out a third interpretation, which avoids the two extremes: which do you prefer?

RSC, 1984

25 **Whitsun morris-dance** *traditional English dance*

26 **idly kinged** badly ruled

27 **Her sceptre ... borne** England is so ridiculously governed

28 **giddy, shallow, humorous** *unstable, lacking depth and unreliable*

29 **attends** accompanies (England does not know fear)

31 **late** recent

34 **modest in exception** restrained and reasonable when raising objections

36 **vanities forespent** past foolish behaviour

37–38 **Brutus** *Lucius Junius Brutus pretended to be stupid* (**Covering discretion with a coat of folly**) *to preserve his life from his uncle, and went on to be a great leader.*

39 **ordure** manure

45–48 **So the proportions ... cloth** if we think the enemy strong, we will put up proper defences; if defences are too skimpy, it will be like a miser who spoils a new coat by not paying for enough cloth

50 **fleshed upon us** trained to fight (*like a hound or hawk*), by being given a taste of our blood

51 **bloody strain** family line which shed our blood

54 **struck** fought

But that defences, musters, preparations,
Should be maintained, assembled and collected,
As were a war in expectation.   20
Therefore, I say, 't is meet we all go forth
To view the sick and feeble parts of France.
And let us do it with no show of fear;
No, with no more than if we heard that England
Were busied with a Whitsun morris-dance;   25
For, my good liege, she is so idly kinged,
Her sceptre so fantastically borne
By a vain giddy, shallow, humorous youth,
That fear attends her not.

CONSTABLE   O peace, Prince Dauphin!
You are too much mistaken in this king.   30
Question your grace the late ambassadors,
With what great state he heard their embassy,
How well supplied with noble counsellors,
How modest in exception, and withal
How terrible in constant resolution,   35
And you shall find his vanities forespent
Were but the outside of the Roman Brutus,
Covering discretion with a coat of folly;
As gardeners do with ordure hide those roots
That shall first spring and be most delicate.   40

DAUPHIN   Well, 't is not so, my lord high constable;
But though we think it so, it is no matter.
In cases of defence 't is best to weigh
The enemy more mighty than he seems;
So the proportions of defence are filled;   45
Which of a weak and niggardly projection
Doth like a miser spoil his coat with scanting
A little cloth.

FRENCH   Think we King Harry strong;
KING   And, princes, look you strongly arm to meet him.
The kindred of him hath been fleshed upon us;   50
And he is bred out of that bloody strain
That haunted us in our familiar paths.
Witness our too much memorable shame
When Cressy battle fatally was struck,
And all our princes captived, by the hand   55
Of that black name, Edward, Black Prince of Wales;

2.4 France: the royal palace at Rouen

As the French King is fearfully recalling the devastation caused in the past by Edward III and his son, the Black Prince, Exeter arrives and formally repeats Henry's claim to the crown of France.

Activities

Plot review (6): Henry's ancestors

Add to your Edward III poster (see the activity on page 16) with details from lines 51–62. The notes on this page, and page 239 will help you with some of the historical details.

Actors' interpretations: the French

What impression to you gain of the French from this photograph of the 1975 production?

RSC, 1975

57 **mountain sire** towering father

59 **heroical seed** heroic offspring

64 **native mightiness and fate of him** the power that he was born with and is destined to use against us

67 **present** immediate

69 **Turn head, and stop pursuit** *an expression from deer-hunting:* turn your antlers to face the pursuing hounds and stop them in their tracks

70 **spend their mouths** make a lot of noise

75 **self-neglecting** not taking care of yourself

76 **brother England** *Henry and the French King are descended from the same ancestor (see page 245).*

79 **divest yourself ... of** strip off

80 **borrowed glories** *Exeter accuses the French King of having taken temporary possession of the glories of kingship properly due to Henry V and his heirs, according to laws devised by God and now part of nature.*

81 **'long** belong

83 **pertain** belong to, are associated with

84 **ordinance of times** time-honoured usage, established practice

Whiles that his mountain sire, on mountain
   standing,
Up in the air, crowned with the golden sun,
Saw his heroical seed, and smiled to see him,
Mangle the work of nature, and deface   60
The patterns that by God and by French fathers
Had twenty years been made. This is a stem
Of that victorious stock; and let us fear
The native mightiness and fate of him.

Enter a Messenger.

MESSENGER   Ambassadors from Harry King of England   65
Do crave admittance to your majesty.

FRENCH   We'll give them present audience. Go, and bring
KING   them.

                       Exeunt Messenger *and certain* Lords

You see this chase is hotly followed, friends.

DAUPHIN   Turn head, and stop pursuit; for coward dogs
Most spend their mouths when what they seem to
   threaten   70
Runs far before them. Good my sovereign,
Take up the English short, and let them know
Of what a monarchy you are the head.
Self-love, my liege, is not so vile a sin
As self-neglecting.   75

Re-enter Lords, *with* EXETER *and train.*

FRENCH   From our brother England?
KING

EXETER   From him; and thus he greets your majesty.
He wills you, in the name of God Almighty,
That you divest yourself, and lay apart
The borrowed glories that by gift of heaven,   80
By law of nature and of nations, 'long
To him and to his heirs; namely, the crown
And all wide-stretchéd honours that pertain
By custom and the ordinance of times
Unto the crown of France. That you may know   85

2.4 France: the royal palace at Rouen

Exeter gives the French King a family tree which supports Henry's claim and threatens violence and destruction if the French refuse to accept it. He then delivers a particular message from Henry to the Dauphin.

Activities

Shakespeare's language: How does Exeter persuade the French?

For language to be powerful and colourful, it does not have to include many adjectives or adverbs: Exeter's threatening speech (lines 98–110) gains most of its effect from strong-sounding verbs and nouns, such as 'rake' (line 99) and 'tempest' (line 100).

1. List the most impressive nouns and verbs and then perform the speech giving them particular emphasis.
2. Copy out some of the most vivid passages and illustrate them (such as Henry attacking like Jupiter, surrounded by tempest and thunder).
3. The speech is not merely a series of threats: what arguments does Exeter use to persuade the French to give in now?
4. Create a wartime poster, using some of Exeter's language, which might be used to encourage people to support the war against the French and join the army.

86 **'Tis no sinister ... raked** it is not an illegitimate or perverse claim dug up out of ancient worm-eaten books or raked up from the dusty old days stretching back before living memory

89 **line** family tree, line of descent

90 **truly demonstrative** demonstrating the truth

91 **Willing you overlook** wishing you to look over

92 **evenly derived** directly descended

95 **indirectly** wrongfully

96 **native** correct, according to descent

challenger claimant to the throne

98 **constraint** force

101 **Jove** *Jupiter, King of the gods, who had thunder as a weapon*

102 **if requiring fail ...** if you do not agree, he will use force

103 **in the bowels ...** in God's name

108 **pining** bereaved, mourning

115 **bear our full intent** carry a message of our complete intentions

119–120 **... may not misbecome ...** *Henry uses any insult which would not reflect badly on Henry himself (the **mighty sender** of the message)*

'T is no siníster nor no awkward claim,
Picked from the worm-holes of long-vanished days,
Nor from the dust of old oblivion raked,
He sends you this most memorable line, (*gives a
    paper*)
In every branch truly demonstrative;   90
Willing you overlook this pedigree:
And when you find him evenly derived
From his most famed of famous ancestors,
Edward the third, he bids you then resign
Your crown and kingdom, indirectly held   95
From him the native and true challenger.

FRENCH   Or else what follows?
KING

EXETER   Bloody constraint; for if you hide the crown
              Even in your hearts, there will he rake for it.
              Therefore in fierce tempest is he coming,   100
              In thunder and in earthquake, like a Jove,
              That, if requiring fail, he will compel.
              And bids you, in the bowels of the Lord,
              Deliver up the crown, and to take mercy
              On the poor souls for whom this hungry war   105
              Opens his vasty jaws; and on your head
              Turning the widows' tears, the orphans' cries,
              The dead men's blood, the pining maidens' groans,
              For husbands, fathers and betrothéd lovers,
              That shall be swallowed in this controversy.   110
              This is his claim, his threatening and my message;
              Unless the Dauphin be in presence here,
              To whom expressly I bring greeting too.

FRENCH   For us, we will consider of this further:
KING   To-morrow shall you bear our full intent   115
              Back to our brother England.

DAUPHIN   For the Dauphin,
              I stand here for him: what to him from England?

EXETER   Scorn and defiance, slight regard, contempt,
              And any thing that may not misbecome
              The mighty sender, doth he prize you at.   120
              Thus says my king: and if your father's highness

2.4 France: the royal palace at Rouen

Exeter threatens revenge for the mocking gift of the tennis-balls, telling the Dauphin how Henry's behaviour changed when he became King. The French King promises to give his response to Henry's claim the following day.

Activities

Character review: the Dauphin (2)

Look back through the scene. What impression do you form of the Dauphin?

1. Note down the statements which reveal him to be (a) practical and sensible; and (b) conceited and lacking in judgement.
2. Improvise the discussion which might take place after Exeter has left, bearing in mind that (a) they have only just learned that Henry and his army have already landed in France; (b) the Dauphin and the Constable have already disagreed with each other.

125–127 **womby vaultages … ordinance** hollow underground caverns will rebuke you for the wrong you have done (**chide your trespass**) and send your mock back to you by echoing our cannon fire (**ordinance**)

128 **render fair return** gives a polite response

130 **odds** argument

131 **Paris balls** tennis-balls (*so called because tennis came to England from France*)

133 **Louvre** French royal palace (*then pronounced like 'lover' – hence the 'mistress' word-play on the next line*)

134 **mistress** (1) chief, (2) see line 133

137 **greener** more inexperienced, less mature

138 **masters** possesses

138–139 **Now he weighs … grain** now he makes use of every second

144 **he is footed** he has a foothold

Do not, in grant of all demands at large,
Sweeten the bitter mock you sent his majesty,
He'll call you to so hot an answer of it,
That caves and womby vaultages of France   125
Shall chide your trespass and return your mock
In second accent of his ordinance.

DAUPHIN   Say, if my father render fair return,
It is against my will; for I desire
Nothing but odds with England. To that end,   130
As matching to his youth and vanity,
I did present him with the Paris balls.

EXETER   He'll make your Paris Louvre shake for it,
Were it the mistress-court of mighty Europe:
And, be assured, you'll find a difference,   135
As we his subjects have in wonder found,
Between the promise of his greener days
And these he masters now. Now he weighs time
Even to the utmost grain; that you shall read
In your own losses, if he stay in France.   140

FRENCH   To-morrow shall you know our mind at full.
KING

EXETER   Dispatch us with all speed, lest that our king
Come here himself to question our delay;
For he is footed in this land already.

FRENCH   You shall be soon dispatched with fair
KING   conditions.   145
A night is but small breath and little pause
To answer matters of this consequence.

Flourish. Exeunt

Exam practice

Actors' interpretations: the French

Imagine you are going to direct 2.4 for your year group. Explain how you want the French to play their parts and what you want to suggest to the audience about the French court.

Before you begin to write, you should think about:
- what you would tell the French King and the Dauphin about how to play their parts
- how you would make clear the differences of opinion between the Dauphin and the Constable
- how you would show the contrasts between the English and the French courts.

Actors' interpretations: English and French scenes

1. *Changing the order*
In some productions of *Henry V*, the scene with Pistol and his companions is moved to the end of Act 1. What advantages and disadvantages might there be in doing that? Before you answer, re-read the Act 2 Chorus speech: what is it mainly about, and where does he say the next scene is to be set?

2. *Showing differences*
If you were directing a production of *Henry V* in the Globe Theatre, how would you show the difference between the English and French courts? Re-read the activities on pages 58, 60 and 64. Then note down ideas about:
- simple scenery
- costumes
- the ways in which the actors behave.

Plot review (7): Henry's family tree

When the French King recalls defeats at the hands of Edward III and calls Henry 'a stem Of that victorious stock' (2.4.62–63), he possibly has in his head a picture of the 'family tree', a common image in Shakespeare's plays and one which his audience would have seen in church windows. Study the version opposite and check that you understand how the main characters in Henry's family are related to each other.

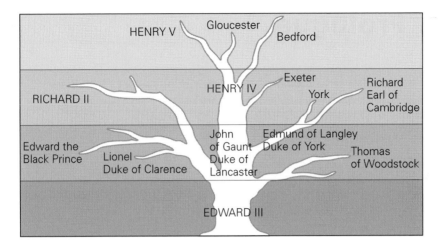

1. How are the following related:
   - Henry V and Edward III?
   - Henry V and Exeter?
   - Henry V, Bedford and Gloucester?
   - Henry's father and Cambridge?

2. Which king was murdered and who had him killed?

3. Which of Henry V's relatives plotted to kill him at Southampton? What relation was he to Henry?

Character review: Henry (10): opinions so far

1. What have you learned about Henry so far? What do you approve of in his behaviour and what do you disapprove of?

2. Write an article about Henry for a tabloid newspaper *The Bugle*. Give it the headline 'The man leading our boys in France' and devote a paragraph to each of the new things you have learned about Henry in Act 2, deciding first whether to write a portrait which is in praise of Henry, critical of him, or a mixture of both views.

   For example, under a sub-heading such as 'Kind or cruel?', you could write about Henry's willingness to pardon a drunk who shouted insults at him but his severe treatment of the traitors. There might also be a paragraph on the death of his old companion Falstaff and another dealing with the message he has sent, through Exeter, to the French. Add anything else you think might interest the readers of *The Bugle*, but make sure that there is evidence in Shakespeare's script for everything you write.

Plot review (8): Falstaff's obituary

Write an article on the death of Sir John Falstaff for *The Chronicle*. Include references to his former friendship with the King and his rejection (see the activity on page 40 and see also page 242), as well as quotations from Mistress Quickly and the others.

3 Prologue

The Chorus relates how, having crossed the English Channel, Henry's army has besieged Harfleur. Henry has rejected the French King's peace terms, which include marriage to the French Princess, and the attack is now at its height.

Activities

Plot review (9): events between Acts 2 and 3

Create a series of newspaper headlines which might accompany reports on all the major events that the Chorus refers to here, including those described in the following sections of the speech:
lines 3–17; 19–24; 25–27; 28–32; 32–34.

Themes: theatre and the imagination (3)

When a verb is used to tell someone what to do ('Go!', 'Pass the sandwiches, please.', 'Have a drink.'), we call this the imperative form. Notice how many times the Chorus uses the imperative form of the verb in this speech (lines 3, 7, 10, 13, 17, 18, 19, 25, 26, 28, 34 and 35). All of these imperative verbs are adding to the theme of theatre and the imagination. What is the Chorus telling or asking the audience to do here? Does this repeated request for us to 'be kind' and help out the performance suggest that Shakespeare was genuinely worried about his theatre's inadequacies, do you think? Or is it simply his way of making sure we visualise exactly what has happened in the story?

1 **imagined wing** the wings of imagination

2 **celerity** speed

6 **streamers ... fanning** pennants fluttering in the face of the morning sun *(Phoebus was the classical sun-god)*

7 **fancies** powers of imagination

8 **hempen tackle** rigging

12 **bottoms** ships

13 **Breasting the lofty surge** moving forwards through the high waves

14 **rivage** shore

15 **inconstant billows** ever-changing waves

18 **Grapple ...** Imagine you are following behind these ships

21 **pith and puissance** strength and power

22–23 **whose chin ...** who are only just getting a beard ...

24 **culled and choice-drawn cavaliers** selected and specially chosen soldiers

26 **ordnance** cannons

27 **girded** besieged, surrounded

30 **to dowry** as a bride's money settlement

32 **likes not** does not please him

33 **linstock** long staff for holding the gunner's match

s.d. ***chambers*** *small guns*

35 **eke out** help out

Act 3

3

Prologue

Enter CHORUS.

CHORUS   Thus with imagined wing our swift scene flies
           In motion of no less celerity
           Than that of thought. Suppose that you have seen
           The well-appointed king at Hampton pier
           Embark his royalty; and his brave fleet   5
           With silken streamers the young Phoebus fanning:
           Play with your fancies, and in them behold
           Upon the hempen tackle, ship-boys climbing;
           Hear the shrill whistle which doth order give
           To sounds confused; behold the threaden sails,   10
           Borne with the invisible and creeping wind,
           Draw the huge bottoms through the furrowed sea,
           Breasting the lofty surge: O do but think
           You stand upon the rivage, and behold
           A city on the inconstant billows dancing;   15
           For so appears this fleet majestical,
           Holding due course to Harfleur. Follow, follow!
           Grapple your minds to sternage of this navy,
           And leave your England, as dead midnight still,
           Guarded with grandsires, babies and old women,   20
           Either past or not arrived to pith and puissance;
           For who is he, whose chin is but enriched
           With one appearing hair, that will not follow
           These culled and choice-drawn cavaliers to France?
           Work, work your thoughts, and therein see a
             siege;   25
           Behold the ordnance on their carriages,
           With fatal mouths gaping on girded Harfleur.
           Suppose the ambassador from the French comes
             back;
           Tells Harry that the king doth offer him
           Katharine his daughter, and with her, to dowry,   30
           Some petty and unprofitable dukedoms.
           The offer likes not: and the nimble gunner
           With linstock now the devilish cannon touches,

Alarum, and chambers go off

           And down goes all before them. Still be kind,
           And eke out our performance with your mind.   35

3.1 France: before the walls of Harfleur

The attack on Harfleur continues and Henry encourages his men in a stirring speech, appealing to their honour and patriotism.

Activities

Character review: Henry (11): the leader in battle

Henry delivers this speech in the middle of battle; the English have made a hole in the city's defences and Henry is exhorting his men to attack again, using every means he can to encourage them.

A How would you make this speech as exciting as possible in a stage production? Think about the use of:
- special effects (such as smoke)
- sound effects, lighting and music
- use of the stage and its different levels
- actors' movements
- costume and make-up.

B Find the parts of the speech in which he:
- refers to his army as equals
- urges them to set aside their peaceful dispositions and be fighters
- calls on his nobles to be worthy of their great warrior ancestors
- challenges them to prove their legitimacy – they were descended from the men who had fought at Crécy
- asks his nobles to be models for the common soldiers to copy
- inspires the farmers and other land-owners to be proud of their English upbringing

continued on page 72

1 **breach** hole in the defences

3 **so becomes** is more fitting for

7 **Stiffen the sinews** tense your muscles

conjure up the blood get it coursing through your veins

8 **Disguise fair nature ...** Hide your usually kind looks

9 **Then lend ...** have a terrible look in your eyes

10 **portage** portholes

16 **bend up** strain to the utmost (*like drawing a bow*)

18 **fet** derived

of war-proof who have proved themselves in war

21 **for lack of argument** when there was no one left to fight

22–23 **Dishonour not ...** Don't bring disgrace upon your mothers: prove (**attest**) that those you call your fathers actually were (**did beget you**)

24 **Be copy ...** be an example to the men who are not nobles

25 **yeomen** farmers

26–27 **show ... The mettle of your pasture** prove how good your up-bringing has been

30 **noble lustre** the gleam of nobility

31 **slips** leashes

33 **upon this charge** possibly: (1) as you charge, or (2) on my word of command

Scene 1

France. Before the gates of Harfleur.

Alarum. Enter KING HENRY, EXETER, BEDFORD, GLOUCESTER,
and Soldiers, *with scaling-ladders.*

KING HENRY Once more unto the breach, dear friends, once more;
Or close the wall up with our English dead.
In peace there's nothing so becomes a man
As modest stillness and humility;
But when the blast of war blows in our ears,   5
Then imitate the action of the tiger;
Stiffen the sinews, conjure up the blood,
Disguise fair nature with hard-favoured rage.
Then lend the eye a terrible aspect.
Let it pry through the portage of the head   10
Like the brass cannon; let the brow o'erwhelm it
As fearfully as doth a galléd rock
O'erhang and jutty his confounded base,
Swilled with the wild and wasteful ocean.
Now set the teeth and stretch the nostril wide,   15
Hold hard the breath and bend up every spirit
To his full height. On, on, you noblest English,
Whose blood is fet from fathers of war-proof!
Fathers that, like so many Alexanders,
Have in these parts from morn till even fought   20
And sheathed their swords for lack of argument.
Dishonour not your mothers; now attest
That those whom you called fathers did beget you.
Be copy now to men of grosser blood,
And teach them how to war. And you, good
    yeomen,   25
Whose limbs were made in England, show us here
The mettle of your pasture. Let us swear
That you are worth your breeding; which I doubt
    not;
For there is none of you so mean and base,
That hath not noble lustre in your eyes.   30
I see you stand like greyhounds in the slips,
Straining upon the start. The game's afoot:
Follow your spirit, and upon this charge
Cry 'God for Harry, England, and Saint George!'

Exeunt. Alarum, and chambers go off

3.2 France: before the walls of Harfleur

Pistol and his cowardly companions are reluctant to join in the attack and try to hold back, but they are driven into the thick of it by the Welsh Captain, Fluellen.

Activities

- suggests that even the lowest born soldiers have the gleam of nobility
- appeals to their patriotism.

Write a letter home from one of the yeomen, describing how the King raised spirits with this speech.

C Watch *either* the Olivier *or* the Branagh film versions of this speech, noting the features referred to in A above and also the use made of camera angles and cutting from one shot to another.

Shakespeare's language: imagery

In lines 9–14 Henry uses two images to let his men know what expressions they should put on when facing the enemy. Draw two cartoons: one to illustrate Henry's advice about what the men's eyes should do (lines 9–11); and another to represent his descriptions of their brows (lines 11–14). The following notes should help: **portage**: portholes; **fearfully**: frighteningly; **gallèd**: eroded; **jutty**: jut out over; **confounded**: demolished; **Swilled with**: swallowed up by; **wasteful**: destructive.

How well do Henry's images help to describe facial expressions, in your opinion?

2 **the knocks are too hot** it's too dangerous

3 **a case** a set (I've only got one life)

4 **the humour of it ...** that's the way it's going

4–5 **very plainsong** simple plain truth (*plainsong: music unadorned by harmonies*)

6 **humours** bad temper and violence

7 **vassals** servants

11 **Would I were** I wish I were

14 **prevail** come true

16 **thither would I hie** that's where I would rush to

17 **truly** (1) honourably, (2) in tune

19 **Avaunt, you cullions!** Go on, you scum!

20 **men of mould** men made of earth, mortal men

21 **Abate** stop

23 **bawcock ... chuck** *terms of endearment (**bawcock** from French: beau coq; **chuck** originally meaning chicken)*

   use lenity be lenient, merciful

26 **These be ... humours** This is a fine way to behave! You're making people angry.

Scene 2

The same.

Enter NYM, BARDOLPH, PISTOL, *and* BOY.

BARDOLPH	On, on, on, on, on! To the breach, to the breach!
NYM	Pray thee, corporal, stay. The knocks are too hot; and for mine own part, I have not a case of lives. The humour of it is too hot; that is the very plain-song of it.

5

PISTOL The plain-song is most just; for humours do abound;

> Knocks go and come; God's vassals drop and die;
> And sword and shield,
> In bloody field,
> Doth win immortal fame. 10

BOY Would I were in an alehouse in London! I would give all my fame for a pot of ale and safety.

PISTOL And I:

> If wishes would prevail with me,
> My purpose should not fail with me, 15
> But thither would I hie.

BOY As duly, but not as truly,
As bird doth sing on bough.

Enter FLUELLEN.

FLUELLEN Up to the breach, you dogs! Avaunt, you cullions!
(*Driving them forward*)

PISTOL Be merciful, great duke, to men of mould. 20
Abate thy rage, abate thy manly rage,
Abate thy rage, great duke!
Good bawcock, bate thy rage! Use lenity, sweet
chuck!

NYM These be good humours! Your honour wins bad 25
humours.

Exeunt all but BOY

3.2 France: before the walls of Harfleur

Describing how boastful, cowardly and dishonest Pistol, Bardolph and Nym are, the Boy decides to leave them and seek out some better company. Fluellen complains to an English Captain, Gower, that the mines dug under the walls of Harfleur are not deep enough.

Activities

Character review: Henry's former companions (2)

1. What is the main point the Boy makes about each of his three companions?

2. Imagine that the Boy's comments on Pistol, Bardolph and Nym were accompanied in a film version by shots which illustrated what he was describing. Pick six comments and draw a storyboard frame for each one.

3. The Boy's descriptions are made vivid by his interesting use of language. Use the notes to explain the word-play in each of the following and show how it adds to our impression of the characters being described or of the Boy himself:
   - 'I am boy to them…man to me' (lines 27–29)
   - 'red-faced…faces it out' (lines 31–32)
   - 'breaks words…keeps whole weapons' (lines 34–35)
   - 'carry coals' (line 47)
   - 'pocketing up of wrongs' (lines 51–52)
   - 'weak stomach…cast it up' (lines 53–54).

28 **swashers** swaggerers, boasters

boy (1) their serving boy, (2) a boy compared to them

30 **antics** clowns

31–32 **white-livered** cowardly

32 **red-faced** (1) apparently courageous, (2) red-faced from drinking *(see 2.1.86 and 2.3.45)*

by the means whereof as a result of which

32–33 **'a faces it out** he blusters

35 **breaks words** (1) starts arguments, (2) breaks promises

43 **purchase** *their euphemism for stolen goods*

46 **filching** stealing

48 **carry coals** (1) do any dirty job for money, (2) put up with insults

50–51 **makes much …** goes against my conscience

52–53 **pocketing up of wrongs** (1) accepting stolen goods, (2) putting up with insults

55 **cast** vomit

56 **presently** immediately

57 **mines** *Besieging armies used to dig under the castle walls and detonate explosives.*

61 **disciplines** accepted practices

62 **concavities … not sufficient** the tunnels are not deep enough

63 **athversary** enemy, adversary

BOY	As young as I am, I have observed these three
	swashers. I am boy to them all three: but all they
	three, though they would serve me, could not be
	man to me; for indeed three such antics do not	30
	amount to a man. For Bardolph, he is white-
	livered and red-faced, by the means whereof 'a
	faces it out, but fights not. For Pistol, he hath a
	killing tongue and a quite sword, by the means
	whereof 'a breaks words, and keeps whole	35
	weapons. For Nym, he hath heard that men of
	few words are the best men, and therefore he
	scorns to say his prayers, lest 'a should be
	thought, a coward: but his few bad words are
	matched with as few good deeds; for 'a never	40
	broke any man's head but his own, and that was
	against a post when he was drunk. They will steal
	anything, and call it purchase. Bardolph stole a
	lute-case, bore it twelve leagues, and sold it for
	three halfpence. Nym and Bardolph are sworn	45
	brothers in filching, and in Calais they stole a fire-
	shovel. I knew by that piece of service the men
	would carry coals. They would have me as
	familiar with men's pockets as their gloves or
	their handkerchers: which makes much against	50
	my manhood, if I should take from another's
	pocket to put into mine, for it is plain pocketing
	up of wrongs. I must leave them, and seek some
	better service. Their villainy goes against my weak
	stomach, and therefore I must cast it up.	55

Exit

Re-enter FLUELLEN, GOWER *following.*

GOWER	Captain Fluellen, you must come presently to the
	mines. The Duke of Gloucester would speak with
	you.

FLUELLEN	To the mines! Tell you the duke, it is not so good
	to come to the mines; for, look you, the mines is	60
	not according to the disciplines of the war. The
	concavities of it is not sufficient; for, look you, th'
	athversary – you may discuss unto the duke –

3.2 France: before the walls of Harfleur

Captain Macmorris enters, an Irishman in charge of digging the mines, with a Scots Captain, Jamy. Macmorris angrily complains that, if they had not been ordered to retreat from the mines, he could have blown up the town in an hour.

Activities

Shakespeare's language: accents and dialects

In portraying the Welsh Fluellen, the Scots Jamy and the Irish Macmorris, Shakespeare has attempted to represent their accents and dialects in his spelling of key words. This is usually no problem for an audience listening to well rehearsed actors, but the strange spellings can cause difficulties when you are trying to read the script on the page. You might find it helpful to complete the following glossary of key examples by writing in the Received Pronunciation (RP) version of the accent features (i.e. the 'neutral' accent, which is not from any one region) and the Standard English versions of the dialect features. Some words have already been noted in the glossary; add others as you find them in later scenes.

Welsh accent	RP
64: Chesu	
64: plow	
77: falorous	
96: voutsafe	

continued on page 78

64–65 is digt … countermines the enemy has dug countermines four yards under our own mines

65 Chesu Jesus

69 i' faith truly (in faith)

72–73 I will verify … beard I will say as much to his face

73–74 He has no more directions … He has no more experience in military science …

75 Roman disciplines *the 'correct' ways in which to fight a war, as laid down by the Romans*

79 falorous valorous, brave

80–81 expedition and knowledge readiness to discuss his knowledge

80 particular personal

85 pristine ancient

86–87 gud-day … God-den good day

89 pioneers *men who dig the mines*

90 Chrish Christ

'T ish ill done it has been badly done

look you, is digt himself four yard under the
countermines. By Cheshu, I think 'a will plow up   65
all, if there is not better directions.

GOWER   The Duke of Gloucester, to whom the order of the
siege is given, is altogether directed by an
Irishman, a very valiant gentlemen, i' faith.

FLUELLEN   It is Captain Macmorris, is it not?   70

GOWER   I think it be.

FLUELLEN   By Cheshu, he is an ass, as in the world. I will
verify as much in his beard. He has no more
directions in the true disciplines of the wars, look
you, of the Roman disciplines, than is a puppy-   75
dog.

Enter MACMORRIS, *and* CAPTAIN JAMY.

GOWER   Here 'a comes, and the Scots captain, Captain
Jamy, with him.

FLUELLEN   Captain Jamy is a marvellous falorous gentleman,
that is certain; and of great expedition and   80
knowledge in the ancient wars, upon my
particular knowledge of his directions. By
Cheshu, he will maintain his argument as well as
any military man in the world, in the disciplines
of the pristine wars of the Romans.   85

JAMY   I say gud-day, Captain Fluellen.

FLUELLEN   God-den to your worship, good Captain James.

GOWER   How now, Captain Macmorris! Have you quit the
mines? Have the pioneers given o'er?

MACMORRIS   By Chrish, la! 'T ish ill done: that work ish give   90
over, the trompet sound the retreat. By my hand, I
swear, and my father's soul, the work ish ill done.
It ish give over. I would have blowed up the town,
so Chrish save me, la, in an hour. O 't ish ill done,
't ish ill done; by my hand, 't ish ill done!   95

FLUELLEN   Captain Macmorris, I beseech you now, will you

3.2 France: before the walls of Harfleur

Fluellen wants a discussion with Macmorris about the correct way in which to fight a war. Macmorris is angry that people are standing around talking when there is still fighting to be done and takes offence when Fluellen makes a remark about his 'nation', the Irish.

Activities

Welsh dialect	Standard English
58: look you	
65: there is…	
140: more better	

Scots accent	RP
84: gud-day	
104: bath	
117: mess	
118: ay'll de	
119: grund	
120: suerly	
121: breff	
121: wad	

Scots dialect	Standard English
122: 'tween you tway	

Irish accent	RP
88: Chrish	
88: ish	
110: beseeched	
111: be Chrish	

Irish dialect	Standard English
91: would have blowed	

97 **voutsafe** promise (vouchsafe)

98 **touching or concerning** *typical of Fluellen's tautology (see the activity on page 124)*

101 **communication** debate

105 **sall … shall**: That will be very good, truly, good captains both (**bath**), and I will answer you, if you will allow me, when the occasion arises. I will certainly do that

107 **marry** indeed (by Mary)

108 **discourse** talk

111 **beseeched** besieged

112 **be Chrish** by Christ

113 **sa'** save

117 **By the mess** By the Mass

118 **slomber** slumber, sleep

ay'll de I'll do

119 **lig 'I the grund** lie in the ground (die)

121 **breff** brief ('That's the long and the short of it')

121–122 **I wad full fain …** I would very much like to hear a discussion between you two (**tway**)

125–127 **Of my nation! …** My nation! What are you going to say about my nation now? Are we all villains, bastards, knaves and rascals?

129 **peradventure** perhaps

130 **affability** friendliness

130–131 **in discretion** if you were to think carefully

voutsafe me, look you, a few disputations with
you, as partly touching or concerning the
disciplines of the war, the Roman wars, in the way
of argument, look you, and friendly   100
communication; partly to satisfy my opinion, and
partly for the satisfaction, look you, of my mind,
as touching the direction of the military
discipline; that is the point.

JAMY   It sall be vary gud, gud feith, gud captains bath,   105
and I sall quit you, with gud leve, as I may pick
occasion. That sall I, marry.

MACMORRIS   It is no time to discourse, so Chrish save me. The
day is hot, and the weather, and the wars, and the
king, and the dukes. It is no time to discourse.   110
The town is beseeched, and the trumpet calls us
to the breach, and we talk, and, be Chrish, do
nothing: 't is shame for us all. So God sa' me, 't is
shame to stand still. It is shame, by my hand, an
there is throats to be cut, and works to be done,   115
and there ish nothing done, so Chrish sa' me, la!

JAMY   By the mess, ere theise eyes of mine take
themselves to slomber, ay 'll de gud service, or ay
'll lig i' the grund for it; ay, or go to death; and
ay 'll pay 't as valorously as I may, that sall I suerly 120
do, that is the breff and the long. Marry, I wad full
fain hear some question 'tween you tway.

FLUELLEN   Captain Macmorris, I think, look you, under your
correction, there is not many of your nation –

MACMORRIS   Of my nation! What ish my nation? Ish a villain,   125
and a bastard, and a knave, and a rascal. What ish
my nation? Who talks of my nation?

FLUELLEN   Look you, if you take the matter otherwise than is
meant, Captain Macmorris, peradventure I shall
think you do not use me with that affability as in   130
discretion you ought to use me, look you; being
as good a man as yourself, both in the disciplines
of war, and in the derivation of my birth, and in
other particularities.

3.3 France: before the gates of Harfleur

Fluellen and Macmorris agree to continue their argument at a more convenient time. Henry threatens the Governor of Harfleur: either they surrender now, or Henry will destroy the town, and its people will be subjected to appalling violence.

Activities

Actors' interpretations: cutting or keeping the scene?

Would you cut the scene with the four captains? Discuss these points:

For keeping the scene:

1. The scene provides some much needed comedy amidst the grimness of the war sequences.
2. It represents the different nations making up the 'English' army and shows its unity.
3. It interestingly shows the disunity within the army.
4. Fluellen and Macmorris represent the old and new ways in which to wage war (without and with gunpowder).
5. It is needed as a 'buffer' to show that time has passed between the renewed assault on Harfleur (3.1) and Henry's ultimatum to the Governor (3.3).

For cutting the scene:

6. It represents Welsh, Scots and Irish as comic stereotypes.
7. It is absurd to represent the Scots as enemies in 1.2 and then show one in the English army.
8. The 'comedy' is no longer amusing.
9. We don't see Jamy or Macmorris again: it is not worth introducing them.

137 **mistake** misunderstand

139 **sounds a parley** a trumpet is sounding, indicating that Harfleur wants to negotiate

140–141 **when there is ...** when a better opportunity arises

1 **How yet resolves ...?** what decision have you made?

2 **latest parle** final negotiation, last peace-talks

4 **proud of destruction** glorying in your deaths

7 **battery** attack

8 **half-achieved** *Henry is half way towards taking the town*

11–14 **And the fleshed ...** and soldiers, experienced in killing, rough and merciless, will be given complete freedom to commit whatever violence they choose, and will have absolutely no conscience about cutting down your young, beautiful virgins and growing children

15 **impious** irreligious *(because, as Henry sees it, the French are fighting against their rightful King)*

16 **Arrayed** dressed

17 **smirched** blackened with smoke

fell feats terrible deeds

MACMOORIS I do not know you so good a man as myself. So   135
           Chrish save me, I will cut off your head.

GOWER   Gentlemen both, you will mistake each other.

JAMY   A, that's a foul fault!

          A parley sounded.

GOWER   The town sounds a parley.

FLUELLEN   Captain Macmorris, when there is more better   140
           opportunity to be required, look you, I will be so
           bold as to tell you I know the disciplines of war;
           and there is an end.

                                                    Exeunt

Scene 3

The same. Before the gates.

The GOVERNOR *and some* Citizens *on the walls; the English forces*
below. Enter KING HENRY *and his train.*

KING HENRY How yet resolves the governor of the town?
           This is the latest parle we will admit.
           Therefore to our best mercy give yourselves,
           Or, like to men proud of destruction,
           Defy us to our worst: for, as I am soldier,   5
           A name that in my thoughts becomes me best,
           If I begin the battery once again,
           I will not leave the half-achieved Harfleur
           Till in her ashes she lie buriéd.
           The gates of mercy shall be all shut up,   10
           And the fleshed soldier, rough and hard of heart,
           In liberty of bloody hand shall range
           With conscience wide as hell, mowing like grass
           Your fresh, fair virgins and your flowering infants.
           What is it then to me, if impious war,   15
           Arrayed in flames like to the prince of fiends,
           Do with his smirched complexion all fell feats
           Enlinked to waste and desolation?
           What is 't to me, when you yourselves are cause,

3.3 France: before the gates of Harfleur

Henry argues that the people of Harfleur will themselves be responsible for their destruction if they refuse to give in now. Let down by the Dauphin, the Governor has no choice but to surrender. Henry decides that, as his army is now stricken with illness, it will be best to spend winter in Calais.

Activities

Character review: Henry (12): a ruthless professional?

A What are the main threats that Henry issues to the Governor of Harfleur? If you were a citizen of Harfleur, which of Henry's threats would you find most terrifying?

B Look again at the end of Henry's speech (lines 33–43) and act it in three different ways: (a) as though you were dreading having to go through with the threats; (b) like a ruthless savage, relishing the prospect of letting your soldiers loose; (c) like a professional soldier who does not particularly like this aspect of warfare, but is confident that it is within the rules and conventions. Which interpretation do you feel best fits the words that he speaks here?

C What evidence can you find in Henry's speech to support Kenneth Branagh's view that Henry is 'a professional killer of chilling ruthlessness… with an awesome personal capacity for violence'?

How do the following help to convey the strength of his message: alliteration; similes; rhetorical questions; personification; onomatopaeia? Look particularly at line 38.

21 **forcing violation** violent rape

22 **licentious** breaking all laws

23 **career** gallop

24 **We may as bootless …** It would be as pointless to try to control our enraged soldiers while they are engaged in plunder, as to …

26 **precepts** written orders

   leviathan enormous whale

30–32 **Whiles yet …** *Henry sees his mercy as a cool wind, blowing away the clouds of war, which rain down a plague of violent murder, looting and wickedness.*

34 **blind** reckless

35 **Defile the locks …** violate the hair

39 **mad** demented with grief

40 **Jewry** the Jewish nation *Henry refers to the Massacre of the Innocents, described in the Bible, when Herod ordered the children of Bethlehem to be slaughtered.*

43 **guilty in defence** *Henry argues that the Governor will be to blame for the slaughter, if he continues to defend the town rather than surrendering.*

45 **whom of succours …** whom we begged for help

46 **Returns us** replies

50 **defensible** able to defend ourselves

58 **addrest** prepared

If your pure maidens fall into the hand   20
Of hot and forcing violation?
What rein can hold licentious wickedness
When down the hill he holds his fierce career?
We may as bootless spend our vain command
Upon the enragéd soldiers in their spoil   25
As send precepts to the leviathan
To come ashore. Therefore, you men of Harfleur,
Take pity of your town and of your people,
Whiles yet my soldiers are in my command,
Whiles yet the cool and temperate wind of grace   30
O'erblows the filthy and contagious clouds
Of heady murder, spoil and villany.
If not, why, in a moment look to see
The blind and bloody soldier with foul hand
Defile the locks of your shrill-shrieking daughters;   35
Your fathers taken by the silver beards,
And their most reverend heads dashed to the walls;
Your naked infants spitted upon pikes,
Whiles the mad mothers with their howls confused
Do break the clouds, as did the wives of Jewry   40
At Herod's bloody-hunting slaughtermen.
What say you? Will you yield, and this avoid,
Or, guilty in defence, be thus destroyed?

GOVERNOR   Our expectation hath this day an end.
The Dauphin, whom of succours we entreated,   45
Returns us that his powers are yet not ready
To raise so great a siege. Therefore, great king,
We yield our town and lives to thy soft mercy.
Enter our gates; dispose of us and ours;
For we no longer are defensible.   50

KING HENRY Open your gates. Come, uncle Exeter,
Go you and enter Harfleur. Three remain,
And fortify it strongly 'gainst the French.
Use mercy to them all. For us, dear uncle,
The winter coming on and sickness growing   55
Upon our soldiers, we will retire to Calais.
To-night in Harfleur we will be your guest;
To-morrow for the the march are we addrest.

Flourish. The KING *and his train enter the town.*

3.4 A room in the royal palace at Rouen

The French Princess Katharine asks her lady-in-waiting Alice to teach her the English words for certain parts of the body.

Activities

Actors' interpretations: learning English

You do not need to speak French to understand what is going on in this scene when it is performed effectively. Lively acting is usually enough to get the meaning across.

Make a list of all the French words which Alice translates for Katharine (*la main*, etc.). Then perform the scene in pairs, using only the French words, but making the meanings clear by the use of:

• gestures
• tone of voice
• movements
• reactions.

It will help if you first decide what the main features of the French accent are. Watch several performances and compare your version with others.

RSC, 1975

1–6   *K: Alice, you have been to England and you speak the language well.*
A: A little, my lady.
K: Please teach me. I have to learn how to speak it. What do you call la main *in English?*

6–11   *A:* La main*? It's called 'de hand'.*
K: 'De hand'. And les doigts*?*
A: Les doigts*? My goodness, I have forgotten* les doigts*; but I will remember. I think they're called 'de fingres'; yes: 'de fingres'.*

12–16   *K:* La main, *'de hand';* les doigts, *'de fingres'. I think I'm a good student: I have learned two English words very quickly. What do you call* les ongles*?*
A: Les ongles*? We call them 'De nails'.*

17–21   *K: 'De nails'. Listen and tell me if I am saying it properly: 'de hand, de fingres' and 'de nails'.*
A: That's very well spoken, my lady. It is extremely good English.
K: Tell me what the English is for le bras.
A: 'De arm', my lady.

22–26   *K: And* le coude*?*
A: 'De elbow'.
K: 'De elbow'. I will repeat all the words that you have taught me so far.
A: I think that will be too difficult, my lady.

84

Scene 4

The FRENCH KING'S *Palace.*

Enter KATHARINE *and* ALICE.

KATHARINE	Alice, tu as été en Angleterre, et tu parles bien le langage.
ALICE	Un peu, madame.
KATHARINE	Je te prie, m'enseignez; il faut que j'apprenne à parler. Comment appelez-vous la main en Anglois?
ALICE	La main? Elle est appelée de hand.
KATHARINE	De hand. Et les doigts?
ALICE	Les doigts? Ma foi, j'oublie les doigts; mais je me souviendrai. Les doigts? Je pense qu'ils sont appelés de fingres; oui, de fingres.
KATHARINE	La main, de hand; les doigts, de fingres. Je pense que je suis le bon écolier; j'ai gagné deux mots d'Anglois vîtement. Comment appelez-vous les ongles?
ALICE	Les ongles? Nous les appelons de nails.
KATHARINE	De nails. Ecoutez; dites-moi, si je parle bien: de hand, de fingres, et de nails.
ALICE	C'est bien dit, madame; il est fort bon Anglois.
KATHARINE	Dites-moi l'Anglois pour le bras.
ALICE	De arm, madame.
KATHARINE	Et le coude?
ALICE	De elbow.
KATHARINE	De elbow. Je m'en fais la répétition de tous les mots que vous m'avez appris dès à présent.
ALICE	Il est trop difficile, madame, comme je pense.

Line numbers: 5, 10, 15, 20, 25

3.4 A room in the royal palace at Rouen

The English lesson continues until Katharine is shocked to learn that the English 'foot' and 'gown' sound like two obscene words in French.

27–35 K: *Excuse me, Alice. Listen: 'de hand, de fingres, de nails, de arma, de bilbow.'*

A: *'De elbow', my lady.*

K: *O Lord God, I forgot! 'De elbow'. What do you call le col?*

A: *'De neck', my lady.*

K: *'De nick'. And le menton?*

A: *'De chin'.*

K: *'De sin'. Le col: 'de nick'; le menton: 'de sin'.*

36–42 A: *Yes. If I may say so, you do indeed pronounce the words exactly like the English themselves.*

K: *I have no doubt that I shall learn, by God's grace, and in a short time.*

A: *Haven't you already forgotten what I have taught you?*

43–50 K: *No, I will recite it all to you: 'de hand, de fingres, de mails –'*

A: *'De nails', my lady.*

K: *'De nails, de arm, de ilbow.'*

A: *If I may correct you: 'de elbow'.*

K: *That's what I said: 'de elbow; de nick' and 'de sin'. What do you call le pied and le robe?*

A: *'De foot', my lady, and 'de coun'.*

51–61 K: *'De foot' and 'de coun'! O Lord God! These are bad, corrupting, rude and shameful words, and not suitable for respectable ladies to use. I would not for all the world speak those words in front of the noblemen of France. Disgusting! 'Le foot' and 'le coun'! All the same, I will go through the whole of my lesson one more time: 'de hand, de fingres, de nails, de arm, de elbow, de nick, de sin, de foot, de coun'.*

A: *Excellent, my lady!*

K: *That's enough for one lesson. Let's go in to dinner.*

Katherine's shock is due to the fact that 'foot' and 'coun' (Alice's pronunciation of 'gown') sound like foutre *and* con, *both obscene words in French (for sexual intercourse and the female genital organs respectively).*

KATHARINE   Excusez-moi, Alice; écoutez: de hand, de fingres,
             de nails, de arma, de bilbow.

ALICE   De elbow, madame.

KATHARINE   O Seigneur Dieu, je m'en oublie! De elbow.   30
             Comment appelez-vous le col?

ALICE   De neck, madame.

KATHARINE   De nick. Et le menton?

ALICE   De chin.

KATHARINE   De sin. Le col, de nick; le menton, de sin.   35

ALICE   Oui. Sauf votre honneur, en vérité, vous
             prononcez les mots aussi droit que les natifs
             d'Angleterre.

KATHARINE   Je ne doute point d'apprendre, par la grace de
             Dieu, et en peu de temps.   40

ALICE   N'avez-vous pas déjà oublié ce que je vous ai
             enseigné?

KATHARINE   Non, je réciterai à vous promptement: de hand,
             de fingres, de mails –

ALICE   De nails, madame.   45

KATHARINE   De nails, de arm, de ilbow.

ALICE   Sauf votre honneur, de elbow.

KATHARINE   Ainsi dis-je; de elbow, de nick, et de sin.
             Comment appelez-vous le pied et la robe?

ALICE   De foot, madame; et de coun.   50

KATHARINE   De foot et de coun! O Seigneur Dieu! Ce sont
             mots de son mauvais, corruptible, gros, et
             impudique, et non pour les dames d'honneur
             d'user. Je ne voudrais prononcer ces mots devant
             les seigneurs de France pour tout le monde. Foh!   55
             Le foot et el coun! Néanmoins, je réciterai une

3.5 The council-chamber in the royal palace at Rouen

Katharine goes through all the words she has learnt. Meanwhile the French nobles express their anger that the English have been allowed to march unopposed half the way from Harfleur to Calais.

5 **Dieu vivant** living God

5–9 **shall a few ... grafters?** *The image is from gardening:* 'Shall a few offshoots (**sprays**) of us, the outpourings of our ancestors' lust (**luxury**), our offspring (**scions**), grafted on to (**put in**) a wild and uncultivated plant (**... savage stock**), grow up so quickly and become taller than their parent plants?' *(The Dauphin thinks of the English as being illegitimate descendants of the Normans.)*

11–14 **Mort de ma vie ... but ...!** If these English are allowed to march on without being fought with, damn me if I don't sell my dukedom and buy a sloppy, filthy farm in that poky little island of Albion (*a poetical name for England*).

14 **nook-shotten** full of corners and sharp turns, poky

15 **Dieu de batailles!** God of battles!

mettle spirit and strength

17 **as in despite** as though defying the wishes of the English

18–20 **Can sodden ...** Can their cold blood be warmed up to give them such courage, by English ale – which tastes like boiled (**sodden**) water, and is used as a medicine (**drench**) for over-ridden clapped out horses (**sur-reined jades**)?

21 **quick** full of life

autre fois ma leçon ensemble: de hand, de fingres,
de nails, de arm, de elbow, de nick, de sin, de
foot, de coun.

ALICE   Excellent, madame!   60

KATHARINE   C'est assez pour une fois: allons-nous à dîner.

Exeunt

Scene 5

The same.

Enter the KING OF FRANCE, *the* DAUPHIN, *the* DUKE OF
BOURBON, *the* CONSTABLE OF FRANCE, *and others.*

FRENCH   'T is certain he hath passed the river Somme.
KING

CONSTABLE   And if he be not fought withal, my lord,
            Let us not live in France; let us quit all,
            And give our vineyards to a barbarous people.

DAUPHIN   O Dieu vivant, shall a few sprays of us,   5
            The emptying of our fathers' luxury,
            Our scions, put in wild and savage stock,
            Spirt up so suddenly into the clouds,
            And overlook their grafters?

BOURBON   Normans, but bastard Normans, Norman
                bastards!   10
            Mort de ma vie! If they march along
            Unfought withal, but I will sell my dukedom,
            To buy a slobbery and a dirty farm
            In that nook-shotten isle of Albion.

CONSTABLE   Dieu de batailles! Where have they this mettle? 15
            Is not their climate foggy, raw and dull,
            On whom, as in despite, the sun looks pale,
            Killing their fruit with frowns? Can sodden water,
            A drench for sur-reined jades, their barley-broth,
            Decoct their cold blood to such valiant heat?   20
            And shall our quick blood, spirited with wine,

3.5 The council-chamber in the royal palace at Rouen

Furious that they are being mocked by their women, the French vow to bring the whole force of their army to bear on the sick and hungry English soldiers.

Activities

Character review: the French (1)

A What do the French in this play dislike about the English? Make notes on their dislikes from lines 1–35.

B Re-read lines 1–60 and then rehearse and perform a brief television war broadcast aimed at the men of France in which the Dauphin, Bourbon and the Constable whip up a hatred against the enemy, using insults ('Norman bastards...') and fear tactics ('Our madams... will give Their bodies to the lust of English youth...').

C Create a war propaganda pamphlet which attempts to frighten and disgust the ordinary French citizen with suggestions that an inferior race are threatening them and that their pure blood will soon be tainted. (There are several references in this scene to the fact that, after the Normans, led by William the Conqueror, had successfully invaded Saxon England in 1066, the resulting 'English' nobility were mainly composed of illegitimate children from Norman–Saxon cross-breeding.) Base your writing on lines 1–60, especially the image of grafting (lines 5–9) and the fear of *miscegenation* – 'race-mixing' (lines 28–31).

23 **roping** hanging like ropes

26 **Poor we may ...** our fields ought to be called 'poor', since they have bred such weak owners

28 **madams** wives and girlfriends

29–31 **Our mettle ... youth.** The males have become weak and the French women say that they now need to breed with the English to create stronger (**bastard**) warriors.

32–35 **They bid ...** Our women tell us to go and become dancing masters in England, where we can teach dances that involve jumping and running (**lavoltas** and **corantos**), saying that we are only good with our feet and make excellent cowards (**lofty runaways**).

39 **hie to the field** hasten to the battlefield

47 **For your great ... shames** For the sake of the great titles you hold, put right these great shames.

48 **Bar** prevent, stand in the way of

49 **pennons** heraldic flags

50–52 **Rush on ... upon** Charge against Henry's army, like an avalanche of melted snow, when the Alps spit and sneeze (**void his rheum**) on the low valleys, as a master does to a servant (**vassal**).

55 **This becomes ...** This is how great people should behave

Seem frosty? O for honour of our land,
Let us not hang like roping icicles
Upon our houses' thatch, whiles a more frosty
   people
Sweat drops of gallant youth in our rich fields! 25
Poor we may call them in their native lords.

DAUPHIN By faith and honour,
Our madams mock at us, and plainly say
Our mettle is bred out and they will give
Their bodies to the lust of English youth, 30
To new-store France with bastard warriors.

BOURBON They bid us to the English dancing-schools,
And teach lavoltas high and swift corantos;
Saying our grace is only in our heels,
And that we are most lofty runaways. 35

FRENCH Where is Montjoy the herald? Speed him hence!
KING Let him greet England with our sharp defiance.
Up, princes, and, with spirit of honour edged
More sharper than your swords, hie to the field!
Charles Delabreth, high constable of France, 40
You Dukes of Orleans, Bourbon, and of Berri,
Alencon, Brabant, Bar, and Burgundy,
Jaques Chatillon, Rambures, Vaudemont,
Beaumont, Grandpré, Roussi, and Fauconberg,
Foix, Lestrale, Bouciqualt, and Charolois, 45
High dukes, great princes, barons, lords and knights,
For your great seats now quit you of great shames.
Bar Harry England, that sweeps through our land
With pennons painted in the blood of Harfleur.
Rush on his host, as doth the melted snow 50
Upon the valleys, whose low vassal seat
The Alps doth spit and void his rheum upon.
Go down upon him, you have power enough,
And in a captive chariot into Rouen
Bring him our prisoner.

CONSTABLE   This becomes the great. 55
Sorry am I his numbers are so few,
His soldiers sick and famished in their march,
For I am sure, when he shall see our army,
He'll drop his heart into the sink of fear

3.6 France: on the route back to Calais

The French King sends his herald Montjoy to discuss ransom terms with Henry. The English meanwhile have captured a bridge which they need to cross on their route to Calais and Fluellen praises the heroic actions of a soldier called Pistol.

60 **for achievement** (1) to conclude the business, (2) as his sole success

offer ... ransom Henry will promise to pay a sum of money to secure his release from prison if he is captured

61 **haste on Montjoy** tell Montjoy to hurry

s.d. **Picardy** *They are still about 50 or 60 miles from Calais (see the map on page 247).*

2 **bridge** *A small force had been sent ahead to capture a bridge which the English would need to cross.*

3–4 **services committed** actions performed

6 **magnanimous** great-hearted

Agamemnon *the leader of the Greek forces at the siege of Troy, perhaps chosen by Fluellen because his name echoes nicely with 'magnanimous'*

11 **pridge** bridge *(see the activity on page 96)*

12 **ancient lieutenant** possibly a sub-lieutenant

15 **Mark Antony** *the Roman general Marcus Antonius (who appears in Shakespeare's* Julius Caesar *and* Antony and Cleopatra*)*

	And for achievement offer us his ransom.	60

FRENCH KING	Therefore, lord constable, haste on Montjoy,
	And let him say to England that we send
	To know what willing ransom he will give.
	Prince Dauphin, you shall stay with us in Rouen.

DAUPHIN	Not so, I do beseech your majesty.	65

FRENCH KING	Be patient, for you shall remain with us.
	Now forth, lord constable and princes all,
	And quickly bring us word of England's fall.

Exeunt

Scene 6

The English camp in Picardy.

Enter GOWER and FLUELLEN, meeting.

GOWER	How now, Captain Fluellen! Come you from the bridge?

FLUELLEN	I assure you, there is very excellent services committed at the bridge?

GOWER	Is the Duke of Exeter safe?	5

FLUELLEN	The Duke of Exeter is as magnanimous as
	Agamemnon, and a man that I love and honour
	with my soul, and my heart, and my duty, and my
	life, and my living, and my uttermost power. He
	is not – God be praised and blessed – any hurt in

10

	the world, but keeps the pridge most valiantly,
	with excellent discipline. There is an ancient
	lieutenant there at the pridge; I think in my very
	conscience he is as valiant a man as Mark Antony;
	and he is a man of no estimation in the world;

15

	but I did see him do as gallant service.

GOWER	What do you call him?

FLUELLEN	He is called Ancient Pistol.

GOWER	I know him not.

3.6 France: on the route back to Calais

Pistol enters and begs Fluellen for his help. Bardolph has been caught stealing from a church and is to be executed, and Pistol wants Fluellen to plead with the Duke of Exeter for his friend's life.

Activities

Character review: Pistol (2)

A Look back at Pistol's earlier appearances (and the activities on pages 36–38 and 74) to remind yourself of the kind of man he is. What do Fluellen's comments (lines 12–18) add to your picture of Pistol?

B Improvise a conversation between Pistol and Nym, in which Pistol describes what he actually did say at the bridge, and how he behaved, to give Fluellen the (false) impression that Pistol was 'as valiant a man as Mark Antony' (line 14). You might get some ideas from the conversation between Fluellen and Gower about the kind of thing Pistol says (lines 64–83).

C 1. Look back at Pistol's final comment in 2.1 and at 2.3.56–57 and discuss what those lines suggest about Pistol's main motivation. Why is he pleading for Bardolph? Does this action show that he is not a total parasite?
2. Annotate lines 21–60 to show what you think Pistol might be thinking and feeling as his conversation with Fluellen progresses and as it is abruptly terminated and he leaves.

26 **buxom** strong, sturdy

27 **giddy Fortune's ...** *The Roman goddess Fortuna was portrayed as a woman, both changeable (***giddy***) and cruel (***furious***), constantly turning a wheel. People fixed to the wheel might find themselves at the top one minute and turned round to the bottom the next, suffering the changes of fortune. She was blindfolded (line 29) to show that she did not choose how to treat particular people, or stood on a round stone (line 30) to represent change and chance.*

31 **muffler** blindfold

34 **moral** symbolic meaning

35 **and mutability ...** and is constantly changing and variable

41 **pax** *either a small picture of the Crucifixion, or a box for carrying the communion wafers (a pix)*

43 **for dog** *animals were sometimes hanged (see* The Merchant of Venice, *4.1.133)*

44 **hemp** the hangman's rope

45 **doom** judgement

48 **vital thread** *In classical mythology, three goddesses known as the Fates were thought to control a person's life: one spun the thread of life, another spun it out and the third cut it to determine the moment of death.*

50 **requite** repay, reward

3.6

Enter PISTOL.

FLUELLEN	Here is the man.	20

PISTOL   Captain, I thee beseech to do me favours.
The Duke of Exeter doth love thee well.

FLUELLEN   Ay, I praise God; and I have merited some love at
his hands.

PISTOL   Bardolph, a soldier, firm and sound of heart,   25
And of buxom valour, hath, by cruel fate,
And giddy Fortune's furious fickle wheel,
That goddess blind,
That stands upon the rolling restless stone –

FLUELLEN   By your patience, Ancient Pistol. Fortune is   30
painted blind, with a muffler afore her eyes, to
signify to you that Fortune is blind; and she is
painted also with a wheel, to signify to you,
which is the moral of it, that she is turning, and
inconstant, and mutability, and variation: and her   35
foot, look you, is fixed upon a spherical stone,
which rolls, and rolls, and rolls: in good truth, the
poet makes a most excellent description of it:
Fortune is an excellent moral.

PISTOL   Fortune is Bardolph's foe, and frowns on him;   40
For he hath stolen a pax, and hanged must be:
A damnéd death!
Let gallows gape for dog; let man go free
And let not hemp his wind-pipe suffocate.
But Exeter hath given the doom of death   45
For pax of little price.
Therefore, go speak; the duke will hear thy voice;
And let not Bardolph's vital thread be cut
With edge of penny cord and vile reproach.
Speak, captain, for his life, and I will thee requite.   50

FLUELLEN   Ancient Pistol, I do partly understand your
meaning.

PISTOL   Why then, rejoice therefore.

FLUELLEN   Certainly, ancient, it is not a thing to rejoice at:

3.6 France: on the route back to Calais

Fluellen refuses to help Bardolph, arguing that discipline has to be maintained. Pistol leaves with an offensive comment and Gower tells Fluellen all about him: Pistol pretends to be a heroic soldier, but it is all a deception.

Character review: Fluellen (1)

What do we learn about Fluellen from this scene with Gower and Pistol? Think about:

(a) the impression he formed of Pistol from his behaviour at the bridge
(b) his words about Fortune
(c) his response to Pistol's plea on Bardolph's behalf
(d) his reaction to Pistol's parting insults
(e) his plans to speak to Pistol in the future.

RSC, 1975

58 & 60 figo ... The fig of Spain! *accompanied by a gesture in which the thumb was thrust between the fingers and jerked upwards, or flicked out from behind the teeth*

62 an arrant counterfeit rascal a complete fake and a crook

63 a bawd, cutpurse a pimp, and a pick-pocket

68 gull *someone easily tricked*

69–70 to grace ... to claim the glory for having been a soldier

71 are perfect in can recite without mistakes

72–73 learn you by rote learn by heart

73 services military exploits

74 sconce fort

74–75 came off proved himself

76 what terms ... what was the condition of the enemy

77 con learn

78 trick up ... decorate with newly-invented oaths

78–81 And what ... And it's amazing to see what effect a beard trimmed like the general's can have, or fearsome battle dress (**horrid suit of the camp**) ...

82 slanders of the age people who bring shame upon the times in which they live

86 ... a hole in his coat if I get the chance to expose him

88 speak with him from give him a report on

	for if, look you, he were my brother, I would desire the duke to use his good pleasure, and put him to execution; for discipline ought to be used.	55

PISTOL   Die and be damned! And figo for thy friendship!

FLUELLEN It is well.

PISTOL   The fig of Spain!   60

Exit

FLUELLEN Very good.

GOWER   Why, this is an arrant counterfeit rascal. I
          remember him now; a bawd, cutpurse.

FLUELLEN I'll assure you, 'a uttered as brave words at the
          bridge as you shall see in a summer's day. But it is   65
          very well; what he has spoke to me, that is well, I
          warrant you, when time is serve.

GOWER   Why, 't is a gull, a fool, a rogue, that now and
          then goes to the wars, to grace himself at his
          return into London under the form of a soldier.   70
          And such fellows are perfect in the great
          commanders' names, and they will learn you by
          rote where services were done; at such and such a
          sconce, at such a breach, at such a convoy; who
          came off bravely, who was shot, who disgraced,   75
          what terms the enemy stood on; and this they
          con perfectly in the phrase of war, which they
          trick up with new-tuned oaths. And what a beard
          of the general's cut and a horrid suit of the camp
          will do among foaming bottles and ale-washed   80
          wits is wonderful to be thought on. But you must
          learn to know such slanders of the age, or else
          you may be marvellously mistook.

FLUELLEN I tell you what, Captain Gower; I do perceive he is
          not the man that he would gladly make show to   85
          the world he is. If I find a hole in his coat, I will
          tell him my mind. (*Drum heard*) Hark you, the
          king is coming, and I must speak with him from
          the pridge.

3.6 France: on the route back to Calais

Henry arrives and Fluellen tells him about the successful capture of the bridge with no loss of life on the English side. When he hears that Bardolph has been condemned to death, Henry confirms that all such wrongdoers must be dealt with severely and the French treated with respect.

Activities °

Character review: Henry (13): the man and the King: leadership

A Why does Bardolph have to be executed? What has he done? Why is it being treated as a serious crime? Why can't Henry pardon him? (Re-read lines 102–118.)

B Henry's reaction to Fluellen's report that Bardolph is to be executed is one of the best examples of a scene which can be interpreted in many different ways. Try acting it first as though Henry is a cool, calm general, whose over-riding concern at this moment is to maintain discipline among his troops. Then act it as though Henry is powerfully affected by the realisation that he has to have his former companion executed. Which of the two interpretations seems to you to work better, bearing in mind what you already know about Henry?

C Following a decision made in the 1984 RSC stage version of *Henry V*, in which he had played the King, Kenneth Branagh decided to show the execution of Bardolph when he filmed the play five years later, even though there is no suggestion in Shakespeare's script that it happens on-stage. What can this add to the scene, and what possible drawbacks are there, in your opinion? (It will help to watch the scene in Branagh's film.)

95 **prave passages** brave fighting

95–96 **was have** did have

101 **perdition** loss

106–107 **bubukles, and whelks ...** sores, boils, pimples, inflammation ...

108 **plue** blue

111 **cut off** executed

113 **compelled** taken by force

115–116 **upbraided ... language** insulted or abused in scornful words

116–118 **for when lenity ... winner** when mercy and cruelty (*personified*) play for a kingdom, the kinder player will win

119 **by my habit** by my clothes (*as the chief herald of France, Montjoy would wear a distinctive tabard – a short-sleeved coat – with the royal arms on*)

Drum and Colours. Enter KING HENRY, GLOUCESTER, *and* Soldiers.

God pless your majesty!   90

KING HENRY How now, Fluellen, cam'st thou from the bridge?

FLUELLEN Ay, so please your majesty. The Duke of Exeter has
very gallantly maintained the pridge. The French
is gone off, look you; and there is gallant and
most prave passages. Marry, th' athversary was   95
have possession of the pridge, but he is enforced
to retire, and the Duke of Exeter is master of the
pridge. I can tell your majesty, the duke is a prave
man.

KING HENRY What men have you lost, Fluellen?   100

FLUELLEN The perdition of th' athversary hath been very
great, reasonable great. Marry, for my part, I think
the duke hath lost never a man, but one that is
like to be executed for robbing a church, one
Bardolph, if your majesty know the man. His face 105
is all bubukles, and whelks, and knobs, and
flames o' fire; and his lips blows at his nose, and
it is like a coal of fire, sometimes plue and
sometimes red; but his nose is executed, and his
fire's out.   110

KING HENRY We would have all such offenders so cut off. And
we give express charge, that in our marches
through the country, there be nothing compelled
from the villages, nothing taken but paid for,
none of the French upbraided or abused in   115
disdainful language; for when lenity and cruelty
play for a kingdom, the gentler gamester is the
soonest winner.

Tucket. Enter MONTJOY.

MONTJOY You know me by my habit.

KING HENRY Well then, I know thee: what shall I know of thee? 120

MONTJOY My master's mind.

3.6 France: on the route back to Calais

Montjoy the herald announces to Henry that the French are now ready to take their revenge on the English. Henry admits that his army is in a poor condition and that he would prefer to march on to Calais unimpeded.

Activities

Character review: Henry (14): the man and the King: loneliness

Talking about Bardolph's death, Kenneth Branagh wrote: 'For me it shed a new light on Henry's loneliness, marking so graphically, as it did, the end of a chapter of events which robbed him of every real friend he had, Falstaff, Scroop, and now symbolically all who remained to remind him of the Boar's Head life. He was now completely alone...Bardolph must die but not, I felt, without intense personal cost to the king...leaving the *man* Henry deeply shaken and the *king* Henry resolved.'

A Remind yourself who Falstaff and Scroop were. How far were they 'real friends' and why did Henry have to lose them?

B Study the scene of Bardolph's death in the Branagh film and talk about the ways in which the actor-director brings out Henry's personal feelings. Write an entry in Henry's private journal in which he writes about Bardolph's death.

C What evidence can you find in the play to support Branagh's view that Henry is (a) 'lonely'; (b) 'completely alone'; and (c) 'deeply shaken' by Bardolph's death? Is there any evidence which actually argues against these interpretations, in your opinion?

124 **did but sleep** were only sleeping

125 **advantage** waiting for the right opportunity

126 **rebuked** beaten

127–128 **not good to bruise ... ripe** we did not want to squeeze the poison from our wound until it was ready

128 **Now we speak upon our cue** now is the right time for us to speak

129 **England** *the King of England*

131 **sufferance** patience

132 **must proportion** must compensate for

134–135 **which in weight ...** compensating us fully for this is beyond his limited resources

136 **exchequer** treasury

effusion pouring out

137 **muster** gathering of forces

142 **So far ...** This is what my King has to say

149 **without impeachment** without being hindered

sooth truth

150 **'t is no wisdom** it is not wise

151 **of craft and vantage** who is strong and can take the initiative

152 **much enfeebled** greatly weakened

158 **air** *with a play on 'heir of France': the Dauphin*

KING HENRY Unfold it.

MONTJOY Thus says my king: Say thou to Harry of England:
Though we seemed dead, we did but sleep:
advantage is a better soldier than rashness. Tell   125
him we could have rebuked him at Harfleur, but
that we thought not good to bruise an injury till it
were full ripe. Now we speak upon our cue, and
our voice is imperial: England shall repent his
folly, see his weakness, and admire our   130
sufferance. Bid him therefore consider of his
ransom, which must proportion the losses we
have borne, the subjects we have lost, the disgrace
we have digested; which in weight to re-answer,
his pettiness would bow under. For our losses, his   135
exchequer is too poor; for the effusion of our
blood, the muster of his kingdom too faint a
number; and for our disgrace, his own person,
kneeling at our feet, but a weak and worthless
satisfaction. To this add defiance: and tell him, for   140
conclusion, he hath betrayed his followers, whose
condemnation is pronounced. So far my king and
master; so much my office.

KING HENRY What is thy name? I know thy quality.

MONTJOY Montjoy.   145

KING HENRY Thou dost thy office fairly. Turn thee back,
And tell thy king I do not seek him now,
But could be willing to march on to Calais
Without impeachment: for, to say the sooth,
Though 't is no wisdom to confess so much   150
Unto an enemy of craft and vantage,
My people are with sickness much enfeebled,
My numbers lessened, and those few I have
Almost no better than so many French;
Who when they were in health, I tell thee, herald,   155
I thought upon one pair of English legs
Did march three Frenchmen. Yet, forgive me, God,
That I do brag thus! This your air of France
Hath blown that vice in me, I must repent.
Go therefore, tell thy master here I am;   160

3.7 France: the French camp near Agincourt

Henry rejects the suggestion of paying a ransom and declares that the English are ready to fight if they have to. As night falls, the English march towards the bridge and prepare to camp on the other side. Near Agincourt, the French nobles long for dawn when they can do battle with the English.

Activities

Character review: Montjoy (1)

Montjoy is the French herald and usually speaks on someone else's behalf. In this scene he is bringing a message from the French King.

1. What are the key points of Montjoy's message?
2. Which features of Montjoy's language suggest that he is delivering a prepared speech, well rehearsed? Match each of the following with examples printed below:
   (a) balanced sentences
   (b) proverbs
   (c) triplets (phrases grouped in threes)
   (d) repeated patterns
   (e) vivid imagery.

   - 'For our losses… satisfaction'
   - 'to bruise an injury… ripe'
   - 'advantage… rashness'
   - 'the losses we have borne… digested'
   - 'Though we seemed… sleep'

161 **trunk** body

169 **tawny** reddish-brown

169–170 **Discolour** *like changing the background* (**ground**) *of a coat of arms from tawny to red*

179 **encamp ourselves** make camp

1 **Would** I wish

3 **an … armour** a suit of armour

My ransom is this frail and worthless trunk,
My army but a weak and sickly guard;
Yet, God before, tell him we will come on,
Though France himself and such another neighbour
Stand in our way. There's for thy labour,   165
    Montjoy. (*Gives a purse of gold*)
Go, bid thy master well advise himself.
If we may pass, we will. If we be hindered,
We shall your tawny ground with your red blood
Discolour. And so, Montjoy, fare you well.   170
The sum of all our answer is but this.
We would not seek a battle, as we are;
Nor, as we are, we say we will not shun it.
So tell your master.

MONTJOY   I shall deliver so. Thanks to your highness.   175

Exit

GLOUCESTER I hope they will not come upon us now.

KING HENRY We are in God's hands, brother, not in theirs.
March to the bridge; it now draws toward night.
Beyond the river we'll encamp ourselves,
And on to-morrow bid them march away.   180

Exeunt

Scene 7

The French camp, near Agincourt.

Enter the CONSTABLE OF FRANCE, *the* LORD RAMBURES,
ORLEANS, DAUPHIN, *with others.*

CONSTABLE   Tut! I have the best armour of the world. Would it
were day!

ORLEANS   You have an excellent armour; but let my horse
have his due.

CONSTABLE   It is the best horse of Europe.   5

ORLEANS   Will it never be morning?

France: the French camp near Agincourt

As the French impatiently await morning, the Dauphin speaks adoringly of his horse: he even once wrote a sonnet in his praise.

Actors' interpretations: contrasting the English and the French

In groups of six, act out the conclusion of Scene 6 and the opening of Scene 7 (from 'I hope…' to '…in the world') in ways that will bring out as many different interpretations as you can. Try each time to contrast the English and the French. For example, the English might be exhausted and the French lively; the English optimistic and the French downbeat; the English full of comradeship, the French bickering among themselves. Show your preferred versions to other groups and discuss which of the contrasts you found most interesting.

11–12 **I will not change …** I would not swap my horse for any which merely treads upon the ground with its hooves (**pasterns**); *the Dauphin implies that his own horse flies (see line 14)*

13–14 **as if his entrails …** as if he were stuffed with hair, like a tennis ball

14 **le cheval volant …** the flying horse, the Pegasus (*a winged horse in Greek mythology*), with nostrils breathing fire

18 **pipe of Hermes** *Hermes, the Greek messenger of the gods, charmed asleep the monster Argus with his pipe*

21 **Perseus** *The Greek hero Perseus was riding Pegasus when he rescued Andromeda.*

21–22 **air and fire …** *these were the light, upward-soaring elements*

25 **jades** poor quality, worn-out horses

28 **palfreys** *the Dauphin rides a lady's horse*

29–30 **his countenance …** his look obliges people to recognise him as their superior

32–33 **from the rising …** from dawn till dusk

33–34 **vary … praise** praise him in a variety of ways

36 **argument** a subject for discussion

37 **reason** debate

DAUPHIN	My Lord of Orleans, and my lord high constable, you talk of horse and armour?
ORLEANS	You are as well provided of both as any prince in the world.

(line) 10

DAUPHIN	What a long night is this! I will not change my horse with any that treads but on four pasterns. Ça, ha! He bounds from the earth, as if his entrails were hairs; le cheval volant, the Pegasus, chez les narines de feu! When I bestride him, I soar, I am a hawk. He trots the air. The earth sings when he touches it. The basest horn of his hoof is more musical than the pipe of Hermes.

15

ORLEANS	He's of the colour of the nutmeg.
DAUPHIN	And of the heat of the ginger. It is a beast for Perseus. He is pure air and fire, and the dull elements of earth and water never appear in him, but only in patient stillness while his rider mounts him. He is indeed a horse, and all other jades you may call beasts.

20

25

CONSTABLE	Indeed, my lord, it is a most absolute and excellent horse.
DAUPHIN	It is the prince of palfreys. His neigh is like the bidding of a monarch and his countenance enforces homage.

30

ORLEANS	No more, cousin.
DAUPHIN	Nay, the man hath no wit that cannot, from the rising of the lark to the lodging of the lamb, vary deserved praise on my palfrey. It is a theme as fluent as the sea. Turn the sands into eloquent tongues, and my horse is argument for them all. 'T is a subject for a sovereign to reason on, and for a sovereign's sovereign to ride on; and for the world, familiar to us and unknown, to lay apart their particular functions and wonder at him. I once writ a sonnet in his praise, and began thus: 'Wonder of nature' –

35

40

3.7 France: the French camp near Agincourt

The Constable and the Dauphin start to bicker with each other and engage in a sharp exchange which involves sexual innuendo about horses and mistresses.

Activities

Shakespeare's language: bawdy word-play

The conversation between the Dauphin and the Constable is full of bawdy word-play, mainly *double-entendres* (double meanings) to do with horses and mistresses, riding and sex.

1. Find all the *double-entendres* and discuss their meanings. How clever are they, in your opinion?
2. Discuss each of the following statements and grade it from 1 (strongly disagree) to 5 (strongly agree):

   The bawdy word-play in this scene is:
   (a) amusing
   (b) not funny, merely smutty – worse than you get in *Carry On* films
   (c) exactly what you might expect from the macho, boastful French as they are portrayed in this play.
3. Finally, decide whether you, as directors, would include this section of the scene or cut it.

45 **courser** swift horse

46 **bears well** carries your weight well. *This begins a series of double entendres (double meanings), where the comments can apply either to horses or to mistresses.*

47 **prescript** appropriate, prescribed

48 **particular** private, exclusively my property

50 **shrewdly** sharply, in a bad temper

52 **bridled** wearing (1) a horse's bridle, (2) a scold's bridle (*worn by 'shrewish' women*)

53 **belike** perhaps

54 **kern** Irish foot soldier

   hose ... breeches

55 **straight strossers** tight trousers (*here:* bare legs)

58 **warily** carefully

60 **I had as lief ...** I would rather have had a **jade** (= (1) old horse, (2) prostitute) for my mistress

61–62 **wears his own hair** doesn't need a wig

65–66 **'Le chien ... '** The dog turns to its own vomit and the sow which was washed to her wallowing in the mire (*from the Epistle of Peter in the New Testament of the Bible*).

69 **so little kin ...** so unrelated to the point you were making

ORLEANS	I have heard a sonnet begin so to one's mistress.
DAUPHIN	Then did they imitate that which I composed to my courser, for my horse is my mistress. 45
ORLEANS	Your mistress bears well.
DAUPHIN	Me well; which is the prescript praise and perfection of a good and particular mistress.
CONSTABLE	Nay, for methought yesterday your mistress shrewdly shook your back. 50
DAUPHIN	So perhaps did yours.
CONSTABLE	Mine was not bridled.
DAUPHIN	O then belike she was old and gentle; and you rode, like a kern of Ireland, your French hose off, and in your strait strossers. 55
CONSTABLE	You have good judgement in horsemanship.
DAUPHIN	Be warned by me, then: they that ride so and ride not warily, fall into foul bogs. I had rather have my horse to my mistress.
CONSTABLE	I had as lief have my mistress a jade. 60
DAUPHIN	I tell thee, constable, my mistress wears his own hair.
CONSTABLE	I could make as true a boast as that, if I had a sow to my mistress.
DAUPHIN	'Le chien est retourné à son propre vomissement, et la truie lavée au bourbier'; thou makest use of anything. 65
CONSTABLE	Yet do I not use my horse for my mistress, or any such proverb so little kin to the purpose.
RAMBURES	My lord constable, the armour that I saw in your tent to-night, are those stars or suns upon it? 70
CONSTABLE	Stars, my lord.

France: the French camp near Agincourt

After the Dauphin has left the tent to put his armour on, Orleans and the Constable discuss him.

Activities

Shakespeare's language: snappy dialogue

The dialogue of rapid short exchanges in this part of the scene is an example of *stichomythia*. This was often found in the plays of the ancient Greeks where it offered a contrast to longer verse speeches and also helped to create excitement or tension.

In pairs, read a section of the dialogue following the Dauphin's exit (lines 90–123) as snappily as you can, to bring out the tense nature of the bickering. A useful technique is cue-biting, in which each actor cuts into the previous speech before it has quite finished.

Rehearse the dialogue several times and discuss what effect on the tone and meaning was achieved by the cue-biting.

74 **... shall not want** will not be short of stars (*implying that he will not lose any honour*)

75–76 **a many superfluously ... away** too many that you don't need (or don't deserve); it would be more honourable if you lost some

77–78 **Even as ... dismounted** It's the same with you praising your horse; he would trot better if you unloaded some of the boasts

79 **his desert** what he deserves

82–83 **faced out of my way** (1) driven away by the enemy faces, (2) made to feel 'put out'

84 **fain** like to

85 **go to hazard ...** have a bet

87 **go yourself to hazard** put yourself in danger

95 **tread out** stamp on

98 **... still be doing** he's always doing something (*ironic*)

DAUPHIN	Some of them will fall to-morrow, I hope.	
CONSTABLE	And yet my sky shall not want.	
DAUPHIN	That may be, for you bear a many superfluously, and 't were more honour some were away.	75
CONSTABLE	Even as your horse bears your praises; who would trot as well, were some of your brags dismounted.	
DAUPHIN	Would I were able to load him with his desert! Will it never be day? I will trot to-morrow a mile, and my way shall be paved with English faces.	80
CONSTABLE	I will not say so, for fear I should be faced out of my way; but I would it were morning; for I would fain be about the ears of the English.	
RAMBURES	Who will go to hazard with me for twenty prisoners?	85
CONSTABLE	You must first go yourself to hazard, ere you have them.	
DAUPHIN	'T is midnight; I'll go arm myself.	

Exit

ORLEANS	The Dauphin longs for morning.	90
RAMBURES	He longs to eat the English.	
CONSTABLE	I think he will eat all he kills.	
ORLEANS	By the white hand of my lady, he's a gallant prince.	
CONSTABLE	Swear by her foot, that she may tread out the oath.	95
ORLEANS	He is simply the most active gentleman of France.	
CONSTABLE	Doing is activity, and he will still be doing.	
ORLEANS	He never did harm, that I heard of.	

3.7 France: the French camp near Agincourt

The Constable alleges that the Dauphin's claim to be a great soldier is mere boastfulness, but Orleans continues to defend the Dauphin's reputation.

Activities

Character review: the Dauphin (3)

Orleans is the Dauphin's cousin and seems to admire him. Imagine that he had written a letter to another relative about the Dauphin's qualities and had then left it lying around in the tent. The Constable finds it and, before sending it off with a messenger, corrects what Orleans has written, adding his own personal views which are not so flattering. In pairs, re-read lines 90–123. Then one person writes Orleans' letter and the other person 'corrects' it in different ink.

109–110 **never any body ...** nobody has ever seen the Dauphin's courage except for his servant (*whom he presumably beats*)

110–111 **'Tis a hooded ...** *expressions from hawking: when the hood is removed from the hawk and it sees its prey, it beats its wings (***bates** = (1) beats, (2) becomes less, *i.e., behaves like a coward*)

112 **Ill will ...** people with a grudge against someone never speak well of them

117 **Well placed ...** what an appropriate proverb: you associate your friend the Dauphin with the devil

120–121 **by how much ... shot** because a fool shoots his arrow too hastily

122 **shot over** gone too far

124 **overshot** outshot, beaten in shooting

CONSTABLE	Nor will do none to-morrow. He will keep that good name still.	100
ORLEANS	I know him to be valiant.	
CONSTABLE	I was told that by one that knows him better than you.	
ORLEANS	What's he?	105
CONSTABLE	Marry, he told me so himself; and he said he cared not who knew it.	
ORLEANS	He needs not; it is no hidden virtue in him.	
CONSTABLE	By my faith, sir, but it is; never any body saw it but his lackey. 'T is a hooded valour, and when it appears, it will bate.	110
ORLEANS	Ill will never said well.	
CONSTABLE	I will cap that proverb with 'There is flattery in friendship'.	
ORLEANS	And I will take up that with 'Give the devil his due'.	115
CONSTABLE	Well placed: there stands your friend for the devil. Have at the very eye of that proverb with 'A pox of the devil.'	
ORLEANS	You are the better at proverbs, by how much 'A fool's bolt is soon shot.'	120
CONSTABLE	You have shot over.	
ORLEANS	'T is not the first time you were overshot.	

Enter a Messenger.

MESSENGER	My lord high constable, the English lie within fifteen hundred paces of your tents.	125
CONSTABLE	Who hath measured the ground?	
MESSENGER	The Lord Grandpré.	

3.7 France: the French camp near Agincourt

The French ridicule the English, claiming that they behave like foolhardy dogs with no sense of danger. Orleans boasts about the hordes of English prisoners they will all take in the morning's battle.

Activities

Character review: the French (3)

Use the French comments on the English (from 'Alas, poor Harry...' to the end of the scene) to compose a pre-battle speech to be delivered by the Constable, encouraging his troops by reminding them what a pathetic and ridiculous army they are facing. If you are feeling confident, you might try composing it in blank verse (see pages 252–253.)

RSC, 1994

131 **peevish** foolish

132 **mope** wander around

 fat-brained stupid

133 **out of his knowledge** (1) away from the world he knows, (2) leaving his common sense behind

134 **apprehension** (1) fear, (2) common sense

140 **mastiffs** *dogs used for bear-baiting (see lines 141–143) and known for their courage*

142 **curs** *an insulting term for a dog*

 winking with their eyes shut

146 **do sympathise with** resemble

147 **in robustious ... coming on** in their boisterous and violent attacks

151 **shrewdly** seriously, severely

153 **stomachs** inclinations

CONSTABLE   A valiant and most expert gentleman. Would it
             were day! Alas, poor Harry of England! He longs
             not for the dawning as we do.   130

ORLEANS   What a wretched and peevish fellow is this King
             of England, to mope with his fat-brained
             followers so far out of his knowledge!

CONSTABLE   If the English had any apprehension, they would
             run away.   135

ORLEANS   That they lack; for if their heads had any
             intellectual armour, they could never wear such
             heavy head-pieces.

RAMBURES   That island of England breeds very valiant
             creatures; their mastiffs are of unmatchable   140
             courage.

ORLEANS   Foolish curs, that run winking into the mouth of
             a Russian bear and have their heads crushed like
             rotten apples! You may as well say, that's a valiant
             flea that dare eat his breakfast on the lip of a lion. 145

CONSTABLE   Just, just; and the men do sympathise with the
             mastiffs in robustious and rough coming on,
             leaving their wits with their wives: and then give
             them great meals of beef and iron and steel, they
             will eat like wolves and fight like devils.   150

ORLEANS   Ay, but these English are shrewdly out of beef.

CONSTABLE   Then we shall find to-morrow they have only
             stomachs to eat and none to fight. Now is it time
             to arm. Come, shall we about it?

ORLEANS   It is not two o'clock: but, let me see, by ten   155
             We shall have each a hundred Englishmen.

                                                    Exeunt

Exam practice

Themes: heroism

In Kenneth Branagh's film version, Pistol, Bardolph and Nym are among the crowd being encouraged by Henry's 'Once more...' speech, but, as the rest of the army attack the breach, they run off in the opposite direction.

A   Not all of this play is about heroism. Note down all the evidence from 3.2.1–55 which shows that Pistol and the others are cowards. Do you sympathise with them or despise them?

B   Act from the end of Henry's speech through to the beginning of the scene which follows (3.1.31–3.2.26) and, if you can, watch the scene as Branagh's film portrays it. Then, in groups, decide how far you agree with the following statements, grading each one from 1 (strongly disagree) to 5 (strongly agree):

1. The opening of Scene 2 shows that Henry's heroic words will not work with everybody.
2. A production of the play ought to make it clear that Pistol and the others are in the minority: most of the army have behaved heroically.
3. The behaviour of Pistol and his cowardly companions should be used in a production to mock Henry's call for courage and patriotism (this mockery is known as 'ironic deflation').
4. There will always be cowards in a war; that should not affect our admiration for Henry and the men who follow him courageously.

C   In many productions the juxtaposition (placing next to each other) of the end of 3.1 and the opening of 3.2 is used to undermine Henry's speech and mock the idea of heroism. Where else in the play so far have you noticed any other interesting juxtapositions? (Look back at the activity on page 104, for example.) You might consider the possible effects on stage of juxtaposing the ends and openings of the following pairs of scenes: 1.1 and 1.2; 2.2 and 2.3; 3.3 and 3.4; 3.4 and 3.5; 3.6 and 3.7. In each case, act out the last few lines of the first scene of the pair and the first few lines of the second. Then discuss the ways in which the second scene might be used to offer a new perspective on the first.

Character review: Henry (15): opinions on his leadership

Three features of Henry's leadership in this Act can be interpreted in very different ways:
- his words to the Governor of Harfleur (3.3): are they tough but fair, or ruthless and savage?
- his reaction to the death sentence on Bardolph (3.6): does Henry come across as disciplined or heartless?
- his response to Montjoy's defiant speech (3.6): is he being honest and frank, or pessimistic and giving too much away?

1. Discuss your own views of each of these in groups of four (looking back at the activities on pages 82 and 98).

2. Then continue the journal entries of Exeter (who praises Henry's actions) and the cynical lord (who questions them), giving each man's view on the three features you have discussed.

Plot review (11): progress of the English and French armies

1. The English newspaper *The Chronicle* decides to publish a supplement updating its readers on the progress of the English army since its arrival in France. In groups, with different people responsible for different sections, create a front page which covers the army's progress from Harfleur to its present position (the latest news is that they have seized the bridge over the River Ternoise at Blangy – see the map on page 88).

   In addition to a clear campaign map, you might include articles on:
   - the French attempts to offer a deal (Prologue 3, 28-32)
   - the siege of Harfleur (3.1)
   - the disputes over tactics (with contrasting opinions from Fluellen and Macmorris: 3.2)
   - Henry's words to the Governor of Harfleur (3.3)
   - the army's progress over the Somme and their capture of the bridge over the Ternoise with no casualties (3.6)
   - discipline in the army and the hanging of Bardolph (3.6)
   - the visit from the French herald (3.6).

2. Other groups might work on the front page of a French newspaper, *Fleur-de-lys*, which is critical of their army's apparent inaction. Include articles in which you:
   - disapprove of the King's offers to the English (Prologue 3, 28–32)
   - are angry at the loss of Harfleur and the Dauphin's lack of readiness (3.3.44–50)
   - wonder whether the French Princess is taking the whole thing seriously enough (3.4)
   - suggest that your leaders are underestimating the enemy (3.5)
   - call upon particular lords to do something (3.5.40–45)
   - are amazed that the English have been allowed to march through France on their way back to Calais, almost unmolested (3.6).

Add a map, more up-to-date than the English one, which shows that the French army are attempting to cut off the English advance and have camped near Agincourt.

Plot review (12): time-chart

Add to the time-chart that you began at the end of Act 1, including the siege of Harfleur.

4 Prologue

The Chorus asks us to imagine the night before Agincourt. While the confident French, impatient for morning, play dice for the prisoners they expect to capture, Henry is walking around the English camp, cheering his men.

Activities

Shakespeare's language: creating atmosphere

The Chorus' speech creates a vivid picture of the night before the battle: darkness, distant sounds and the contrasting spirits of the two armies. Read the whole speech aloud.

1. Find words to describe the atmosphere that Shakespeare creates here.
2. How does the language help to create that atmosphere? Talk about (a) the onomatopoeic effects of the *m* and *s* sounds (lines 1–7); (b) the effect of the rhythm of line 13; (c) the effect of the assonance in line 15.
3. Imagine a film in which the speech was heard over a sequence of different visual images. Sketch roughly a series of frames to represent appropriate shots and label them to show where in the speech they should appear. (Don't forget the possibilities of 'panning', where the camera moves across a scene in a single shot.)
4. In groups, create freeze-frames for the lines which represent (a) the French; (b) the English around their camp-fires; and (c) Henry encouraging his men. Form into the tableaux as the speech is read.

1 **entertain conjecture** allow yourselves to imagine
2 **poring dark** tiring darkness
3 **wide vessel** vast container
5 **stilly** softly
6 **fixed sentinels** guards at posts
8 **paly** (1) pale, (2) in vertical lines
9 **umbered** dark-coloured, shadowed
12 **accomplishing** completing the armouring of
14 **note** (1) sound, (2) notification
17 **secure** over-confident
18 **over-lusty** over-cheerful
19 **Do ... play at dice** *The French are gambling, with the English prisoners they will capture as their stakes.*
20–22 **chide** complain at; the night is slow-moving (**tardy-gaited**), and compared to an ugly witch
23 **watchful** used by the men who are (1) keeping watch, (2) awake
24 **inly ruminate** inwardly 'chew over', think about
25 **gesture** bearing; appearance and behaviour
26 **Investing** consisting of
32 **host** army
35 **note** sign
37–38 **Nor doth he ... night** neither have his cheeks lost any of their colour, even though he is tired, having been awake all night

Act 4

4

Prologue

Enter CHORUS.

CHORUS   Now entertain conjecture of a time
When creeping murmur and the poring dark
Fills the wide vessel of the universe.
From camp to camp, through the foul womb of night,
The hum of either army stilly sounds,   5
That the fixed sentinels almost receive
The secret whispers of each other's watch.
Fire answers fire, and through their paly flames
Each battle sees the other's umbered face.
Steed threatens steed, in high and boastful neighs   10
Piercing the night's dull ear, and from the tents
The armourers, accomplishing the knights,
With busy hammers closing rivets up,
Give dreadful note of preparation.
The country cocks do crow, the clocks do toll,   15
And the third hour of drowsy morning name.
Proud of their numbers and secure in soul,
The confident and over-lusty French
Do the low-rated English play at dice;
And chide the cripple tardy-gaited night   20
Who, like a foul and ugly witch, doth limp
So tediously away. The poor condemnéd English,
Like sacrifices, by their watchful fires
Sit patiently and inly ruminate
The morning's danger, and their gesture sad,   25
Investing lank-lean cheeks and war-worn coats,
Presenteth them unto the gazing moon
So many horrid ghosts. O now, who will behold
The royal captain of this ruined band
Walking from watch to watch, from tent to tent, 30
Let him cry 'Praise and glory on his head!'
For forth he goes and visits all his host,
Bids them good morrow with a modest smile
And calls them brothers, friends and countrymen.
Upon his royal face there is no note   35
How dread an army hath enrounded him;
Nor doth he dedicate one jot of colour
Unto the weary and all-watchéd night,
But freshly looks and over-bears attaint

4.1 France: the English camp near Agincourt

The Chorus completes the picture of Henry visiting his men the night before the battle and he enters, explaining to his brother Gloucester that there is always some good to be derived from a bad situation.

39–40 **overbears attaint ... semblance** he hides any sign of tiredness by looking cheerful

42 **Beholding him ...** as soon as they see him, they are comforted by his appearance

43–44 **A largess ... one** Henry looks at everybody and generously provides the same kind of universal gift (**largess**) as the sun does.

45 **mean and gentle** common people and nobles

46 **as may unworthiness define** as far as our unworthy efforts (as actors) can show it

47 **touch** impression

50 **foils** light swords used in the theatre

53 **Minding** calling to mind

mockeries poor imitations

5 **... observingly distil it out** if men would look for the essential goodness in it and extract it

7 **husbandry** management

9 **admonishing** warning us

10 **dress us fairly ...** prepare ourselves properly for what is to come (**our end**)

12 **make a moral of ...** find some good lesson in

15 **churlish turf** rough ground

16 **This lodging ...** I prefer this accommodation

With cheerful semblance and sweet majesty;   40
That every wretch, pining and pale before,
Beholding him, plucks comfort from his looks.
A largess universal like the sun
His liberal eye doth give to every one,
Thawing cold fear, that mean and gentle all,   45
Behold, as may unworthiness define,
A little touch of Harry in the night.
And so our scene must to the battle fly;
Where – O for pity! – we shall much disgrace
With four or five most vile and ragged foils,   50
Right ill-disposed in brawl ridiculous,
The name of Agincourt. Yet sit and see,
Minding true things by what their mockeries be.

Exit

Scene 1

The English camp at Agincourt.

Enter KING HENRY, BEDFORD, *and* GLOUCESTER.

KING HENRY   Gloucester, 't is true that we are in great danger;
The greater therefore should our courage be.
Good morrow, brother Bedford. God Almighty!
There is some soul of goodness in things evil,
Would men observingly distil it out,   5
For our bad neighbour makes us early stirrers,
Which is both healthful and good husbandry.
Besides, they are our outward consciences,
And preachers to us all, admonishing
That we should dress us fairly for our end.   10
Thus may we gather honey from the weed,
And make a moral of the devil himself.

Enter ERPINGHAM.

Good morrow, old Sir Thomas Erpingham!
A good soft pillow for that good white head
Were better than a churlish turf of France.   15

ERPINGHAM   Not so, my liege. This lodging likes me better,
Since I may say 'Now lie I like a king.'

4.1 France: the English camp near Agincourt

Having disguised himself in Sir Thomas Erpingham's cloak, Henry is not recognised by Pistol, who questions him about his rank.

Activities

Actors' interpretations: Henry and Pistol

Many productions use Henry's encounter with Pistol as an opportunity to inject some lightness and comedy into the dark and tense opening moments of Act 4.

1. Read the scene in pairs and decide which aspects of it could be comic. Think about:
   - Pistol creeping about in the middle of the night (is he up to no good?)
   - Henry fumbling with his cloak so that he won't be recognised by his old companion
   - Henry perhaps struggling to think up a name and inspirationally coming up with Harry le Roy
   - Pistol's ignorance of French ('A Cornish name.')
   - a possibly dramatic exit by Pistol.

   Act the scene out as comically as you can.

2. Now look through the scene again to discover how it might be played more seriously.
   - Might Pistol be stealing from a sleeping comrade when Henry stumbles upon him?

continued on page 122

18 **pains** discomforts

19 **Upon example** to use the experience as something to learn from (and refer to later in some formal speech)

20–23 **And when the mind ...** When our brain is enlivened (**quickened**), our other organs – though previously deadened (**defunct**) with sleep – throw off their drowsiness and take on a new lightness (**legerity**), like a snake after it has cast its old skin (**slough**)

25 **Commend me to** send my greeting to

26 **anon** immediately

27 **pavilion** army tent

31 **I and my bosom ...** I have to be alone with my thoughts

34 **God-a-mercy** may God be merciful to you ('God have mercy')

35 **Qui va là?** Who goes there?

38 **popular** an ordinary person (*'of the people'*)

39 **gentleman of a company** a gentleman volunteer

40 **Trail'st thou ...** Are you an infantryman? *Soldiers would carry their pikes by trailing them along the ground*

puissant powerful

44 **bawcock ... heart of gold** a fine person *(see 3.2.23)* ... a perfect man

KING HENRY 'T is good for men to love their present pains
Upon example; so the spirit is eased:
And when the mind is quickened, out of doubt,   20
The organs, though defunct and dead before,
Break up their drowsy grave and newly move,
With casted slough and fresh legerity.
Lend me thy cloak, Sir Thomas. Brothers both,
Commend me to the princes in our camp;   25
Do my good morrow to them, and anon
Desire them all to my pavilion.

GLOUCESTER We shall, my liege.

ERPINGHAM Shall I attend your grace?

KING HENRY   No, my good knight;
Go with my brothers to my lords of England.   30
I and my bosom must debate awhile,
And then I would no other company.

ERPINGHAM The Lord in heaven bless thee, noble Harry!

KING HENRY God-a-mercy, old heart! Thou speak'st cheerfully.

Exeunt all but KING.

Enter PISTOL.

PISTOL Qui va là?   35

KING HENRY A friend.

PISTOL Discuss unto me; art thou officer?
Or art thou base, common, and popular?

KING HENRY I am a gentleman of a company.

PISTOL Trail'st thou the puissant pike?   40

KING HENRY Even so. What are you?

PISTOL As good a gentleman as the emperor.

KING HENRY Then you are a better than the king.

PISTOL The king's a bawcock, and a heart of gold,

4.1 France: the English camp near Agincourt

Still not realising who he is speaking to, Pistol expresses his affection for the King. The disguised Henry introduces himself as Harry le Roy, a Welshman, and Pistol leaves, threatening revenge on Fluellen.

Activities

- Does Pistol suddenly become sincere when he speaks affectionately about Henry as 'a bawcock...'?
- How does Henry react to hearing such affectionate words from an old friend he rejected when he became King?

  Bring out all these elements as you act the scene again, this time seriously.

3. Discuss which of the two versions you prefer: which one fits your overall interpretation of the play. Could it work to mix the two interpretations, making the scene part-comic, part-serious?

Actors' interpretations: staging the scene

The first part of this scene (lines 1–34) involves Henry and his nobles; the second part (lines 35–63), Henry and Pistol; the third (lines 64–85), Fluellen and Gower.

Look at the design of Shakespeare's stage on page 238 and discuss these questions:

- On which parts of the stage might the three sections take place?
- Where might Pistol appear from?
- Where could Fluellen and Gower be, so that they do not see Henry but he hears them?

45 **imp of fame** fame's child

48 **bully** another term of affection, like bawcock *(see A Midsummer Night's Dream, 4.2.18)*

49 **Harry le Roy** le roi *in French means 'the king'; Pistol thinks it sounds Cornish*

51 **a Welshman** *Henry, formerly the Prince of Wales, was born in Monmouth. Shakespeare might have been flattering his Tudor Queen with her Welsh ancestors (see 4.7.93–110).*

52 **Know'st thou** Do you know ...?

54–55 **... his leek ...** *As one of the national emblems of Wales, Welshmen would wear a leek on Saint David's (Davy's) day (1 March).*

54 **pate** head

59 **kinsman** relative; or fellow Welshman

60 **The figo** 'the fig of Spain!' *(see 3.6.58)*

63 **it sorts well with** it suits, it goes well with

65 **fewer** more quietly

65–66 **It is the greatest ...** It is the most amazing thing

67 **prerogatifes** correct principles

69–70 **Pompey the Great** *Gnæus Pompeius (106–48 BC) was a great Roman general.*

70 **I warrant you** I assure you

71 **tiddle taddle ...** nattering

	A lad of life, an imp of fame;	45
	Of parents good, of fist most valiant.	
	I kiss his dirty shoe, and from heart-string	
	I love the lovely bully. What is thy name?	

KING HENRY   Harry le Roy.

PISTOL   Le Roy? A Cornish name. Art thou of Cornish crew?   50

KING HENRY   No, I am a Welshman.

PISTOL   Know'st thou Fluellen?

KING HENRY   Yes.

PISTOL   Tell him, I'll knock his leek about his pate
Upon Saint Davy's day.   55

KING HENRY   Do not you wear your dagger in your cap that
day, lest he knock that about yours.

PISTOL   Art thou his friend?

KING HENRY   And his kinsman too.

PISTOL   The figo for thee, them!   60

KING HENRY   I thank you. God be with you!

PISTOL   My name is Pistol called.

KING HENRY   It sorts well with your fierceness.

Exit PISTOL

Enter FLUELLEN *and* GOWER *from different sides.*

GOWER   Captain Fluellen!

FLUELLEN   So! In the name of Jesu Christ, speak fewer. It is   65
the greatest admiration in the universal world,
when the true and ancient prerogatifes and laws
of the wars is not kept. If you would take the
pains but to examine the wars of Pompey the
Great, you shall find, I warrant you, that there is   70
no tiddle taddle or pibble pabble in Pompey's

4.1 France: the English camp near Agincourt

Overhearing Fluellen's comments to Gower about maintaining discipline and quiet in the army, Henry privately praises the Welshman and then, still disguised, encounters three English soldiers, Bates, Court and Williams.

Activities

Character review: Fluellen (2)

Henry describes Fluellen's words and behaviour as 'a little out of fashion' (line 83). Look at the exchange with Gower (lines 64–82) and at Fluellen's earlier appearances and find evidence to support the idea that Fluellen prefers the old ways of doing things (such as fighting wars) and represents the traditional, old-fashioned values, such as loyalty and discipline. Look particularly at:

- 3.2.19 (his attitude to the cowards)
- 3.2.59–104 (his belief that wars should be fought following the Roman model)
- 3.6.1–16 (his admiration for courageous leaders)
- 3.6.54–57 (his support of strict discipline)
- 4.1.65–80 (his dislike of undisciplined troops).

What other qualities have you observed in him?

74 **sobriety** seriousness, orderliness

modesty correct behaviour

77–78 **prating coxcomb** chattering idiot

83 **out of fashion** odd, quaint, unconventional

96 **good old commander** *Erpingham was in his late 50s, commander of the bowmen.*

98 **estate** situation

camp I warrant you, you shall find the ceremonies
of the wars, and the cares of it, and the forms of
it, and the sobriety of it, and the modesty of it, to
be otherwise.   75

GOWER   Why, the enemy is loud; you hear him all night.

FLUELLEN   If the enemy is an ass and a fool and a prating
coxcomb, is it meet, think you, that we should
also, look you, be an ass and a fool and a prating
coxcomb? In your own conscience now?   80

GOWER   I will speak lower.

FLUELLEN   I pray you and beseech you that you will.

Exeunt GOWER *and* FLUELLEN

KING HENRY Though it appear a little out of fashion,
There is much care and valour in this
Welshman.   85

Enter three soldiers, JOHN BATES, ALEXANDER COURT, *and* MICHAEL
WILLIAMS.

COURT   Brother John Bates, is not that the morning
which breaks yonder?

BATES   I think it be; but we have no great cause to desire
the approach of day.

WILLIAMS   We see yonder the beginning of the day, but I   90
think we shall never see the end of it. Who goes
there?

KING HENRY A friend.

WILLIAMS   Under what captain serve you?

KING HENRY Under Sir Thomas Erpingham.   95

WILLIAMS   A good old commander and a most kind
gentleman. I pray you, what thinks he of our
estate?

4.1 France: the English camp near Agincourt

Discussing their likely fate in the coming battle, Henry makes the point that the King experiences the same emotions as ordinary men, including fear. Soon they begin to discuss whether they are fighting for a just cause.

Activities

Character review: Henry (16): the man and the King

Re-read Henry's speech which begins '...the king is but a man, as I am' (lines 103–115).

1. Note down the examples he gives to support his claim that, once he has removed all the trappings of royalty, he is like ordinary men.

2. What do you think he means by his statement that the King's 'affections are higher mounted' (lines 108–109) than ordinary people's? Do you agree with him?

3. Find moments from earlier in the play to support Henry's claim that he experiences the same emotions as ordinary people.

99–100 **Even as ... day** Just like men shipwrecked on a sand-bank who expect to be washed off it by the next tide

102 **nor it is not meet** and it would not be the right thing (for him to tell the King)

105 **the element shows** the sky appears

106 **conditions** properties

106–108 **His ceremonies ...** When he removes all the trappings of royalty ...

109–110 **when they stoop ...** *An expression from hawking: when the King experiences baser emotions, they are just like common people's.*

112 **... of the same relish** The king experiences fears in the same way as ordinary people.

113 **no man should possess him** the King should not be caught looking frightened

119 **at all adventures** whatever the risks

119–120 **so we were quit here** so long as we were out of this

121 **By my troth** In all honesty, I will say what I truly believe (**my conscience**) about the King

125 **ransomed** captured and freed after paying a sum of money

129 **Methinks** It seems to me

130–131 **his cause being young** given that he is fighting for a just cause

4.1

KING HENRY	Even as men wrecked upon a sand, that look to be washed off the next tide. 100
BATES	He hath not told his thought to the king?
KING HENRY	No; nor it is not meet he should. For, though I speak it to you, I think the king is but a man, as I am. The violet smells to him as it doth to me. The element shows to him as it doth to me. All 105 his senses have but human conditions. His ceremonies laid by, in his nakedness he appears but a man; and though his affections are higher mounted than ours, yet, when they stoop, they stoop with the like wing. Therefore when he sees 110 reason of fears, as we do, his fears, out of doubt, be of the same relish as ours are. Yet, in reason, no man should possess him with any appearance of fear, lest he, by showing it, should dishearten his army. 115
BATES	He may show what outward courage he will; but I believe, as cold a night as 't is, he could wish himself in Thames up to the neck; and so I would he were, and I by him, at all adventures, so we were quit here. 120
KING HENRY	By my troth, I will speak my conscience of the king. I think he would not wish himself any where but where he is.
BATES	Then I would he were alone! So should he be sure to be ransomed, and a many poor men's lives 125 saved.
KING HENRY	I dare say you love him not so ill, to wish him here alone, howsoever you speak this to feel other men's minds. Methinks I could not die anywhere so contented as in the king's company, his cause 130 being just and his quarrel honourable.
WILLIAMS	That's more than we know.
BATES	Ay, or more than we should seek after; for we know enough, if we know we are the king's

4.1 France: the English camp near Agincourt

Replying to an argument of Williams', Henry argues that a king cannot be held responsible for the souls of those soldiers who die without having repented of their sins.

Activities

Themes: duty and responsibility

The argument between Williams and Henry is on the important theme of duty and responsibility and goes something like this:

- *Williams* (lines 137–150): If the King's cause is not a good one, he bears a heavy responsibility for the deaths of the men who die fighting for him. These men have no choice: they have to follow him because it is their duty.
- *Henry* (lines 151–163): No, the King is not responsible for people being damned if they are sinners and die in the King's service.
  (lines 164–182) War is a way of punishing sinners who have escaped punishment in the law courts; and the King can't be held responsible for their damnation.
  (lines 183–193) Every subject has a patriotic duty to look after the King; but he has a spiritual duty to look after his own soul. That's why everybody going to war has to make sure that they are free of sin, and God might let them survive so that they can show others how to prepare for death.

1. Re-read the argument to make sure that you have followed Henry's logic.

continued on page 130

138 **hath a heavy reckoning to make** will have to answer to heaven for a serious sin

140 **latter day** Day of Judgement

144 **rawly left** left suddenly

145–147 **how can they charitably ... argument** how can they generously settle anything through the shedding of blood?

149–150 **all proportion ...** all the rightful duties of a subject

151–152 **sent about merchandise** sent off on a voyage as a merchant

152 **do sinfully miscarry** dies after having committed sins

153 **imputation of** responsibility for

157 **in many irreconciled iniquities** with many sins that he has not yet atoned for

159 **author of** reason for

160 **answer** answer for, take responsibility for

162 **purpose not** do not offer

165 **arbitrement of swords** settling things by fighting

166 **unspotted** innocent

167 **peradventure** perhaps

168 **beguiling** deceiving ... by lies

170 **bulwark** shield, 'cover'

171 **gored** violently harmed

173 **outrun native punishment** escaped punishment in their own country

175 **beadle** officer of the law

subjects. If his cause be wrong, our obedience to   135
the king wipes the crime of it out of us.

WILLIAMS   But if the cause be not good, the king himself
hath a heavy reckoning to make, when all those
legs and arms and heads, chopped off in a battle,
shall join together at the latter day and cry all   140
'We died at such a place'; some swearing, some
crying for a surgeon, some upon their wives left
poor behind them, some upon the debts they owe,
some upon their children rawly left. I am afeared
there are few die well that die in a battle; for how   145
can they charitably dispose of anything, when
blood is their argument? Now, if these men do not
die well, it will be a black matter for the king that
led them to it; whom to disobey were against all
proportion of subjection.   150

KING HENRY   So, if a son that is by his father sent about
merchandise, do sinfully miscarry upon the sea,
the imputation of his wickedness, by your rule,
should be imposed upon his father that sent him.
Or if a servant, under his master's command   155
transporting a sum of money, be assailed by
robbers and die in many irreconciled iniquities,
you may call the business of the master the
author of the servant's damnation. But this is not
so. The king is not bound to answer the particular   160
endings of his soldiers, the father of his son, nor
the master of his servant; for they purpose not
their death, when they purpose their services.
Besides, there is no king, be his cause never so
spotless, if it come to the arbitrement of swords,   165
can try it out with all unspotted soldiers. Some
peradventure have on them the guilt of premeditated
and contrived murder; some, of beguiling
virgins with the broken seals of perjury; some,
making the wars their bulwark, that have before   170
gored the gentle bosom of peace with pillage and
robbery. Now, if these men have defeated the law
and outrun native punishment, though they can
outstrip men, they have no wings to fly from God.
War is his beadle, war is his vengeance; so that   175

4.1 France: the English camp near Agincourt

The men agree with Henry's argument that every man is responsible for his own soul, but Henry becomes angry when Williams mocks him over the idea of trusting the King's word and an argument develops between them.

Activities

2. Do you think he answered Williams' initial point successfully? Look carefully at lines 147–163.

3. Is Henry trying to evade his responsibilities here? Where else in the play might Henry be accused of shifting responsibility for his deeds on to other people? Is he doing that in the following scenes with:
   - the Archbishop (1.2)?
   - the French Ambassador (1.2)?
   - the traitors (2.2)?
   - the Governor of Harfleur (3.3)?

4. Henry says (line 198) 'I myself heard the King say he would not be ransomed.' Look back at the note to 3.5.60 and check that you understand how the ransom system worked.
   - Why is it important that Henry has publicly refused to be ransomed?
   - What is Williams' view of Henry's statement about ransom?
   - Does Williams have a point, in your opinion?

176 **before-breach** previous law-breaking

180 **unprovided** unprepared (with their sins not absolved)

182 **impieties ... visited** the sins for which they are now being punished

186 **mote** speck (of dust)

188 **blessedly lost** wasted in a good cause

189–193 **it were not sin ... prepare** it isn't sinful to believe that, since the man had made God such a complete (**free**) offer, God had allowed him to survive, as an example to show others how to prepare for death

194–195 **every man that dies ill ...** if a man dies, having committed sins, that's his responsibility, not the King's

197 **lustily** strongly and enthusiastically

203 **You pay him then!** (*sarcastically*) you pay him out; you punish him (for breaking his word)

203–205 **That's a perilous shot out of an elder gun ... monarch** an ordinary person's grudge against the King carries as much weight as a bullet fired from a pop-gun! (*Children made pop-guns from hollowed-out elder wood.*)

209 **your reproof ...** you made that point rather too bluntly

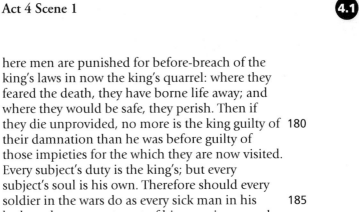

here men are punished for before-breach of the
king's laws in now the king's quarrel: where they
feared the death, they have borne life away; and
where they would be safe, they perish. Then if
they die unprovided, no more is the king guilty of   180
their damnation than he was before guilty of
those impieties for the which they are now visited.
Every subject's duty is the king's; but every
subject's soul is his own. Therefore should every
soldier in the wars do as every sick man in his   185
bed, wash every mote out of his conscience: and
dying so, death is to him advantage; or not dying,
the time was blessedly lost wherein such
preparation was gained: and in him that escapes, it
were not sin to think that, making God so free an   190
offer, He let him outlive that day to see His
greatness and to teach others how they should
prepare.

WILLIAMS   'T is certain, every man that dies ill, the ill upon his
              own head, the king is not to answer it.   195

BATES   I do not desire he should answer for me; and yet I
              determine to fight lustily for him.

KING HENRY   I myself heard the king say he would not be ransomed.

WILLIAMS   Ay, he said so, to make us fight cheerfully. But
              when our throats are cut, he may be ransomed,   200
              and we ne'er the wiser.

KING HENRY   If I live to see it, I will never trust his word after.

WILLIAMS   You pay him them! That's a perilous shot out of
              an elder-gun, that a poor and private displeasure
              can do against a monarch! You may as well go   205
              about to turn the sun to ice with fanning in his
              face with a peacock's feather. You'll never trust his
              word after! Come, 't is a foolish saying.

KING HENRY   Your reproof is something too round. I should be
              angry with you, if the time were convenient.   210

WILLIAMS   Let it be a quarrel between us, if you live.

4.1 France: the English camp near Agincourt

Henry and Williams angrily agree to fight if they survive the battle and they exchange gloves as a challenge. When the three soldiers depart, Henry is left alone to ponder the responsibilities and worries of a king.

Activities

Actors' interpretations: tension and argument

Annotate the build-up to the challenge between Henry and Williams (lines 196–229) with director's notes.

Show how the tension increases as each man becomes angrier and less in control by writing notes on (a) their changing feelings, and (b) their movements, gestures and facial expressions.

Finally, rehearse the scene with props (two pairs of gloves) and act it out. Remember the technique of cue-biting (see the activity on page 108) to add tension and realism.

214 **gage** *an item (often a glove) thrown down as a challenge to a fight*

221 **take thee a box** ... give you a punch

228 **enow** enough

230 **lay** bet

   crowns (1) French gold coins, (2) heads

231–232 **they bear them** ... they carry them the heads on their shoulders (i.e. they outnumber us)

232–233 **to cut French crowns ... clipper** *Cutting (or 'clipping') gold out of coins was treason; but tomorrow the King will be a clipper of French* **crowns** (= (1) coins, (2) heads, (3) royal crowns).

235 **Upon the King!** It's all the King's responsibility!

236 **careful** anxious (full of care)

238 **condition** state (of being King)

239 **subject to** ... kings have to put up with the words (**breath**) of every fool who cannot feel more than his own aches and pains (**wringing**)

241 **hearts-ease** rest and relaxation

243 **privates** ordinary people

KING HENRY I embrace it.

WILLIAMS How shall I know thee again?

KING HENRY Give me any gage of thine, and I will wear it in my
bonnet. Then, if ever thou darest acknowledge it,   215
I will make it my quarrel.

WILLIAMS Here 's my glove. Give me another of thine.

KING HENRY There.

WILLIAMS This will I also wear in my cap. If ever thou come
to me and say, after to-morrow, 'This is my glove',   220
by this hand, I will take thee a box on the ear.

KING HENRY If ever I live to see it, I will challenge it.

WILLIAMS Thou darest as well be hanged.

KING HENRY Well, I will do it, though I take thee in the king's
company.   225

WILLIAMS Keep thy word. Fare thee well.

BATES Be friends, you English fools, be friends. We have
French quarrels enow, if you could tell how to
reckon.

KING HENRY Indeed, the French may lay twenty French crowns   230
to one, they will beat us; for they bear them on
their shoulders. But it is no English treason to cut
French crowns, and to-morrow the king himself
will be a clipper.

Exeunt Soldiers

Upon the king! Let us our lives, our souls,   235
Our debts, our careful wives,
Our children and our sins lay on the king!
We must bear all. O hard condition,
Twin-born with greatness, subject to the breath
Of every fool, whose sense no more can feel   240
But his own wringing! What infinite heart's-ease
Must kings neglect that private men enjoy!
And what have kings that privates have not too,

4.1 France: the English camp near Agincourt

Henry reflects on the fact that the only thing that distinguishes a king from ordinary men is 'ceremony', which itself has no practical use. What is more, kings have so many cares that they are unable to enjoy a peaceful night's sleep.

Activities

Character review: Henry (17): the King and 'ceremony'

In lines 265–266, Henry lists the objects which indicate Kingship: **balm** (oil for anointing the King's head at a coronation), **sceptre, ball** (royal orb: a sphere with a cross on top), **sword, mace** and **crown**.

A What does Henry mean by 'ceremony'? If you were in Henry's court, what features of 'ceremony' might you be aware of? (Think about the official costume a King wears and the ceremonies he performs.)

B List (a) the drawbacks to 'ceremony' as Henry sees them; (b) the things that ceremony prevents him from doing; (c) the things that ceremony is incapable of doing or helping with; and (d) the advantages of being an ordinary person.

C Kenneth Branagh thought that the 'Upon the king' soliloquy emerges because of the 'terrible certainty of what Williams has said'. Look back at Henry's conversation with Williams and decide which aspects of the conversation might have led to Henry's thoughts in the soliloquy.

244 **ceremony** *all the trappings of a king: clothes and crowns, rituals, customs, etc.*

246–247 **that suffer'st more ... worshippers** kings suffer more griefs than ordinary people

248 **rents ... comings in** what rent or income do you receive?

250 **soul of adoration** real nature of the worship offered to you

251 **Art thou aught else ...** Are you anything else but social position, rank and order (**place, degree and form**)?

253 **Wherein thou art ...** and in doing that you are ...

255 **homage** respect due to a king

258–259 **Thinkst thou ... adulation** Do you think you can put out a king's fever by blowing the breath of flatterers at him?

260 **flexure** bowing (of flatterers)

263 **subtly** cleverly

268 **farcéd** inflated, overdone

271 **thrice-** three times

275 **distressful bread** food earned through hard work

277 **lackey** servant

278 **Phoebus** *classical sun-god*

279 **Elysium** *in Greek mythology, a place of happiness for the dead*

280 **Hyperion** *father of the sun-god*

284 **Winding up** filling up

285 **Had the forehand ...** would have an advantage over ...

Save ceremony, save general ceremony?
And what art thou, thou idol ceremony?   245
What kind of god art thou, that suffer'st more
Of mortal griefs than do thy worshippers?
What are thy rents? What are thy comings in?
O ceremony, show me but thy worth!
What is thy soul of adoration?   250
Art thou aught else but place, degree and form,
Creating awe and fear in other men,
Wherein thou art less happy being feared
Than they in fearing?
What drinkst thou oft, instead of homage sweet, 255
But poisoned flattery? O, be sick, great greatness,
And bid thy ceremony give thee cure!
Thinkst thou the fiery fever will go out
With titles blown from adulation?
Will it give place to flexure and low bending?   260
Canst thou, when thou commandst the beggar's
    knee,
Command the heath of it? No, thou proud dream,
That playst so subtly with a king's repose;
I am a king that find thee, and I know
'T is not the balm, the sceptre and the ball,   265
The sword, the mace, the crown imperial,
The intertissued robe of gold and pearl,
The farcéd title running 'fore the king,
The throne he sits on, nor the tide of pomp
That beats upon the high shore of this world,   270
No, not all these, thrice-gorgeous ceremony,
Not all these, laid in bed majestical,
Can sleep so soundly as the wretched slave,
Who with a body filled and vacant mind
Gets him to rest, crammed with distressful bread; 275
Never sees horrid night, the child of hell;
But, like a lackey, from the rise to set,
Sweats in the eye of Phoebus and all night
Sleeps in Elysium; next day after dawn,
Doth rise and help Hyperion to his horse,   280
And follows so the ever-running year,
With profitable labour, to his grave.
And, but for ceremony, such a wretch,
Winding up days with toil and nights with sleep,
Had the forehand and vantage of a king.   285

4.1 France: the English camp near Agincourt

Erpingham comes to tell Henry that his nobles have been looking for him. Promising to meet them all in his tent, Henry stays behind for a moment and prays. He asks God to remove fear from his men's hearts and not to think about the fact that his father killed Richard II to gain the crown.

Activities

Plot review (13): Henry's father and Richard

Read page 239 and the activity on page 66 and check that you know the answers to the following questions:

1. Who was Henry's father?
2. What was 'the fault' Henry's 'father made in compassing the crown'?
3. Who was Richard?
4. Why should Henry have Richard's body re-buried, and then shed tears over it?
5. What were the 'forcéd drops of blood'?

Character review: Henry (18): 'O God of battles...'

1. Act out the speech in as many different moods as you can: for example, terrified, defiant or pleading. Show your preferred version to someone else and explain why you think it is the appropriate one.
2. In the Olivier film, Henry was shown silently praying while his words were heard in 'voice-over'. In the Branagh film, Henry speaks his prayer aloud, after the others have left and leans against a cart in which a soldier is sleeping. In many theatre productions, Henry is alone. How would you stage this scene?

286 **member of** person who shares

287 **in gross brain ...** his stupid brain knows (**wots**) little of

289 **Whose hours ...** it is the peasant who benefits most from the king's hours of lying awake

290 **jealous of** anxious about

294 **steel** harden

296 **reckoning** ability to count

298–299 **the fault my father made ...** *Henry IV had taken the crown from Richard II, who was then murdered (see page 240).*

299 **compassing** obtaining

300 **interréd new** reburied in a new place

301 **contrite** repentant

302 **Than from it ...** than the drops of blood which were forced out of Richard's body when he was murdered

305 **to pardon blood** to beg God to forgive the murder

306 **chantries** chapels

307 **still** continuously

308–310 **nothing worth ...** *Henry worries that all his penitent actions are worth nothing, since his repentance comes after the murder and, although he is praying for pardon, he is still holding on to the crown for which Richard was killed.*

312 **thy errand** your reason for calling me

The slave, a member of the country's peace,
Enjoys it; but in gross brain little wots
What watch the king keeps to maintain the peace,
Whose hours the peasant best advantages.

Enter ERPINGHAM.

ERPINGHAM   My lord, your nobles, jealous of your absence,   290
Seek through your camp to find you.

KING HENRY   Good old knight,
Collect them all together at my tent.
I'll be before thee.

ERPINGHAM   I shall do 't, my lord.

Exit

KING HENRY [*Kneels*] O God of battles, steel my soldiers' hearts!
Possess them not with fear; take from them now   295
The sense of reckoning, if the opposéd numbers
Pluck their hearts from them. Not to-day, O Lord,
O, not to-day, think not upon the fault
My father made in compassing the crown!
I Richard's body have interréd new;   300
And on it have bestowed more contrite tears
Than from it issued forcéd drops of blood.
Five hundred poor I have in yearly pay,
Who twice a day their withered hands hold up
Toward heaven, to pardon blood; and I have built 305
Two chantries, where the sad and solemn priests
Sing still for Richard's soul. More will I do;
Though all that I can do is nothing worth,
Since that my penitence comes after all,
Imploring pardon.   310

Enter GLOUCESTER, *calling.*

GLOUCESTER My liege!

KING HENRY   My brother Gloucester's voice? (*rises*) Ay;
I know thy errand, I will go with thee.
The day, my friends and all things stay for me.

Exeunt

137

4.2 France: the French camp near Agincourt

The Dauphin and his nobles eagerly mount their horses, mockingly complaining that the feeble English army will not offer enough sport for all the assembled French.

Activities

Character review: the French (4)

1. To capture the French nobles' excitement and optimism, perform lines 1–15, choosing only one word from each line. Act out the scene quickly and with plenty of volume.
2. How would you stage this scene (a) in a film; and (b) in the theatre?

RSC, 1997

1 **gild** turn to gold

2–6 **Montez ...** Mount your horses ... You, slave, servant ... Away (**Via!**), over water and land. Nothing more? What about air and fire (**Rien puis ...**) Yes, heaven itself! (**Ciel!**)

8 **for present ...** they neigh to be used immediately

9 **make incision** prick their sides with your spurs

11 **dout them ...** extinguish them with excess courage (in the overflowing blood)

14 **embattled** formed up in line of battle

17 **fair show** impressive appearance

18 **shales** shells

21 **curtle-axe** cutlass

23 **for lack of sport** *because there will not be enough English to enjoy using their weapons on*

24 **vapour of our valour** the mere smell of our bravery will defeat them

25 **positive 'gainst ...** definite, without any objections ...

26 **superfluous lackeys** extra servants, not needed for the battle

Scene 2

The French camp.

Enter the DAUPHIN, ORLEANS, RAMBURES, *and others.*

ORLEANS	The sun doth gild our armour. Up, my lords!
DAUPHIN	Montez à cheval! My horse! Varlet! Lacquais! Ha!
ORLEANS	O brave spirit!
DAUPHIN	Via! Les eaux et la terre.
ORLEANS	Rien puis? L'air et le feu?

5

DAUPHIN   Ciel, cousin Orleans.

Enter CONSTABLE.

       Now, my lord constable!

CONSTABLE   Hark, how our steeds for present service neigh!

DAUPHIN   Mount them, and make incision in their hides,
That their hot blood may spin in English eyes,   10
And dout them with superfluous courage, ha!

RAMBURES   What, will you have them weep our horses' blood?
How shall we, then, behold their natural tears?

Enter Messenger.

MESSENGER   The English are embattled, you French peers.

CONSTABLE   To horse, you gallant princes, straight to horse!   15
Do but behold yon poor and starvéd band,
And your fair show shall suck away their souls,
Leaving them but the shales and husks of men.
There is not work enough for all our hands;
Scarce blood enough in all their sickly veins   20
To give each naked curtle-axe a stain,
That our French gallants shall to-day draw out,
And sheathe for lack of sport. Let us but blow on
     them,
The vapour of our valour will o'erturn them.
'T is positive 'gainst all exceptions, lords,   25
That our superfluous lackeys and our peasants,

4.2 France: the French camp near Agincourt

Grandpré spurs the French nobles into action, describing how pathetic the English look. With a joke from the Dauphin that they ought to send the English some food before they fight, the French nobles rush off impatiently to join battle.

Activities

Character review: the French (5)

Use the words of the nobles in this scene to write an article for the French newspaper *Fleur-de-lys*. After its initial doubts (see the activity on page 115), it is now supporting the French army wholeheartedly and the article should express total confidence and optimism. Describe the pitiful state of the English army, as the French see it, and refer to the fact that the French army is so big that there will hardly be enough work for them all to do.

28–29 **enow To purge ...** enough to rid this battlefield of such a pitiful-looking (**hilding**) enemy

30 **mountain's basis** hill's foot

31 **Took stand ...** stood by as idle on-lookers

35 **tucket sonance** trumpet call

36 **dare** paralyse with fear

37 **couch down** cower

39 **carrions, desperate of their bones** living corpses, in despair of saving their lives

40 **Ill-favouredly become ...** look ugly in the morning light

41 **curtains** banners

42 **passing** extremely

43–44 **Big Mars ...** The great god of war has lost all his magnificence in their poor army (**host**) and peeps pathetically through their rusty visors

46 **jades** worn-out horses

48 **down-roping** trickling down

49 **gimmal bit** two-part mouthpiece of the bridle

51 **executors** *people who make arrangements about a dead person's possessions*

53–55 **Description ...** Words do not have the power to give a *life-like* description of the English army (**battle**), since it is *life-less*

58 **fasting** starving

provender food

60 **guidon** banner

Who in unnecessary action swarm
About our squares of battle, were enow
To purge this field of such a hilding foe,
Though we upon this mountain's basis by   30
Took stand for idle speculation:
But that our honours must not. What's to say?
A very little little let us do,
And all is done. Then let the trumpets sound
The tucket sonance and the note to mount;   35
For our approach shall so much dare the field
That England shall couch down in fear, and yield.

Enter GRANDPRÉ

GRANDPRÉ   Why do you stay so long, my lords of France?
Yon island carrions, desperate of their bones,
Ill-favouredly become the morning field.   40
Their ragged curtains poorly are let loose,
And our air shakes them passing scornfully.
Big Mars seems bankrupt in their beggared host
And faintly through a rusty beaver peeps.
The horsemen sit like fixéd candlesticks,   45
With torch-staves in their hand; and their poor jades
Lob down their heads, dropping the hides and hips,
The gum down-roping from their pale-dead eyes,
And in their pale dull mouths the gimmal bit
Lies foul with chewed grass, still and motionless;   50
And their executors, the knavish crows,
Fly o'er them, all impatient for their hour.
Description cannot suit itself in words
To demonstrate the life of such a battle
In life so lifeless as it shows itself.   55

CONSTABLE   They have said their prayers, and they stay for death.

DAUPHIN   Shall we go send them dinners and fresh suits
And give their fasting horses provender,
And after fight with them?

CONSTABLE   I stay but for my guidon. To the field!   60
I will the banner from a trumpet take,
And use it for my haste. Come, come, away!
The sun is high, and we outwear the day.

Exeunt

4.3 France: the English camp near Agincourt

In the English camp, the nobles weigh up the frightening odds against them, but Henry encourages them with the view that, because their numbers are so small, each man's share of honour will be that much greater.

2 **battle** army

3 **three score thousand** 60,000. *Exeter's comment (line 3) implies that there were 12,000 English, but recent historians believe that there might have been as few as 6,000, most of whom were archers.*

18 **work** *This often meant 'fighting' in Shakespeare's plays.*

20–22 **If we are marked ...** If we are fated to die, our country will not have suffered too great a loss by our small numbers ...

Scene 3

The English camp.

Enter GLOUCESTER, BEDFORD, EXETER, ERPINCHAM, *with the English army;* SALISBURY *and* WESTMORELAND.

GLOUCESTER Where is the king?

BEDFORD The king himself is rode to view their battle.

WEST-
MORELAND Of fighting men they have full three score thousand.

EXETER There's five to one; besides, they all are fresh.

SALISBURY God's arm strike with us! 'T is a fearful odds.   5
God be wi' you, princes all; I'll to my charge.
If we no more meet till we meet in heaven,
Then, joyfully, my noble Lord of Bedford,
My dear Lord Gloucester, and my good Lord Exeter,
And my kind kinsman, warriors all, adieu!   10

BEDFORD Farewell, good Salisbury, and good luck go with thee!

EXETER Farewell, kind lord; fight valiantly to-day.
And yet I do thee wrong to mind thee of it,
For thou art framed of the firm truth of valour.

Exit SALISBURY

BEDFORD He is as full of valour as of kindness;   15
Princely in both.

Enter KING HENRY.

WEST-   O that we now had here
MORELAND But one ten thousand of those men in England
That do no work to-day!

KING HENRY   What's he that wishes, so?
My cousin Westmoreland? No, my fair cousin.
If we are marked to die, we are enow   20
To do our country loss; and if to live,
The fewer men, the greater share of honour.
God's will, I pray thee, wish not one man more.

4.3 France: the English camp near Agincourt

As the battle is about to start, Henry lifts his army's spirits. Using the smallness of their numbers to encourage a feeling of brotherhood, he predicts that in years to come they will recall as old men the deeds they performed on Saint Crispin's Day.

Activities

Character review: Henry (19): Saint Crispin's Day

What methods does Henry use in his reply to Westmoreland and in the St Crispin's Day speech (lines 19-67) to encourage his men?

1. In pairs, find the lines in which Henry:
   - stresses his confidence in the size of the English army
   - makes his men feel proud to be a part of history
   - makes them feel that, although they are mostly ordinary men, their deeds will always be remembered
   - makes them feel good about being only a few
   - stresses the brotherhood of the army, whether high or low born
   - promises that common soldiers will be made gentlemen by their actions in the battle
   - makes them feel that others will feel envious because they were not part of the glory
   - appeals to the soldiers' masculinity.

2. Which of Henry's qualities as a leader can be seen at work here?

3. Do you admire Henry's leadership here, or is he being dishonest (since he must know they are likely to be wiped out)?

24 **covetous** greedy

25 **upon my cost** at my expense

26 **It yearns me not** it doesn't bother me if people wear my clothes; I am not interested in such superficial things

30 **coz** cousin

35 **stomach** 'guts'

38–39 **We would not die** I do not want to die alongside any man who is afraid to die in my company

40–67 *This part of Henry's address is often called 'the St Crispin's Day speech'. (Crispin and Crispian were shoemakers in Rome, put to death for their Christian faith; they became patron saints of shoemakers, their day being 25 October).*

45 **the vigil** *the evening before the saint's day*

49 **yet ... forgot** and even if the time comes when everything else is forgotten ...

50 **advantages** exaggerations

55 **in their flowing cups ...** they will be remembered in toasts

62 **be he ne'er so vile ...** however humble and low-born he might be, this day will turn him into a gentleman

By Jove, I am not covetous for gold,
Nor care I who doth feed upon my cost;   25
It yearns me not if men my garments wear;
Such outward things dwell not in my desires.
But if it be a sin to covet honour,
I am the most offending soul alive.
No, faith, my coz, wish not a man from England.   30
God's peace! I would not lose so great an honour
As one man more, methinks, would share from me
For the best hope I have. O, do not wish one more!
Rather proclaim it, Westmoreland, through my host,
That he which hath no stomach to this fight,   35
Let him depart. His passport shall be made
And crowns for convoy put into his purse.
We would not die in that man's company
That fears his fellowship to die with us.
This day is called the feast of Crispian.   40
He that outlives this day, and comes safe home,
Will stand a tip-toe when this day is named,
And rouse him at the name of Crispian.
He that shall live this day, and see old age,
Will yearly on the vigil feast his neighbours,   45
And say 'To-morrow is Saint Crispian.'
Then will he strip his sleeve and show his scars,
And say 'These wounds I had on Crispin's day.'
Old men forget; yet all shall be forgot,
But he'll remember, with advantages   50
What feats he did that day. Then shall our names,
Familiar in his mouth as household words,
Harry the king, Bedford and Exeter,
Warwick and Talbot, Salisbury and Gloucester,
Be in their flowing cups freshly remembered.   55
This story shall the good man teach his son;
And Crispin Crispian shall ne'er go by,
From this day to the ending of the world,
But we in it shall be rememberéd:
We few, we happy few, we band of brothers;   60
For he to-day that sheds his blood with me
Shall be my brother; be he ne'er so vile,
This day shall gentle his condition.
And gentlemen in England now a-bed
Shall think themselves accursed they were not
    here.   65

4.3 France: the English camp near Agincourt

As news comes that the French are ready to charge, Montjoy arrives for a final time to ask if Henry will agree to be ransomed. Henry rejects the suggestion, as he has done before.

Activities

Character review: Montjoy (2)

1. Which features of Montjoy's speech (lines 79–88) seem to be emphasising (a) certain defeat for the English; and (b) the need for the English to repent of their sins?

2. Try acting his speech (a) mockingly and arrogantly; and (b) sympathetically and pityingly. Which interpretation do you prefer? What effect does each one have on the way in which Henry begins his reply (lines 90–92)?

3. If you have the opportunity, study the different ways in which the two Montjoys deliver this speech in the 1944 and 1989 films and decide which of the interpretations in 2 (above) each one comes closest to.

66 **hold their manhoods cheap** consider themselves to be not real men

69 **bravely ...** looking impressive in their line of battle

70 **expedience** speed

74 **would** I wish

76 **unwished** wished away

80 **compound** agree terms

83 **englutted** swallowed up

84 **mind** remind

86 **retire** retreat

91 **achieve** overcome

93–94 **The man that once ...** *One of Æsop's fables tells of a man who over-confidently sold a bear's skin before he had killed the animal, and was then nearly killed himself in hunting it.*

And hold their manhoods cheap, whiles any speaks
That fought with us upon Saint Crispin's day.

Re-enter SALISBURY.

SALISBURY   My sovereign lord, bestow yourself with speed.
              The French are bravely in their battles set,
              And will with all expendience charge on us.   70

KING HENRY   All things are ready, if our minds be so.

WEST   Perish the man whose mind is backward now!
MORELAND

KING HENRY   Thou dost not wish more help from England, coz?

WEST   God's will, my liege, would you and I alone,
MORELAND   Without more help, could fight this royal battle!   75

KING HENRY   Why, now thou hast unwished five thousand men;
              Which likes me better than to wish us one.
              You know your places. God be with you all!

Tucket. Enter MONTJOY.

MONTJOY   Once more I come to know of thee, King Harry,
              If for thy ransom thou wilt now compound,   80
              Before thy most assuréd overthrow.
              For certainly thou art so near the gulf,
              Thou needs must be englutted. Besides, in mercy,
              The Constable desires thee thou wilt mind
              Thy followers of repentance; that their souls   85
              May make a peaceful and a sweet retire
              From off these fields, where, wretches, their poor
                 bodies
              Must lie and fester.

KING HENRY   Who hath sent thee now?

MONTJOY   The Constable of France.

KING HENRY   I pray thee, bear my former answer back: 90
              Bid them achieve me and then sell my bones.
              Good God, why should they mock poor fellows thus?
              The man that once did sell the lion's skin

4.3 France: the English camp near Agincourt

Henry tells Montjoy that, if the English are killed, their corpses will cause a plague in France. His soldiers might look ragged, he says, but they are full of courage, and Montjoy leaves with the repeated message that Henry is refusing to be ransomed.

Activities

Shakespeare's language: the plight of the English

1. Find the parts of Henry's reply to Montjoy in which he admits that the English (a) will not in many cases survive the battle; and (b) are in a sorry state.

2. Somehow Henry manages to turn the English plight to his advantage. Draw a series of cartoons to accompany the vivid pictures he creates in this speech. Focus especially on lines:
   • 93–94
   • 95–97
   • 98–107 (perhaps more than one cartoon here)
   • 108–114
   • 115–119.

   Write Henry's words underneath each cartoon and display them.

3. Look back at question 3 on page 144. What does Henry's reply to Montjoy add to your opinion of him as a leader?

96 **native** in their own country

97 **witness ... in brass** engraved as epitaphs on brass plates

100–103 **the sun shall ...** as the sun causes unpleasant vapours to rise from the dead, so will the soldiers' honours be drawn up to heaven, while the decaying remains cause plague

102 **clime** climate, country

104 **abounding** (1) abundant, (2) rebounding (it will bounce back to harm you)

107 **Killing in relapse ...** killing you, (1) while they are decaying; (2) by a deadly rebound

109 **for the working day** in a practical, workaday spirit (they 'mean business')

110–111 **Our gayness and our gilt ...** our decorations and gold ornaments are all made dirty

112 **feather** plume (*for decorating their helmets*)

114 **slovenry** sloppiness, untidiness

115 **in the trim** (1) smartly dressed, (2) in good shape

117 **in fresher robes** (1) in better clothes (by taking new ones from the French), (2) in the clothes you wear in heaven

119 **And turn them ...** dismiss them from their master's service

130 **vaward** vanguard

While the beast lived, was killed with hunting him.
A many of our bodies shall no doubt   95
Find native graves; upon the which, I trust,
Shall witness live in brass of this day's work.
And those that leave their valiant bones in France,
Dying like men, though buried in your dunghills,
They shall be famed; for there the sun shall greet
    them,   100
And draw their honours reeking up to heaven;
Leaving their earthly parts to choke your clime,
The smell whereof shall breed a plague in France.
Mark then abounding valour in our English,
That being dead, like to the bullet's grazing,   105
Break out into a second course of mischief,
Killing in relapse of mortality.
Let me speak proudly: tell the Constable
We are but warriors for the working-day;
Our gayness and our gilt are all besmirched   110
With rainy marching in the painful field.
There's not a piece of feather in our host –
Good argument, I hope, we will not fly –
And time hath worn us into slovenry.
But, by the mass, our hearts are in the trim;   115
And my poor soldiers tell me, yet ere night
They'll be in fresher robes, or they will pluck
The gay new coats o'er the French soldiers' heads
And turn them out of service. If they do this –
As, if God please, they shall – my ransom then   120
Will soon be levied. Herald, save thou thy labour;
Come thou no more for ransom, gentle herald.
They shall have none, I swear, but these my joints;
Which if they have as I will leave 'em them,
Shall yield them little, tell the Constable.   125

MONTJOY   I shall, King Harry. And so fare thee well.
Thou never shalt hear herald any more.

KING HENRY I fear thou'lt once more come again for ransom.

    Enter YORK.

YORK   My lord, most humbly on my knee I beg
The leading of the vaward.   130

4.4 France: the battlefield of Agincourt

As the conflict is about to start, Henry grants York's request to lead the vanguard and leaves the outcome of the fight in God's hands. On the field of battle, Pistol encounters a cowardly and frightened French gentleman and threatens to cut his throat unless he promises to pay an enormous ransom.

Activities

Character review: Henry (20): his leadership before battle

Write the journal entries of (a) Exeter, and (b) the cynical lord (see the activities on pages 28 and 52), in which they express their views of both the Saint Crispin's day speech and Henry's reply to Montjoy. Exeter admires the qualities of leadership that Henry has displayed in adverse circumstances. The cynical lord might well take the view that Henry is manipulating his men: he knows that they are in serious trouble and is not being honest with them.

Then hot-seat Henry and find out what he really feels about the coming battle, and what was in his mind when he gave the troops his 'Saint Crispin's Day' speech and when he replied to Montjoy.

s.d. **Alarum. Excursions.** *Trumpet-calls; soldiers run on stage and off, to give an impression of battle*

1 **Yield, cur!** Surrender, dog!

2–3 **Je pense ...** I think you are a high-born gentleman

4 **Qualtitie ...** *a nonsense reply, echoing the Frenchman's words*

6 **O Seigneur Dieu!** O lord God! *Pistol misunderstands and thinks his surname is Dew.*

8 **Perpend** Listen

9 **fox** sword

10 **Except** unless

11 **Egregious** enormous, extraordinary

12 **O, prenez ...** O, have mercy, take pity on me! *Again (line 13), Pistol misunderstands and takes 'moi' to be a coin (a 'moy')*

13 **... shall not serve** will not be enough

14 **rim** midriff (insides)

16 **Est-il impossible ...** is it impossible to escape your arm's strength?

17 **Brass** *'Bras' would have sounded like 'brass' in the French of that time.*

18 **luxurious** lecherous

20 **O pardonnez moi!** O, pardon me!

KING HENRY Take it, brave York. Now, soldiers, march away;
And how thou pleasest, God, dispose the day!

Exeunt

Scene 4

The field of battle.

Alarum. Excursions. Enter PISTOL, French Soldier, *and* Boy.

PISTOL Yield, cur!

FRENCH SOLDIER Je pense que vous êtes gentilhomme de bonne qualité.

PISTOL Qualtitie calmie custure me! Art thou a gentleman?
What is thy name? Discuss.   5

FRENCH SOLDIER O Seigneur Dieu!

PISTOL O, Signieur Dew should be a gentleman.
Perpend my words, O Signieur Dew,
    and mark;
O Signieur Dew, thou diest on point of fox,
Except, O signieur, thou do give to me   10
Egregious ransom.

FRENCH SOLDIER O, prenez miséricorde! Ayez pitié de moi!

PISTOL Moy shall not serve; I will have forty moys;
Or I will fetch thy rim out at thy throat
In drops of crimson blood.   15

FRENCH SOLDIER Est-il impossible d'échapper la force de ton bras?

PISTOL Brass, cur!
Thou damnéd and luxurious mountain goat,
Offer'st me brass?

FRENCH SOLDIER O pardonnez moi!   20

4.4 France: the battlefield of Agincourt

Translating for Pistol, the Boy explains that the Frenchman is called Monsieur le Fer and is a gentleman from a good family. Pistol happily agrees to control his fury and accept the offer of two hundred crowns in ransom money.

Activities

Actors' interpretations: Pistol and le Fer

A Imagine you were filming this scene. Sketch out four frames of a storyboard which will show the funniest moments.

B Write director's notes to 4.4.1–66, showing what the actors do to show:
- the comedy in Pistol's misunderstandings due to his lack of French
- the comedy in le Fer's cowardice
- the role played by the Boy and his attitude to what is going on.

Give advice on:
- movements and actions (what weapons are they carrying?)
- how to speak the lines
- facial expressions
- the characters' feelings.

Add notes on how you think Pistol and le Fer ought to be dressed in this scene.

C Some productions of the play choose to play down the comedy in this scene. If you wished to do this, which darker aspects could you focus on? What would the actors do in order to bring them out? What effect would (a) a comic, and (b) a darker interpretation have on the battle sequence as a whole (4.4 to 4.7)? How ominous should the Boy's speech at the end be made to sound?

24 **Écoutez ...** Listen: what is your name?

25 **le Fer** Fer *is French for iron.*

27 **I'll fer him ...** *Pistol plays on the sound of the word 'fer': firk means to beat.*

32 **Que dit-il ...** What is he saying, sir?

32–35 **Il me commande ...** He orders me to tell you to prepare yourself, because this soldier here is ready to cut your throat immediately

36 **Owy, cuppele gorge, permafoy** 'Oui, couper la gorge, par ma foi' – yes, cut the throat, by my faith

39–41 **O je vous supplie ...** O, I beg you, for the love of God, pardon me! I am a gentleman of a good family. Preserve my life and I will give you two hundred crowns.

48 **Petit monsieur ...** Young gentleman, what does he say?

PISTOL	Sayst thou me so? Is that a ton of moys? Come hither, boy. Ask me this slave in French What is his name.
BOY	Écoutez. Comment êtes-vous appelé?
FRENCH SOLDIER	Monsieur le Fer. 25
BOY	He says his name is Master Fer.
PISTOL	Master Fer! I'll fer him, and firk him, and ferret him. Discuss the same in French unto him.
BOY	I do not know the French for fer, and ferret, and firk. 30
PISTOL	Bid him prepare, for I will cut his throat.
FRENCH SOLDIER	Que dit-il, monsieur?
BOY	Il me commande de vous dire que vous faites vous prêt; car ce soldat ici est disposé tout à cette heure de couper votre gorge. 35
PISTOL	Owy, cuppele gorge, permafoy, Peasant, unless thou give me crowns, brave crowns; Or mangled shalt thou be by this my sword.
FRENCH SOLDIER	O je vous supplie, pour l'amour de Dieu, me pardonner! Je suis gentilhomme de bonne maison. 40 Gardez ma vie, et je vous donnerai deux cents écus.
PISTOL	What are his words?
BOY	He prays you to save his life. He is a gentleman of a good house; and for his ransom he will give you two hundred crowns. 45
PISTOL	Tell him my fury shall abate, and I The crowns will take.
FRENCH SOLDIER	Petit monsieur, que dit-il?

4.4 France: the battlefield of Agincourt

Pistol leads off the grateful le Fer and the Boy observes that, despite Pistol's heroic language, he is actually a coward. The Boy adds that the army's baggage train is vulnerable to attack, as there are only boys guarding it.

Activities

Actors' interpretations: the death of Nym

The Boy reports that Nym has been hanged (lines 69–73). Some actors feel that, since we have become interested in Nym, it is disappointing to hear of his death in this second-hand way. In the Branagh film, we actually see Nym being killed, but not by hanging: he is stabbed by a French soldier while robbing a corpse on the field of battle.

If you were directing the play, how would you answer the actor playing Nym if he asked you (a) 'Why was I hanged? What crime did I commit?' and (b) 'Can we change the way I die and show my death on-stage?'

In giving your answers, you might like to consider why Shakespeare made the decision not to tell us what crime Nym had been hanged for, and to have his death reported in this way.

49 **Encore qu'il est ...** Once again that it is against his oath to pardon any prisoner; nevertheless for the crowns you have promised him, he is happy to give you your liberty: your freedom

53–57 **Sur mes genoux ...** On my knees, I give you a thousand thanks and consider myself fortunate to have fallen into the hands of a knight who I consider to be the bravest, most valiant and distinguished lord in England

64 **I will some mercy show** *This is against the rules of war: he ought to take le Fer to his commanding officer.*

66 **Suivez-vous ...** follow the great captain

70–71 **roaring devil ...** *Pistol is like a devil in medieval plays, who would roar out when beaten by a wooden dagger (see* Twelfth Night, *4.2.128–132).*

72–73 **both hanged** *This is the first we hear about Nym's death; Bardolph's was reported in 3.6 (102–105).*

73 **durst** dared

74 **lackeys** servants

BOY	Encore qu'il est contre son jurement de pardonner aucun prisonnier, néanmoins, pour les 50 écus que vous l'avez promis, il est content de vous donner la liberté, le franchisement.
FRENCH SOLDIER	Sur mes genoux je vous donne mille remerciements; et je m'estime heureux que je suis tombé entre les mains d'un chevalier, je pense, le plus 55 brave, vaillant, et trés distigué seigneur d'Angleterre.
PISTOL	Expound unto me, boy.
BOY	He gives you, upon his knees, a thousand thanks; and he esteems himself happy that he hath fallen 60 into the hands of one, as he thinks, the most brave, valorous, and thrice-worthy signieur of England.
PISTOL	As I suck blood, I will some mercy show. Follow me! 65
BOY	Suivez-vous le grand capitaine.

Exeunt PISTOL *and French* Soldier

I did never know so full a voice issue from so
empty a heart: but the saying is true, 'The empty
vessel makes the greatest sound.' Bardolph and
Nym had ten times more valour than this roaring 70
devil i' the old play, that every one may pare his
nails with a wooden dagger: and they are both
hanged; and so would this be if he durst steal any
thing adventurously. I must stay with the lackeys,
with the luggage of our camp. The French might 75
have a good prey of us, if he knew of it; for there
is none to guard it but boys.

Exit

4.5 Another part of the battlefield

The French army has collapsed in total disorder, even though they still outnumber the English, and the desperate nobles prepare to die in battle rather than live on in shame and dishonour.

Activities

Character review: the French (6)

A Re-read 4.2 (before the battle) and 4.5 (near the end of the battle) and list the main differences between the ways in which the French nobles are behaving. Look particularly at the things they say about the English. Draw two cartoons which will illustrate the main differences.

B Select sections from 4.2 and 4.5 to bring out most effectively the contrasts between the two scenes; then perform them, one after the other. Annotate the two sections you have chosen with directors' notes to show how you would bring out these contrasts in a film version. Your notes should refer to (a) what the actors are doing (tone of voice, gestures, movements, etc), and (b) the use of sound effects, visual effects and music.

C Look carefully at the language used by the French nobles in 4.2 and then in 4.5. What differences do you notice? Look, for example, at: the different tone of the exclamations; vocabulary to do with honour and with shame; the imagery used of the English in 4.2 (lines 43–52) and of the French themselves in 4.5 (lines 12–16); the contrast between order and disorder; the different kinds of 'haste' in the two scenes.

1–3 **O diable! ...** O, the devil! O lord! The day is lost! All is lost! My life's death!

Confounded lost

5 **plumes** the feathers worn on their helmets seem to mock them with their shames

O méchante fortune O, evil fortune

7 **perdurable** long-lasting

13 **with his cap ...** begging

14 **pandar** pimp

15 **no gentler** no more noble

17 **spoiled** ruined

friend befriend

19 **enow** enough

20 **throngs** crowds

Scene 5

Another part of the field.

Enter CONSTABLE, ORLEANS, BOURBON, DAUPHIN, *and* RAMBURES.

CONSTABLE	O diable!
ORLEANS	O Seigneur, le jour est perdu, tout est perdu!
DAUPHIN	Mort de ma vie! All is confounded, all!

DAUPHIN   Mort de ma vie! All is confounded, all!
Reproach and everlasting shame
Sits mocking in our plumes. O méchante fortune!   5
Do not run away. (*A short alarum*).

CONSTABLE   Why, all our ranks are broke.

DAUPHIN   O perdurable shame! Let's stab ourselves.
Be these the wretches that we played at dice for?

ORLEANS   Is this the king we sent to for his ransom?

BOURBON   Shame and eternal shame, nothing but shame!   10
Let us die in honour: once more back again;
And he that will not follow Bourbon now,
Let him go hence, and with his cap in hand,
Like a base pander, hold the chamber-door
Whilst by a slave, no gentler than my dog,   15
His fairest daughter is contaminated.

CONSTABLE   Disorder, that hath spoiled us, friend us now!
Let us on heaps go offer up our lives.

ORLEANS   We are enow yet living in the field
To smother up the English in our throngs,   20
If any order might be thought upon.

BOURBON   The devil take order now! I'll to the throng.
Let life be short, else shame will be too long.

Exeunt

4.6 Another part of the battlefield

Henry senses victory but realises that all is not over yet. Exeter reports the deaths of the Duke of York and the Earl of Suffolk.

8 **Larding** enriching

9–10 **Yoke-fellow … lies** *Suffolk and York are joined together by the companionship of their honourable* (**honour-owing** = honour-owning) *wounds.*

11 **haggled over** hacked and mangled

12 **insteeped** soaked

15 **Tarry** wait

19 **in our chivalry** as knights

21 **raught me his hand** reached out to me

22 **gripe** grip

26 **espoused** married

28 **pretty** beautiful

29 **waters** tears

31 **all my mother …** all the tender feelings inherited from my mother

33 **compound** come to terms

Scene 6

Another part of the field.

Alarums. Enter KING HENRY *and forces,* EXETER, *and others.*

KING HENRY	Well have we done, thrice valiant countrymen,
	But all's not done; yet keep the French the field!

EXETER	The Duke of York commends him to your majesty.

KING HENRY Lives he, good uncle? Thrice within this hour
I saw him down; thrice up again, and fighting;   5
From helmet to the spur all blood he was.

EXETER In which array, brave soldier, doth he lie,
Larding the plain; and by his bloody side,
Yoke-fellow to his honour-owing wounds,
The noble Earl of Suffolk also lies.   10
Suffolk first died: and York, all haggled over,
Comes to him, where in gore he lay insteeped,
And takes him by the beard, kisses the gashes
That bloodily did yawn upon his face,
And cries aloud. 'Tarry, dear cousin Suffolk!   15
My soul shall thine keep company to heaven.
Tarry, sweet soul, for mine, then fly abreast,
As in this glorious and well-foughten field
We kept together in our chivalry!'
Upon these words I came and cheered him up: 20
He smiled me in the face, raught me his hand,
And, with a feeble gripe, says 'Dear my lord,
Commend my service to my sovereign.'
So did he turn and over Suffolk's neck
He threw his wounded arm and kissed his lips,   25
And so exposed to death, with blood he sealed
A testament of noble-ending love.
The pretty and sweet manner of it forced
Those waters from me which I would have stopped,
But I had not so much of man in me,   30
And all my mother came into mine eyes
And gave me up to tears.

KING HENRY   I blame you not;
For, hearing this, I must perforce compound
With mistful eyes, or they will issue too. (*Alarum*)

4.7 Another part of the battlefield

Believing that the French are re-grouping for a further attack, Henry orders his men to kill their prisoners. Fluellen and Gower express their anger at the French who have killed the luggage boys while fleeing from the battle.

37 **kill his prisoners** *as a small army, the English could not risk suffering a renewed attack while trying to control large numbers of prisoners who might rise up against them*

1 **poys** boys *(The French had killed the boys guarding the baggage; see 4.4.75–77).*

2 **arrant** notorious

3 **knavery** wickedness

   offert offered

10 **to cut his prisoner's throat** *Either these are different prisoners from those killed at the end of Scene 6, or Gower believes that Henry's order was in response to the death of the boys.*

12 **porn** born *(Fluellen is proud that Henry was born in Monmouth, on the Welsh border.)*

14 **Pig** big *(Fluellen compares Henry with Alexander the Great: see 3.1.19.)*

18 **magnanimous** great-hearted

19 **variations** varied; differently expressed

24 **'orld** world

But, hark! What new alarum is this same?   35
The French have reinforced their scattered men.
Then every soldier kill his prisoners;
Give the word through.

Exeunt

Scene 7

Another part of the field.

Enter FLUELLEN *and* GOWER.

FLUELLEN   Kill the poys and the luggage! 'T is expressly
against the law of arms. 'T is as arrant a piece of
knavery, mark you now, as can be offert. In your
conscience, now, is it not?

GOWER   'T is certain there's not a boy left alive, and the   5
cowardly rascals that ran from the battle ha' done
this slaughter. Besides, they have burned and
carried away all that was in the king's tent,
wherefore the king, most worthily, hath caused
every soldier to cut this prisoner's throat. O 't is a   10
gallant king!

FLUELLEN   Ay, he was porn at Monmouth, Captain Gower.
What call you the town's name where Alexander
the Pig was born?

GOWER   Alexander the Great.   15

FLUELLEN   Why, I pray you, is not pig great? The pig, or the
great, or the mighty, or the huge, or the
magnanimous, are all one reckonings, save the
phrase is a little variations.

GOWER   I think Alexander the Great was born in Macedon.   20
His father was called Philip of Macedon, as I take it.

FLUELLEN   I think it is in Macedon where Alexander is porn.
I tell you, captain, if you look in the maps of the
'orld, I warrant you sall find, in the comparisons
between Macedon and Monmouth, that the   25

4.7 Another part of the battlefield

Suggesting similarities between Henry and Alexander the Great, Fluellen points out that both men caused the deaths of their best friend, in Henry's case, Sir John Falstaff. Henry enters, angry at the massacre of the boys.

Activities

Character review: Henry (21): Henry and Alexander

Fluellen's attempt to compare Henry with Alexander the Great seems to puzzle Gower.

1. What parallels between the two men does Fluellen find, in terms of (a) their exploits; (b) geography; and (c) their 'best friends'?
   How convincing do you find parallels (a), (b) or (c)?

2. To remind yourself about Henry's relationship with Falstaff, look at pages 240–244. Why might Shakespeare want his audience to be reminded of Henry's rejection of Falstaff at this point? In pairs, discuss each of these possible reasons:

   The reminder of Falstaff at this point shows us that:
   - all great men have flaws
   - Henry's glorious rise and successes are at the expense of his old friends
   - Henry is ruthless and will use people to get what he wants
   - Henry has a fierce temper
   - whereas the death of Cleitus was a crime caused by Alexander's drunkenness, the rejection of Falstaff was a sensible action brought about by good judgement.

29 **prains** brains

33 **is come after it ...** follows it fairly (**indifferent**) closely

34 **figures** parallels, comparisons

36 **wraths ... cholers** angers ... bad moods

38 **intoxicates in his prains** drunk

40 **Cleitus** when he was drunk (**intoxicates in his prains**), *Alexander killed his foster-brother, Cleitus*

46–47 **in his ales and his cups** drunk

49 **doublet** *jacket, originally made with double-thickness*

50 **gipes** jokes

   knaveries bad deeds

57 **trumpet** trumpeter

60 **void the field** clear the battlefield

situations, look you, is both alike. There is a river in
Macedon, and there is also, moreover, a river at
Monmouth. It is called Wye at Monmouth; but it
is out of my prains what is the name of the other
river; but 't is all one, 't is alike as my fingers is to   30
my fingers, and there is salmons in both. If you
mark Alexander's life well, Harry of Monmouth's
life is come after it indifferent well, for there is
figures in all things. Alexander, God knows, and
you know, in his rages, and his furies, and his   35
wraths, and his cholers, and his moods, and his
displeasures, and his indignations, and also being
a little intoxicates in his prains, did, in his ales
and his angers, look you, kill his best friend,
Cleitus.   40

GOWER   Our king is not like him in that. He never killed
any of his friends.

FLUELLEN   It is not well done, mark you now, to take the tales
out of my mouth, ere it is made and finished. I
speak but in the figures and comparisons of it. As   45
Alexander killed his friend Cleitus, being in his
ales and his cups, so also Harry Monmouth, being
in his right wits and his good judgements, turned
away the fat knight with the great-belly doublet: he
was full of jests, and gipes, and knaveries, and   50
mocks; I have forgot his name.

GOWER   Sir John Falstaff.

FLUELLEN   That is he: I'll tell you there is good men porn at
Monmouth.

GOWER   Here comes his majesty.   55

Alarum. Enter KING HENRY *and forces;* WARWICK, GLOUCESTER, EXETER,
and others:

KING HENRY   I was not angry since I came to France
Until this instant. Take a trumpet, herald;
Ride thou unto the horsemen on yon hill:
If they will fight with us, bid them come down,
Or void the field; they do offend our sight.   60

4.7 Another part of the battlefield

Henry is threatening to kill the remaining prisoners unless the last of the French horsemen leave the battlefield, when Montjoy enters to announce that the French have acknowledged defeat and to ask for permission to bury their dead.

Activities

Shakespeare's language: anger

Hearing news of the killing of the boys, Henry enters angrily and the language reveals the strength of his feelings.

Read the speech through, noticing the large number of words with one syllable (line 59 is totally monosyllabic). Perform the speech, emphasising the 'punchy' monosyllabic lines to help to convey Henry's emotions.

Character review: Montjoy (3)

1. What are Montjoy's main statements here?
2. Find words to describe his mood.
3. Compare this appearance of Montjoy with his last one (4.3.79–127). What differences might a stage or film production bring out through:
   - his tone of voice
   - his 'body language'
   - his costume
   - any other aspects of his appearance or voice?

62 **skirr** scurry

63 **Assyrian slings** *slings were a favourite weapon of the ancient Assyrians*

70 **fined** staked, wagered *(see 4.3.120–125)*

74 **book** make a record of

79–80 **steeds Fret fetlock deep in gore** horses struggle in blood to the tops of their hoofs

81 **Yerk out** lash out

86 **peer** appear

If they'll do neither, we will come to them,
And make them skirr away, as swift as stones
Enforcéd from the old Assyrian slings.
Besides, we'll cut the throats of those we have,
And not a man of them that we shall take   65
Shall taste our mercy. Go and tell them so.

Exit Herald

Enter MONTJOY.

EXETER   Here comes the herald of the French, my liege.

GLOUCESTER His eyes are humbler than they used to be.

KING HENRY How now! What means this, herald? Know'st thou
                   not
                 That I have fined these bones of mine for ransom?   70
                 Comest thou again for ransom?

MONTJOY   No, great king:
                 I come to thee for charitable licence,
                 That we may wander o'er this bloody field
                 To book our dead, and then to bury them,
                 To sort our nobles from our common men.   75
                 For many of our princes – woe the while! –
                 Lie drowned and soaked in mercenary blood;
                 So do our vulgar drench their peasant limbs
                 In blood of princes; and their wounded steeds
                 Fret fetlock deep in gore, and with wild rage   80
                 Yerk out their arméd heels at their dead masters,
                 Killing them twice. O give us leave, great king,
                 To view the field in safety and dispose
                 Of their dead bodies!

KING HENRY   I tell thee truly, herald,
                 I know not if the day be ours or no;   85
                 For yet a many of your horsemen peer
                 And gallop o'er the field.

MONTJOY   The day is yours.

KING HENRY Praiséd be God, and not our strength, for it!
                 What is this castle called that stands hard by?

4.7 Another part of the battlefield

Henry names the battle after the nearby castle, Agincourt, and Fluellen proudly reminds the King of his Welsh connections. Heralds are dispatched to find out how many have died on each side.

Activities

Actors' interpretations: reactions to the news

Henry does not fully realise that the English have won the battle until Montjoy informs him 'The day is yours' (line 87).

1. In groups, work out some silent reactions (from Gloucester, Exeter, Fluellen and any others who might be on stage). Think about:
   - facial expressions
   - gestures and movements
   - a possible pause before or after Henry's line 'Praiséd be God...'.
2. Freeze frame the moment Montjoy informs them that they have won.

Character review: Fluellen (3)

1. What does Fluellen say to Henry about (a) Henry's famous ancestors; and (b) the Welsh?
2. Why do you think he chooses (a) to approach Henry at all at this point; and (b) to raise these topics? (It will help to think first about how Henry might be feeling at this moment, just after the news that the English have won the battle.)
3. Write an entry in Fluellen's private journal in which he explains what was in his mind at this point and why he said the things he did.

92 **Crispin Crispianus** *see note to 4.3.40*

93 **your grandfather** *Fluellen means great-grandfather (Edward III; see page 66).*

101–102 **where leeks did grow** *In fact, the wearing of leeks is supposed to commemorate a British victory over the Saxons in AD 540.*

102 **Monmouth caps** *tall, brimless hats*

105 **Saint Tavy's day** *Saint David's day (1 March, see note to 4.1.54–55)*

108 **Wye** *the river flowing through Monmouth*

109 **plood** *As well as being born in Monmouth, Henry had a Welsh great-grandmother.*

MONTJOY	They call it Agincourt.	90

KING HENRY Then call we this the field of Agincourt,
Fought on the day of Crispin Crispianus.

FLUELLEN Your grandfather of famous memory, an 't please
your majesty, and your great-uncle Edward, the
Plack Prince of Wales, as I have read in the 95
chronicles, fought a most prave pattle here in
France.

KING HENRY They did, Fluellen.

FLUELLEN Your majesty says very true. If your majesties is
remembered of it, the Welshmen did good service 100
in a garden where leeks did grow, wearing leeks in
their Monmouth caps, which, your majesty know,
to this hour is an honourable badge of the service;
and I do believe your majesty takes no scorn to
wear the leek upon Saint Tavy's day. 105

KING HENRY I wear it for a memorable honour;
For I am Welsh, you know, good countryman.

FLUELLEN All the water in Wye cannot wash your majesty's
Welsh plood out of your pody, I can tell you that.
God pless and preserve it, as long as it pleases his 110
grace, and his majesty too!

KING HENRY Thanks, good my countryman.

FLUELLEN By Jeshu, I am your majesty's countryman, I care
not who know it. I will confess it to all the 'orld. I
need not to be ashamed of your majesty, praised 115
be God, so log as your majesty is an honest man.

KING HENRY God keep me so! Our heralds go with him;
Bring me just notice of the numbers dead
On both our parts.

Exeunt Heralds *with* MONTJOY

Call yonder fellow hither.

(Points to WILLIAMS*)*

4.7 Another part of the battlefield

Henry calls Williams to him and asks him why he is wearing a glove in his hat. Williams explains and Fluellen supports the soldier's determination to keep his promise and fight with the man who challenged him, whoever he might be.

Activities

Plot review (14): Williams and the glove

In pairs, one person explains to the other who Williams is and why he is wearing a glove in his cap (see 4.1.86–229), and the second person explains Fluellen's opinion in this scene on whether Williams ought to keep his word (lines 135–147).

Shakespeare's language: dramatic irony

Look back at the activity on page 44 to remind yourself about dramatic irony. Then pick out the dramatic irony in this exchange between Henry, Williams and Fluellen. How do you feel at these moments (when you know something that Williams and Fluellen do not know)? Why do you think Shakespeare included dramatic irony here?

122 **WILLIAMS** *This is the soldier who exchanged gloves with the disguised Henry in 4.1 (211–217).*

An 't if it

123 **withal** with

125 **swaggered** behaved arrogantly, boasted

127–128 **take him a box** strike him

133 **craven** coward

135 **of great sort** of high rank

136 **quite from the answer ... of** such high rank that he cannot in honour accept a challenge from someone as low-born as a common soldier

138 **Lucifer and Beelzebub** *high-ranking devils in hell*

140 **be perjured** breaks his word

141 **arrant** notorious

Jacksauce impudent person

149–150 **is good knowledge and literatured** is knowledgeable and well-read

Exeter	Soldier, you must come to the king.	120
King Henry	Soldier, why wearest thou that glove in thy cap?	
Williams	An 't please your majesty, 't is the gage of one that I should fight withal, if he be alive.	
King Henry	An Englishman?	
Williams	An 't please your majesty, a rascal that swaggered with me last night; who, if 'a live and ever dare to challenge this glove, I have sworn to take him a box o' th' ear: or if I can see my glove in his cap – which he swore, as he was a soldier, he would wear if alive – I will strike it out soundly.	125
		130
King Henry	What think you, Captain Fluellen, is it fit this soldier keep his oath?	
Fluellen	He is a craven and a villain else, an 't please your majesty, in my conscience.	
King Henry	It may be his enemy is a gentleman of great sort, quite from the answer of his degree.	135
Fluellen	Though he be as good a gentleman as the devil is, as Lucifer and Belzebub himself, it is necessary, look your grace, that he keep his vow and his oath. If he be perjured, see you now, his reputation is as arrant a villain and a Jacksauce as ever his black shoe trod upon God's ground and his earth, in my conscience, la!	140
King Henry	Then keep thy vow, sirrah, when thou meetest the fellow.	
		145
Williams	So I will, my liege, as I live.	
King Henry	Who servest thou under?	
Williams	Under Captain Gower, my liege.	
Fluellen	Gower is a good captain, and is good knowledge and literatured in the wars.	150
King Henry	Call him hither to me, soldier.	

4.7 Another part of the battlefield

Having sent Williams out of the way, Henry asks Fluellen to wear a glove. It is of course Williams', but Henry claims to have taken it from the Duke of Alençon in battle, adding that anyone who challenges it is a friend of Alençon's and must be arrested.

153 **this favour** the glove which he had been given by Williams

154–158 **Alençon** Henry is making up this story about his fight with the Duke of Alençon, so that the patriotic Fluellen will be keen to challenge anybody wearing the matching glove.

158 **apprehend** arrest

162 **aggriefed at** (aggrieved at), offended by

163 **fain** like to

172 **haply** perhaps

179 **touched with choler** short tempered

WILLIAMS I will, my liege.

Exit

KING HENRY Here, Fluellen, wear thou this favour for me and
stick it in thy cap. When Alençon and myself were
down together, I plucked this glove from his helm. 155
If any man challenge this, he is a friend to Alençon,
and an enemy to our person. If thou encounter any
such, apprehend him, an thou dost me love.

FLUELLEN Your grace doos me as great honours as can be
desired in the hearts of his subjects. I would fain   160
see the man, that has but two legs, that shall find
himself aggriefed at this glove. That is all; but I
would fain see it once, an please God of his grace
that I might see.

KING HENRY Knowest thou Gower?   165

FLUELLEN He is my dear friend, an please you.

KING HENRY Pray thee, go seek him, and bring him to my tent.

FLUELLEN I will fetch him.

Exit

KING HENRY My Lord of Warwick, and my brother Gloucester,
Follow Fluellen closely at the heels.   170
The glove which I have given him for a favour
May haply purchase him a box o' th' ear.
It is the soldier's; I by bargain should
Wear it myself. Follow, good cousin Warwick.
If that soldier strike him, as I judge   175
By his blunt bearing he will keep his word,
Some sudden mischief may arise of it;
For I do know Fluellen valiant
And, touched with choler, hot as gunpowder,
And quickly will return an injury.   180
Follow, and see there be no harm between them.
Go you with me, uncle of Exeter.

Exeunt

4.8 Another part of the battlefield

When Williams comes back, he immediately notices the glove in Fluellen's cap and challenges it by striking him. Recalling Henry's words, Fluellen orders Williams' arrest as a friend of Alençon's and a traitor.

Activities

Shakespeare's language: *in medias res*

Many of Shakespeare's scenes begin with characters entering in the middle of a conversation. When this happens, we say that the scene opens *in medias res* (pronounced 'in meddy-ass rays' – a Latin expression simply meaning 'in the middle of things').

In pairs, improvise the imagined conversation from the point where Williams finds Gower up to their entrance at the beginning of the scene.

1   **I warrant** I assure you

3   **apace** quickly

4   **peradventure** perhaps

10 **arrant** notorious, outrageous

13 **forsworn** *Williams is determined not to break the promise he gave in 4.1 (214–227) and which Fluellen himself agreed that he should keep in 4.7 (129–134).*

15 **plows** blows

17 **a lie in thy throat** a deliberate lie

22 **contagious** catching (it will spread)

23 **as you shall desire** as you could wish to see

Scene 8

Before KING HENRY'S *pavilion.*

Enter GOWER *and* WILLIAMS.

WILLIAMS   I warrant it is to knight you, captain.

Enter FLUELLEN.

FLUELLEN   (*To* GOWER) God's will and his pleasure, captain, I
beseech you now, come apace to the king. There is
more good toward you peradventure than is in
your knowledge to dream of.   5

WILLIAMS   Sir, know you this glove? (*shows his second glove,
which matches the one in Fluellen's cap*)

FLUELLEN   Know the glove! I know the glove is a glove.

WILLIAMS   I know this (*Points to* FLUELLEN's *cap*) and thus I
challenge it. (*Strikes him*)

FLUELLEN   'S blood! An arrant traitor as any is in the universal 10
world, or in France, or in England!

GOWER   How now, sir! (*To* WILLIAMS) You villain!

WILLIAMS   Do you think I'll be forsworn?

FLUELLEN   Stand away, Captain Gower! I will give treason his
payment into plows, I warrant you.   15

WILLIAMS   I am no traitor.

FLUELLEN   That's a lie in thy throat, [*To* GOWER] I charge you in
his majesty's name, apprehend him! He's a friend
of the Duke Alençon's.

Enter WARWICK *and* GLOUCESTER.

WARWICK   How now, how now! What's the matter?   20

FLUELLEN   My Lord of Warwick, here is – praised be God for
it! – a most contagious treason come to light, look
you, as you shall desire in a summer's day.
Here is his majesty.

4.8 Another part of the battlefield

Henry arrives on the scene and, having listened to their explanations, reveals that he was the man Williams had challenged the night before the battle. Williams defends himself by claiming that he meant no offence: as far as he had been aware, he was challenging an ordinary common man.

Activities

Actors' interpretations: sorting out the gloves

1. In the 1999 StageGraft production, the actors took some time to work out exactly how the gloves are used in this scene. Find two pairs of gloves and act out the challenge between Henry and Williams which took place in 4.1. (lines 90–234). Then work out which gloves are being referred to in the following lines: 6; 8; 29 (two gloves here); 40 (two again).
   Perform the scene, using the gloves correctly and showing Williams' dawning realisation that he is in deep trouble.

2. The Branagh film did not include this incident, cutting from 4.7.120 to 4.8.74. What is (a) gained; and (b) lost, if the sequence is cut?

36–37 **is pear me testimony ...** will bear (**pear**) me witness

37 **will avouchment** will acknowledge

40 **the fellow** the other one of the pair

45 **martial law** *law enforced in wartime*

46 **make me satisfaction** put this right, satisfy my honour

50 **abuse** insult

Enter KING HENRY *and* EXETER.

KING HENRY	How now! What's the matter? 25

FLUELLEN   My liege, here is a villain and a traitor, that, look
your grace, has struck the glove which your majesty
is take out of the helmet of Alençon.

WILLIAMS   My liege, this was my glove: here is the fellow of it;
and he that I gave it to in change promised to wear 30
it in his cap: I promised to strike him, if he did. I
met this man with glove in his cap, and I have
been as good as my word.

FLUELLEN   Your majesty, hear now, saving your majesty's
manhood, what an arrant, rascally, beggarly, lousy 35
knave it is: I hope your majesty is pear me
testimony and witness, and will avouchment, that
this is the glove of Alençon, that your majesty is
give me; in your conscience now?

KING HENRY   Give me thy glove, soldier; look, here is the fellow 40
of it.
'T was I, indeed, thou promisedst to strike;
And thou hast given me most bitter terms.

FLUELLEN   An please your majesty, let his neck answer for it, if
there is any martial law in the world. 45

KING HENRY   How canst thou make me satisfaction?

WILLIAMS   All offences, my lord, come from the heart. Never
came any from mine that might offend your
majesty.

KING HENRY   It was ourself thou didst abuse. 50

WILLIAMS   Your majesty came not like yourself: you appeared
to me but a common man; witness the night, your
garments, your lowliness; and what your highness
suffered under that shape, I beseech you take it for
your own fault and not mine: for had you been as I 55
took you for, I made no offence; therefore, I beseech
your highness, pardon me.

4.8 Another part of the battlefield

Henry orders Williams' glove to be filled with gold coins and Fluellen also makes his peace with the soldier. Lists brought in by a herald reveal that over fifteen hundred French have been taken prisoner in addition to ten thousand killed.

Activities

Character review: Williams (1)

A What do you think Williams is feeling when Henry reveals that he was the man Williams challenged? What could happen to Williams at this point?

B Perform Williams' response to Henry's question ('How canst thou make me satisfaction?') in different ways, for example either terrified and begging for forgiveness, or defiant and confident in the rightness of his excuse. Which version seems more in keeping with his behaviour in 4.1?

C Hot-seat Williams, asking him how he feels now that the incident with the gloves is all over. Question him in particular about how he feels about (a) Henry disguising himself the night before the battle; and (b) the money given to him by Henry and by Fluellen. Is he delighted with his good fortune, for example; or does he feel 'bought off' and patronised by those in power, like the Williams in the 1976 RSC production?

63 **mettle** courage and spirit
66 **prawls and prabbles** brawls and squabbles
71 **wherefore** why
72 **pashful** bashful, reluctant
76 **good sort** high rank
80 **besides** in addition to
84 **bearing banners** wearing coats of arms
86 **esquires** gentlemen
88 **dubbed knights** knighted
90 **mercenaries** professional soldiers fighting for money

KING HENRY Here, uncle Exeter, fill this glove with crowns,
And give it to this fellow. Keep it, fellow;
And wear it for an honour in thy cap   60
Till I do challenge it. Give him the crowns:
And, captain, you must needs be friends with him.

FLUELLEN By this day and this light, the fellow has mettle
enough in his belly. Hold, there is twelve pence for
you; and I pray you to serve Got, and keep you out 65
of prawls, and prabbles, and quarrels, and
dissensions, and, I warrant you, it is the better for
you.

WILLIAMS I will none of your money.

FLUELLEN It is with a good will; I can tell you, it will serve you 70
to mend your shoes. Come, wherefore should you
be so pashful? Your shoes is not so good. 'T is a
good silling, I warrant you, or I will change it.

      Enter an English Herald.

KING HENRY Now, herald, are the dead numbered?

HERALD Here is the number of the slaughtered French.   75

KING HENRY What prisoners of good sort are taken, uncle?

EXETER Charles Duke of Orleans, nephew to the king;
John Duke of Bourbon, and Lord Bouciqualt:
Of other lords and barons, knights and squires,
Full fifteen hundred, besides common men.   80

KING HENRY This note doth tell me of ten thousand French
That in the field lie slain: of princes, in this
    number,
And nobles bearing banners, there lie dead
One hundred twenty-six: added to these,   85
Of knights, esquires, and gallant gentlemen,
Eight thousand and four hundred; of the which,
Five hundred were but yesterday dubbed knights:
So that, in these ten thousand they have lost,
There are but sixteen hundred mercenaries.   90
The rest are princes, barons, lords, knights, squires,
And gentlemen of blood and quality.

4.8 Another part of the battlefield

The English losses have been very slight: York and Suffolk, two named gentlemen and only twenty-five common soldiers. Giving credit for the victory to God, Henry orders that the appropriate religious ceremonies should take place.

Activities

Plot review (15): casualties of Agincourt

A Imagine you were filming *Henry V* and had decided to show some flashback shots to accompany the reading of the French and English dead. Draw three or four frames of scenes from earlier in the play which might be effective. For example, you might show the confident Constable (who is one of the dead) boasting about the coming French victory (4.2), or York (also killed in battle) asking to lead the attack (4.3.129–131).

B Use lines 76–103 to write the front page report for the French newspaper, the *Fleur-de-lys*. Include a statement about what went wrong (see pages 248–250) and, in particular, devote sections to comments on the Constable (who has been killed) and Orléans (taken prisoner).

Then, in contrast, compose two headlines for English newspapers (one a tabloid, the other a broadsheet).

C 1. If you read Shakespeare's main source, Holinshed's *Chronicles*, you will find that he has repeated Holinshed's lists of names and statistics almost word-for-word. Why might Shakespeare have

continued on page 180

---

101 **lusty** lively

109 **but five and twenty** only twenty-five. *Recent historians have estimated that between 7,000 and 10,000 French died at Agincourt (with a further 1,500 taken prisoner) and 400 to 500 English (see page 183).*

111 **... Ascribe we all** *Henry gives all the credit of the victory to God.*

111–114 **When without stratagem ... other?** When was there ever a battle in which, without any trickery, but in straightforward hand-to-hand fighting, the losses were so high on one side and so low on the other? Take the credit, God, for it is due to no one but You.

125 **Do ... rites** Let us perform all the appropriate religious ceremonies

126 **'Non nobis' and 'Te Deum'** *hymns praising God; 'Non nobis' asks God to take all the glory Himself, rather than giving it to us*

The names of those their nobles that lie dead:
Charles Delabreth, High Constable of France;   95
Jaques of Chatillon, Admiral of France;
The Master of the Cross-bows, Lord Rambures;
Great Master of France, the brave Sir Guichard
　　Dolphin.
John Duke of Alençon, Anthony Duke of Brabant,
The brother to the Duke of Burgundy,   100
And Edward Duke of Bar: of lusty earls,
Grandpré and Roussi, Fauconberg and Foix,
Beaumont and Marle, Vaudemont and Lestrale.
Here was a royal fellowship of death!
Where is the number of our English dead?   105
(Herald *shows him another paper*)
Edward the Duke of York, the Earl of Suffolk,
Sir Richard Ketley, Davy Gam, esquire:
None else of name; and of all other men
But five and twenty. O God, thy arm was here;
And not to us, but to thy arm alone,   110
Ascribe we all! When without stratagem,
But in plain shock and even play of battle,
Was ever known so great and little loss
On one part and on th' other? Take it, God,
For it is none but thine!

EXETER　　　　　　　　　　　　　'T is wonderful!   115

KING HENRY　Come, go we in procession to the village:
And be it death proclaiméd through our host
To boast of this or take that praise from God
Which is his only.

FLUELLEN　Is it not lawful, an please your majesty, to tell how   120
many is killed?

KING HENRY　Yes, captain; but with this acknowledgement,
That God fought for us.

FLUELLEN　Yes, my conscience, he did us great good.

KING HENRY　Do we all holy rites;   125
Let there be sung 'Non nobis' and 'Te Deum';

Henry announces that, after hymns have been sung and they have buried their dead, they will set off for Calais and then England.

Activities

felt it important to use Holinshed in that way; and what is the effect of these long lists of names?

2. A particular detail which comes from Holinshed is the number of the English dead (twenty-five). We now know that between 400 and 500 English died: would you agree with those productions which change 'But five and twenty' to 'But five and twenty score'? What are the arguments (a) for making the change; and (b) for leaving the number as it is?

Actors' interpretations: after Agincourt

As Act 4 draws to a close and the Agincourt sequence is concluded, Henry calls for the dead to be buried and hymns to be sung. In the Branagh film there follows a long sequence in which, in a continuous camera shot accompanied by the 'Non nobis', we see Henry carrying the body of the Boy through the battlefield, trudging past many of the characters who have fought and the bodies of those who have died (including Pistol mourning over the dead Nym). What are the advantages of ending the Act in this way? How would you end the Act in a stage production?

127 **charity** Christian burial
128 **Calais** *see the map on page 247*
129 **ne'er** never

The dead with charity enclosed in clay.
And then to Calais; and to England then;
Where ne'er from France arrived more happy men.

Exeunt

Exam practice

Character review: Montjoy (4)

Imagine you are Montjoy, the French herald. Write down your thoughts as you walk through the battlefield and rejoin the French survivors. You could begin: *I cannot believe that we could have suffered such a disastrous defeat ...*

Before you begin to write, you should think about Montjoy's impressions of:
- what Henry told him about the state of the English army when he saw them on the march (3.6)
- the confidence of the French nobles before the battle (3.7 and 4.2)
- Henry's response to the final offer of ransom (4.3)
- the behaviour of the French during the battle, including the slaughter of the English baggage boys (4.5 and 4.7)
- the French defeat and their heavy casualties (4.7.67–92 and 4.8.75–104).

Themes: war (5)

A Williams' description of men who have died in battle appearing at the Day of Judgement (4.1.137–144) is a grim reminder of the horrors of war and we learn how devastating it can be when Henry reads the lists of the French dead in 4.8. Try to capture some of this by creating a collage of photographs of modern wars taken from newspapers and magazines. Williams' and Henry's words might be incorporated into the design or printed alongside it.

B In a group, plan and perform a news programme (for either English or French television) following the battle of Agincourt. After a brief report, you could interview Henry or one of his commanders, a soldier from each side, Montjoy or someone like Williams. Try to show the unique perspective that each of these characters has.

C In pairs, improvise a discussion between two priests who have overheard Henry's prayer and argue about whether or not it will be answered. Should God assist the English in battle, rather than the French? Or turn a blind eye to the fact that Henry's father was a usurper? Will the building of chantries help Henry to receive God's pardon for his father's actions? How genuinely penitent *is* Henry?

Plot review (16): Shakespeare's battle statistics

4.3 and 4.8 give an idea of the overwhelming odds facing the English and the nature of their victory. The exact size of the French army is still not known: the latest estimates vary between 20,000 and 150,000, 60 per cent of whom were men-at-arms (knights and well-armed soldiers). The English army almost certainly totalled 6,000 men, of whom 5,000 were archers and the rest men-at-arms.

Different writers offer their own opinions on the relative sizes of the two armies and it is interesting to compare (a) Holinshed (whose account of English and Scottish history Shakespeare seems to have read), (b) Shakespeare himself and (c) recent historians.

Draw up the following table:

	Holinshed	Shakespeare	Recent historians
Size of French army	60,000		20,000–150,000
Size of English army	15,000		6,000
French dead	10,000		7,000–10,000 (+1,500 prisoners)
English dead	25		400–500

1. Fill in the middle column with the figures that Shakespeare supplies.
2. How different is Shakespeare's calculation of the odds at the start of the battle (4.3.4) to the calculations of recent historians?
3. Update your time-chart (see pages 28 and 115) with details of the march through France and the battle of Agincourt.

Character review: Henry (23): opinions on Agincourt, Williams and God

Write further entries in the journals of Exeter and the cynical lord. Include comments from both on:
- Henry's leadership in battle (did he win the battle of Agincourt, or did the French lose it?)
- the business with Williams and the gloves (light-hearted fun or thoughtless and selfish?)
- Henry's repeated references to God, especially 4.7.88 and 4.8.109–129 (a sign of genuine piety or hypocrisy?).

5 Prologue

The Chorus once again apologises that the actors cannot represent everything on their limited stage, and describes Henry's triumphant return to England.

Activities

Plot review (16): between Agincourt and Henry's return to France

Although the Chorus does not make it clear, the 'interim' described (line 43) actually covered five years: 1415–1420.

A Note down the six main events recounted by the Chorus: lines 6–7; 8–13; 13–22; 22–35; 38–39; 40.

B In groups, form freeze-frames to represent the six events listed in A and give each one a newspaper headline.

C Look at the verbs in the Chorus' speech. What effects are achieved by the widespread use of (a) the imperative form (see page 68), and (b) the present tense? Think especially about these verbs' contribution to the theme of theatre and the imagination.

1 **vouchsafe** grant, agree

3 **admit the excuse** excuse us in the way we treat

9 **Athwart** across

10 **Pales in the flood** encloses, fences in the sea

12 **whiffler** *an official who clears the way for a royal procession*

21–22 **Giving full ...** all the trophies and any signs or displays (**ostent**) of victory are shown in praise of God, not himself

23 **quick forge** *imagination is described as a forge where thoughts are hammered out*

25 **brethren in best sort** aldermen and nobles of the highest rank

27 **plebeians** common people

29–32 **As, by a lower ...** *The comparison is made with the return of the Earl of Essex, who had been sent to Ireland by Queen Elizabeth I (**our gracious empress**) to put down a rebellion; the parallel is more humble (**lower**), but, in their affection, people hope he will return triumphantly, with the rebellion defeated, spitted (**broachéd**) on his sword.*

34–35 **Much more ...** Many more people turned out to welcome Henry (than for Caesar or Essex), and with better reason

36–37 **As yet ...** because, as the French are still mourning their defeat, Henry has no reason to leave England

184

Act 5

Prologue

Enter CHORUS.

CHORUS   Vouchsafe to those that have not read the story,
That I may prompt them: and of such as have,
I humbly pray them to admit the excuse
Of time, of numbers and due course of things,
Which cannot in their huge and proper life   5
Be here presented. Now we bear the king
Toward Calais: grant him there; there seen,
Heave him away upon your wingéd thoughts
Athwart the sea. Behold, the English beach
Pales in the flood with men, with wives and boys,   10
Whose shouts and claps out-voice the
    deep-mouthed sea,
Which like a mighty whiffler 'fore the king
Seems to prepare his way. So let him land,
And solemnly see him set on to London.
So swift a pace hath thought that even now   15
You may imagine him upon Blackheath;
Where that his lords desire him to have borne
His bruiséd helmet and his bended sword
Before him through the city. He forbids it,
Being free from vainness and self-glorious pride;   20
Giving full trophy, signal and ostent
Quite from himself to God. But now behold,
In the quick forge and working-house of thought,
How London doth pour out her citizens!
The mayor and all his brethren in best sort,   25
Like to the senators of the antique Rome,
With the plebeians swarming at their heels,
Go forth and fetch their conquering Caesar in:
As, by a lower but loving likelihood,
Were now the general of our gracious empress,   30
As in good time he may, from Ireland coming,
Bringing rebellion broachéd on his sword,
How many would the peaceful city quit,
To welcome him! Much more, and much more
    cause,
Did they this Harry. Now in London place him –   35
As yet the lamentation of the French
Invites the King of England's stay at home;

5.1 France: the English camp

Five years have passed and the Chorus reports that, after some political negotiations, Henry is once more in France. Fluellen is telling Gower that Pistol had mocked his wearing of a leek and that he is now bent on revenge, when Pistol himself swaggers in.

Activities

Character review: Fluellen (4)

In pairs, improvise the imagined scene in which Pistol brings Fluellen bread and salt and bids him eat his leek. Discuss Fluellen's reactions and then write a letter from Fluellen to a friend or relative at home in Wales in which he recounts the episode and vows revenge. If you want a challenge, represent some of Fluellen's dialect in the letter.

38 **The emperor** *the Holy Roman Emperor, Sigismund*

42–43 **played The interim** I have represented everything that has happened in between, by reminding you that it is in the past

44 **brook abridgement** put up with this summarising

45 **straight back again** *In fact, the Chorus moves the action forward five years to 1420, when Henry has returned to France to sign a peace treaty (see 5.2.1).*

4 **asse** as

5 **scald** scabby

6 **pragging** bragging

9 **yesterday** *presumably 1 March, Saint David's day*

11 **... breed no contention** could not start an argument with him

15 **swelling** strutting, full of himself

19 **bedlam** mad (*after the Bedlam – or Bethlehem – hospital in London*)

Trojan *for some reason an insulting term here*

20 **Parca's fatal web** *The Parcae were the three Fates in classical mythology (see 3.6.49); Pistol means: 'Do you want me to kill you?'*

21 **qualmish** sick

The emperor's coming in behalf of France,
To order peace between them – and omit
All the occurrences, whatever chanced,   40
Till Harry's back-return again to France:
There must we bring him; and myself have played
The interim, by remembering you 't is past.
Then brook abridgement, and your eyes advance,
After your thoughts, straight back again to France.   45

Exit

Scene 1

France. The English camp.

Enter FLUELLEN *and* GOWER.

GOWER   Nay, that 's right; but why wear you your leek
to-day? Saint Davy's day is past.

FLUELLEN   There is occasions and causes why and wherefore
in all things. I will tell you, asse my friend,
Captain Gower: the rascally, scald, beggarly, lousy,   5
pragging knave, Pistol, which you and yourself
and all the world know to be no petter than a
fellow, look you now, of no merits, he is come to
me and prings me pread and salt yesterday, look
you, and bid me eat my leek. It was in a place   10
where I could not breed no contention with him;
but I will be so bold as to wear it in my cap till I see
him once again, and then I will tell him a little
piece of my desires.

Enter PISTOL.

GOWER   Why, here he comes, swelling like a turkey-cock.   15

FLUELLEN   'T is no matter for his swellings nor his turkey-
cocks. God pless you, Ancient Pistol! You scurvy,
lousy knave, God pless you!

PISTOL   Ha, art thou bedlam? Dost thou thirst, base Trojan,
To have me fold up Parca's fatal web?   20
Hence! I am qualmish at the smell of leek.

5.1 France: the English camp

Fluellen beats Pistol with his cudgel and forces him to eat some leek.

Activities

Actors' interpretations: Pistol and the leek

A Perform the scene (up to Fluellen's exit) without dialogue, like a silent movie, trying to bring out the visual humour.

B Annotate the scene with director's advice on how it could be performed, including references to:
- movements and actions
- how to speak the lines
- where to pause
- facial expressions
- how the characters are feeling.

C 1. Note down the opportunities to play this scene (a) for broad comedy; and (b) to bring out the crueller aspects. Which is more effective at this point in the play, in your opinion?
2. This is another scene which is often cut, leaving only Pistol's soliloquy. What is (a) gained, and (b) lost, if all the business with the leek is cut?

22 **peseech** beseech, beg

28 **Cadwallader** *a Welsh warrior, the last of the British kings*

goats *Pistol implies that Welshmen are all goat farmers.*

34 **victuals** food

35 **mountain-squire ...** gentleman who owns worthless land (*which cannot be farmed*)

36 **low** (1) low-born, (2) low in contrast to mountain-high (line 35)

39 **astonished** stunned

41 **peat his pate** beat his head

42 **green** raw

42–43 **ploody coxcomb** bloody head ('cock's comb': *the fool's cap worn by a jester. See* Twelfth Night, *5.1.172*).

51 **cudgel** club

52 **do you** may it do you

FLUELLEN   I peseech you heartily, scurvy, lousy knave, at my
           desires, and my requests, and my petitions, to eat,
           look you, this leek; because, look you, you do not
           love it, nor your affections and your appetites and   25
           your digestions does not agree with it, I would
           desire you to eat it.

PISTOL   Not for Cadwallader and all his goats.

FLUELLEN   There is one goat for you. (*Strikes him*) Will you
           be so good, scald knave, as eat it?   30

PISTOL   Base Trojan, thou shalt die.

FLUELLEN   You say very true, scald knave, when God's will is.
           I will desire you to live in the mean time, and eat
           your victuals. Come, there is sauce for it. (*Strikes
           him*) You called me yesterday mountain-squire;   35
           but I will make you to-day a squire of low degree.
           I pray you, fall to: if you can mock a leek, you can
           eat a leek.

GOWER   Enough, captain: you have astonished him.

FLUELLEN   I say, I will make him eat some part of my leek, or   40
           I will peat his pate four days. Bite, I pray you; it is
           good for your green wound and your ploody
           coxcomb.

PISTOL   Must I bite?

FLUELLEN   Yes, certainly, and out of doubt and out of   45
           question too, and ambiguities.

PISTOL   By this leek, I will most horribly revenge:
           (FLUELLEN *strikes him*) I eat and eat, I swear –

FLUELLEN   Eat, I pray you. Will you have some more sauce to
           your leek? There is not enough leek to swear by.   50
           (*Cudgels him*)

PISTOL   Quiet thy cudgel; thou dost see I eat.

FLUELLEN   Much good do you, scald knave, heartily. Nay,
           pray you, throw none away; the skin is good for

5.1 France: the English camp

Fluellen throws Pistol a small coin and departs, leaving Gower to lecture Pistol for being a fraud and for mocking the Welshman. Pistol is now alone: he has received news that his wife is dead, and he feels old and tired.

Activities

Character review: Pistol (3)

A What has happened to all the other former companions of the King: Falstaff, Bardolph, Nym, the Boy and, most recently, Mistress Quickly? You can check by looking up the following references: 2.3.1–6; 3.6.101–110; 4.4.69–73; 4.7.1; and 5.1.84–85.

B Write an article for a magazine headed 'Where are they now?' about what has become of the King's former friends. End with speculations on Pistol's whereabouts, reporting that the last we heard he had been involved in an incident with a Welshman in France and had been seen sailing to England...

C 1. What different moods is it possible to capture with Pistol's soliloquy?
2. On Shakespeare's stage, it was easy to show Pistol exiting as Henry entered for the opening of 5.2. What effects can be gained by the juxtaposition of Pistol's exit and Henry's 5.2. entrance? In the 1999 StageGraft production, Pistol was leaving when Henry entered, alone. Pistol looked at the King without expression and then turned and left. What point might the director have been trying to make? How would you stage Pistol's exit?

58 **groat** coin worth four pence
60 **Me a groat!** *Pistol is insulted by the offer.*
61 **verily** truly
63 **in earnest of** as a down-payment on the revenge I will take
69 **counterfeit** false, fake
71 **respect** reason
72 **predeceased valour** bravery of men who are now dead
72–73 **dare not avouch ...** you dare not back up your words with actions
74 **gleeking and galling** mocking and irritating
76 **garb** manner (*literally:* clothing)
80 **Doth Fortune ...** *fortune is now being fickle, behaving like a hussy (***huswife***) to Pistol (see note to 3.6.27)*
81 **Nell** *Mistress Quickly, Pistol's wife*
   spital hospital
82 **malady of France** venereal disease
83 **my rendezvous** my 'retreat' (*a place to return to*)
84 **wax** grow
85 **bawd** pimp

your broken coxcomb. When you take occasions
to see leeks hereafter, I pray you, mock at 'em;   55
that is all.

PISTOL   Good.

FLUELLEN   Ay, leeks is good. Hold you, there is a groat to
heal your pate.

PISTOL   Me a groat!   60

FLUELLEN   Yes, verily and in truth, you shall take it; or I have
another leek in my pocket, which you shall eat.

PISTOL   I take thy groat in earnest of revenge.

FLUELLEN   If I owe you anything, I will pay you in cudgels.
You shall be a woodmonger, and buy nothing of   65
me but cudgels. God b' wi' you, and keep you,
and heal your pate.

Exit

PISTOL   All hell shall stir for this.

GOWER   Go, go; you are a counterfeit cowardly knave! Will
you mock at an ancient tradition, begun upon an   70
honourable respect, and worn as a memorable
trophy of predeceased valour and dare not
avouch in your deeds any of your words? I have
seen you gleeking and galling at this gentleman
twice or thrice. You thought, because he could not 75
speak English in the native garb, he could not
therefore handle an English cudgel: you find it
otherwise; and henceforth let a Welsh correction
teach you a good English condition. Fare ye well.

Exit

PISTOL   Doth Fortune play the huswife with me now?   80
News have I that my Nell is dead i' the spital
Of malady of France;
And there my rendezvous is quite cut off.
Old do I wax, and from my weary limbs
Honour is cudgelled. Well, bawd I'll turn,   85

5.2 France: the royal palace at Troyes

Pistol decides to return to England. He will become a pimp and a pick-pocket, and pretend that the wounds inflicted by Fluellen are battle-scars. In the palace, the English and French courts meet to sign a peace treaty.

Activities

Actors' interpretations: moving the scene

Many productions move 5.1 to the end of Act 4: what are the advantages and disadvantages? Think about the following possible advantages and find a counter-argument for each one:

- It is neater to follow the Act 5 Chorus with just the scene in the French palace: the Chorus implies that Act 5 will be about Henry and political matters.
- There is no logical reason for Pistol to have returned to France: the war has finished.
- The feud between Pistol and Fluellen starts on the march from Harfleur; it is more logical to bring it to a close a few days later, just after Agincourt, rather than resurrect it five years later.
- If the leek incident comes just after Williams and the glove, we can compare the two as acts in which honour is at stake.

86 **and something lean ...** with a leaning towards being a nimble-fingered pickpocket (**cutpurse ...**)

89 **Gallia** French *(beggars commonly used to pretend that they were old soldiers, wounded in battle)*

1 **Peace to ...** Peace – the reason why we are met here – be to this meeting (*It is five years after the battle of Agincourt – May 1420 – and they have met to sign the Treaty of Troyes.*)

2 **our sister** the French Queen Isabel

5–6 **a branch and member ... contrived** *The Duke of Burgundy, who has brought everyone together, was related to both the French and English royal houses.*

12–14 **So happy ... eyes** may the outcome (**issue**) of this meeting be as successful as we are happy to see your eyes ...

16 **bent** gaze

17 **fatal balls** (1) deadly cannon-balls, (2) deadly eye-balls

basilisks (1) large cannons, (2) *mythical reptiles, whose looks could kill, hatched by a serpent from a cockerel's egg*

18 **venom** poison

And something lean to cutpurse of quick hand.
To England will I steal, and there I'll steal:
And patches will I get unto these cudgelled scars,
And swear I got them in the Gallia wars.

Exit

Scene 2

France. A royal palace.

Enter, at one door, KING HENRY, EXETER, BEDFORD,
GLOUCESTER, WARWICK, WESTMORELAND, *and other Lords; at
another, the* FRENCH KING, QUEEN ISABEL, *the* PRINCESS
KATHARINE, ALICE, *and other* Ladies; *the* DUKE OF BURGUNDY,
and his train.

KING HENRY	Peace to this meeting, wherefore we are met!
	Unto our brother France, and to our sister,
	Health and fair time of day; joy and good wishes
	To our most fair and princely cousin Katharine;
	And, as a branch and member of this royalty, 5
	By whom this great assembly is contrived,
	We do salute you, Duke of Burgundy;
	And, princes French, and peers, health to you all!

FRENCH   Right joyous are we to behold your face,
KING   Most worthy brother England; fairly met!   10
            So are you, princes English, every one.

QUEEN   So happy be the issue, brother England,
ISABEL   Of this good day and of this gracious meeting,
            As we are now glad to behold your eyes;
            Your eyes, which hitherto have borne in them   15
            Against the French, that met them in their bent,
            The fatal balls of murdering basilisks.
            The venom of such looks, we fairly hope,
            Have lost their quality, and that this day
            Shall change all griefs and quarrels into love.   20

KING HENRY   To cry amen to that, thus we appear.

QUEEN   You English princes all, I do salute you.
ISABEL

5.2 France: the royal palace at Troyes

The Duke of Burgundy, acting as mediator, describes the destructive effects that war has had upon the French countryside and the population.

Activities

Themes: war (6)

Peace is personified (lines 34–37) as an injured woman, whose job as nurse is to nourish all the good things in life. Burgundy asks why she should not be allowed to show her face again in the fertile countryside of France.

A List the effects that war has had, according to Burgundy, on (a) hedges (42–44); (b) meadows (48–53); and (c) the people themselves (54–62)

B Create a collage from images cut from newspapers and magazines to represent the effects of war upon the countryside, incorporating extracts from Burgundy's vivid speech (lines 23–67).

C People who interpret *Henry V* as an attack upon war, rather than a glorification of it, often cite Burgundy's speech, and particularly lines 54–62, in which he describes the effects of war on the civilian population. Discuss how such an interpretation might be supported by:
- the reference to soldiers growing like savages (lines 59–61) and the link with children (line 56)
- the choice of the word 'unnatural' (line 62) – in Shakespeare's plays, this tends to mean something as strong as 'against the rules of nature'.

27 **bar** judgement place

29 **my office ...** my job has been successful in so far as

31 **congreeted** exchanged greetings

33 **rub** obstacle

37 **put up ... visage** show her face

39 **husbandry** crops

40 **corrupting ...** rotting because of its own richness

42 **even-pleached** evenly layered

44 **fallow leas** arable land left uncultivated

45 **darnel ...** *types of weed*

46 **coulter** the blade of a plough

47 **deracinate** root up

48 **even mead** flat meadow

erst once, in the old days

50 **Wanting the scythe** needing to be cut

rank rotten, choked with weeds

51–53 **Conceives by idleness ... utility** because people have not bothered to tend the land, nothing grows abundantly except for weeds, ugly and useless

55 **Defective in their natures** because it is in their nature to become corrupt

58 **sciences that should become ...** the learning which should adorn our country

61 **diffused attire** untidy clothing

BURGUNDY   My duty to you both, on equal love,
Great Kings of France and England! That I have
    laboured
With all my wits, my pains and strong
    endeavours,   25
To bring your most imperial majesties
Unto this bar and royal interview,
Your mightiness on both parts best can witness.
Since, then, my office hath so far prevailed
That, face to face and royal eye to eye,   30
You have congreeted, let it not disgrace me,
If I demand, before this royal view,
What rub or what impediment there is,
Why that the naked, poor and mangled Peace,
Dear nurse of arts, plenties and joyful births,   35
Should not in this best garden of the world
Our fertile France, put up her lovely visage?
Alas, she hath from France too long been chased,
And all her husbandry doth lie on heaps,
Corrupting in its own fertility.   40
Her vine, the merry cheerer of the heart,
Unprunéd dies; her hedges even-pleached,
Like prisoners wildly overgrown with hair,
Put forth disordered twigs; her fallow leas
The darnel, hemlock and rank fumitory   45
Doth root upon, while that the coulter rusts
That should deracinate such savagery;
The even mead, that erst brought sweetly forth
The freckled cowslip, burnet and green clover,
Wanting the scythe, all uncorrected, rank,   50
Conceives by idleness, and nothing teems
But hateful docks, rough thistles, kecksies, burs,
Losing both beauty and utility.
And as our vineyards, fallows, meads and hedges,
Defective in their natures, grow to wildness,   55
Even so our houses and ourselves and children,
Have lost, or do not learn for want of time,
The sciences that should become our country;
But grow like savages – as soldiers will
That nothing do but meditate on blood, –   60
To swearing and stern looks, diffused attire
And every thing that seems unnatural.
Which to reduce into our former favour

5.2 France: the royal palace at Troyes

Henry points out that peace depends upon the French consenting to his demands. The French King agrees to study the details of the peace treaty in the company of Queen Isabel, Burgundy and the English nobles. Henry asks for Katharine to be left with him.

Activities

Actors' interpretations: Henry's terms

What is the French King thinking when he enters? Is he undecided about whether to accept Henry's terms or has he already made up his mind?

Rehearse and perform lines 68–98, firstly as though everybody is co-operating and knows that an agreement will be reached; then much more edgily, perhaps with Henry adopting a threatening tone, the French King being extremely defensive and Queen Isabel doing her best to mediate. In both cases, decide how Katharine should react when Henry refers to her as 'our capital demand' (line 96) – is she amused to be referred to in that way or offended?

63–64 **Which to reduce** and you are met here to return France to its former appearance

65 **let** obstacle

68–70 **If ... cited** If you want a return to the peace, the lack (**want**) of which gives rise to all the imperfections you have quoted

71 **accord** agreement

72 **tenours** main points

73 **enscheduled** listed

77–78 **I have but with a cursitory eye O'erglanced ...** I have only skimmed over

79 **presently** immediately

80–81 **with better heed To re-survey them** to look through them more carefully

81 **suddenly** without delay

82 **Pass our accept** give our acceptance and final answer

86 **free** full

ratify formally confirm

87 **Augment** add to

88 **advantageable for our dignity** to the advantage of our honour

90 **consign thereto** agree to it

93 **Haply** perhaps

94 **When articles ...** when people are being too particular in insisting upon unimportant items of detail

96 **capital** main

comprised included

You are assembled: and my speech entreats
That I may know the let, why gentle Peace   65
Should not expel these inconveniences
And bless us with her former qualities.

KING HENRY   If, Duke of Burgundy, you would the peace,
Whose want gives growth to the imperfections
Which you have cited, you must buy that peace   70
With full accord to all our just demands;
Whose tenours and particular effects
You have, enscheduled briefly, in your hands.

BURGUNDY   The king hath heard them; to the which as yet
There is no answer made.

KING HENRY   Well then, the peace,   75
Which you before so urged, lies in his answer.

FRENCH   I have but with a cursitory eye
KING   O'erglanced the articles: pleaseth your grace
To appoint some of your council presently
To sit with us once more, with better heed   80
To re-survey them, we will suddenly
Pass our accept and peremptory answer.

KING HENRY   Brother, we shall. Go, uncle Exeter,
And brother Clarence, and you, brother Gloucester,
Warwick and Huntingdon, go with the king;   85
And take with you free power to ratify,
Augment, or alter, as your wisdoms best
Shall see advantageable for our dignity,
Anything in or out of our demands,
And we'll consign thereto. Will you, fair sister,   90
Go with the princes, or stay here with us?

QUEEN   Our gracious brother, I will go with them:
ISABEL   Haply a woman's voice may do some good,
When articles too nicely urged be stood on.

KING HENRY   Yet leave our cousin Katharine here with us.   95
She is our capital demand, comprised
Within the fore-rank of our articles.

QUEEN   She hath good leave.
ISABEL

Despite the language difficulties, Henry begins his courtship of Katharine, but claims not to be a very eloquent wooer.

Activities

Character review: Henry and Katharine (1)

Form a group of eight. Two people, who will be Henry and Katharine, sit apart from the group and look back through the play to decide how they might be feeling at this moment. Meanwhile the remaining members of the group devise some questions which can be put to both characters concerning (a) their emotions as the rest of the court leave them alone together; (b) their feelings about each other; (c) their attitudes to the idea of a political marriage to unite the two kingdoms.

Divide into two groups, three people hot-seating Katharine, three Henry, and ask them each the same list of questions, recording their responses. Finally, re-form into the group of eight and compare Henry's and Katharine's responses to the same questions. Where were the greatest differences in their responses? How do you account for them?

99 **vouchsafe** agree

101 **love-suit** request for a woman's love

104 **soundly** (1) strongly, (2) unbrokenly (see line 106)

106 **brokenly** *a play on (1) 'broken' English, (2) the opposite of 'soundly' (line 104)*

108 **Pardonnez-moi** excuse me

vat what

111–112 **Que dit-il? ...** What does he say? That I am like the angels? Yes, really, saving your grace, that's what he says.

115 **O bon Dieu! ...** O good God! Men's tongues are full of deceit.

121 **the better Englishwoman** *because she prefers people to speak plainly*

127 **mince it** speak in a roundabout way (*not plainly*)

129 **I wear out my suit** I use up all the words I have in which to plead for your love

Act 5 Scene 2

Exeunt all except KING HENRY, KATHARINE, *and* ALICE

KING HENRY   Fair Katharine, and most fair,
Will you vouchsafe to teach a soldier terms
Such as will enter at a lady's ear   100
And plead his love-suit to her gentle heart?

KATHARINE   Your majesty shall mock at me; I cannot speak
your England.

KING HENRY O fair Katharine, if you will love me soundly with
your French heart, I will be glad to hear you   105
confess it brokenly with your English tongue. Do
you like me, Kate?

KATHARINE   Pardonnez-moi, I cannot tell vat is 'like me'.

KING HENRY An angel is like you, Kate, and you are like an
angel.   110

KATHARINE   Que dit-il? Que je suis semblable à les anges?

ALICE   Oui, vraiment, sauf votre grace, ainsi dit-il.

KING HENRY I said so, dear Katharine; and I must not blush to
affirm it.

KATHARINE   O bon Dieu! Les langues des hommes sont   115
pleines de tromperies.

KING HENRY What says she, fair one? That the tongues of men
are full of deceits?

ALICE   Oui, dat de tongues of de mans is be full of
deceits: dat is de princess.   120

KING HENRY The princess is the better Englishwoman. I' faith,
Kate, my wooing is fit for thy understanding. I
am glad thou canst speak no better English; for,
if thou couldst, thou wouldst find me such a
plain king that thou wouldst think I had sold   125
my farm to buy my crown. I know no ways to
mince it in love, but directly to say 'I love you';
then if you urge me farther than so say 'Do you
in faith?' I wear out my suit. Give me your

5.2 France: the royal palace at Troyes

Henry admits that he lacks all the accomplishments expected of a courtier, but argues that his very plainness is an attractive quality: he has a true heart and will always remain faithful.

Activities

Character review: Henry (24): '...such a plain king'

Use Henry's self-critical comments as the basis for an article in a magazine such as *Hello*, entitled 'Our dull King', which takes the view that Henry has few attractive qualities. Then write a letter which appears in the magazine a week later, pointing out that this is just a surface view: when you get to know him, he is talented and good company, even if he does run himself down. (Use what you have seen of Henry throughout the play as evidence for the points in your letter.)

Which of the two views do you prefer? Is he dull or interesting?

130 **clap hands** shake on it

134 **undid** would ruin

135–137 **measure** 135: talent to write poetry; 136: ability to dance rhythmically; 137: quantity

141 **might buffet** could box

143 **lay on** fight

143–144 **jack-an-apes** monkey

145 **greenly** lovesick, sheepish

146 **cunning in protestation** skill in expressing myself

147 **I never use ...** I never use oaths until I am forced to and never break them even if someone tries to force me

148 **temper** make-up, character

151 **be thy cook** 'cook me up' into something better looking

156 **uncoined constancy** faithfulness which has not been passed around among other women

157 **perforce must do thee right** will have to be faithful to you

159 **of infinite tongue** with the ability to talk smoothly to all sorts of women

159–161 **that can rhyme ... again** men who write poetry to gain a woman's favour, soon lose it when they have to talk sense

162 **prater** someone who talks rubbish

164 **curled pate** head of curly hair

165 **wax hollow** grow sunken

answer; i' faith, do: and so clap hands and a   130
bargain. How say you, lady?

KATHARINE   Sauf votre honneur, me understand vell.

KING HENRY   Marry, if you would put me to verses or to dance
for your sake, Kate, why you undid me: for the
one, I have neither words nor measure, and for   135
the other, I have no strength in measure, yet a
reasonable measure in strength. If I could win a
lady at leap-frog, or by vaulting into my saddle
with my armour on my back, under the
correction of bragging be it spoken, I should   140
quickly leap into a wife. Or if I might buffet for
my love, or bound my horse for her favours, I
could lay on like a butcher and sit like a jack-an-
apes, never off. But, before God, Kate, I cannot
look greenly nor gasp out my eloquence, nor I   145
have no cunning in protestation; only downright
oaths, which I never use till urged, nor never
break for urging. If thou canst love a fellow of this
temper, Kate, whose face is not worth sun-
burning, that never looks in his glass for love of   150
anything he sees there, let thine eye be thy cook. I
speak to thee plain soldier: if thou canst love me
for this, take me; if not, to say to thee that I shall
die, is true; but for thy love, by the Lord, no; yet I
love thee too. And while thou livest, dear Kate,   155
take a fellow of plain and uncoined constancy;
for he perforce must do thee right because he
hath not the gift to woo in other places: for these
fellows of infinite tongue, that can rhyme
themselves into ladies' favours, they do always   160
reason themselves out again. What! A speaker is
but a prater; a rhyme is but a ballad. A good leg
will fall; a straight back will stoop; a black beard
will turn white; a curled pate will grow bald; a fair
face will wither; a full eye will wax hollow: but a   165
good heart, Kate, is the sun and the moon; or,
rather, the sun, and not the moon; for it shines
bright and never changes, but keeps his course
truly. If thou would have such a one, take me; and
take me, take a soldier; take a soldier, take a king. 170

5.2 France: the royal palace at Troyes

Katharine does not see how she could love the enemy of France, and Henry tries to persuade her in his imperfect French.

Activities

Character review: Henry (25): does he love Katharine?

'...for I love France so well that I will not part with a village of it...' (lines 178–179).

Divide the class into two, one half arguing that Henry genuinely wants to marry Katharine, the other arguing that he is only interested in acquiring land, titles and power. You will need to look back through the play from the beginning to find supporting evidence (especially to 1.2 and the Act 3 Chorus, lines 28–32).

Branagh, 1989

185–188 **Je quand ... mienne** *A bad French version of his statement in lines 179–180*

187 **Saint Denis** *the patron saint of France*

be my speed help me

192–193 **Sauf votre honneur ...** If I may say so, your French is better than my English

195 **truly-falsely** expressing his true love, but in bad French

196 **at one** (1) on the same level, (2) in sympathy

204 **dispraise those parts ...** criticise the features in me

And what sayest thou then to my love? Speak, my
fair, and fairly, I pray thee.

KATHARINE   Is it possible dat I should love de enemy of
France?

KING HENRY   No, it is not possible you should love the enemy   175
of France, Kate; but, in loving me, you should
love the friend of France; for I love France so well
that I will not part with a village of it; I will have
it all mine: and, Kate, when France is mine and I
am yours, then yours is France and you are mine.   180

KATHARINE   I cannot tell vat is dat.

KING HENRY   No, Kate? I will tell thee in French; which I am
sure will hang upon my tongue like a new-
married wife about her husband's neck, hardly to
be shook off. Je quand sur le possession de   185
France, er quand vous avez le possession de moi,
– let me see, what then? Saint Denis be my speed!
– donc votre est France et vous êtes mienne. It is
as easy for me, Kate, to conquer the kingdom as
to speak so much more French. I shall never   190
move thee in French, unless it be to laugh at me.

KATHARINE   Sauf votre honneur, le François que vous parlez, il
est meilleur que l'Anglois lequel je parle.

KING HENRY   No, faith, is't not, Kate: but thy speaking of my
tongue, and I thine, most truly-falsely, must needs   195
be granted to be much at one. But, Kate, dost
thou understand thus much English, canst thou
love me?

KATHARINE   I cannot tell.

KING HENRY   Can any of your neighbours tell, Kate? I'll ask   200
them. Come, I know thou lovest me: and at night,
when you come into your closet, you'll question
this gentlewoman about me; and I know, Kate,
you will to her dispraise those parts in me that
you love with your heart: but, good Kate, mock   205
me mercifully; the rather, gentle princess, because

5.2 France: the royal palace at Troyes

Henry continues his wooing, looking ahead to the time when they have a son. He claims that, although he is unattractive in appearance now, he will improve with age.

Activities

Shakespeare's language: Henry's skill with words

It has often been pointed out that, despite Henry's claim not to be able to use language with any great skill ('I have no cunning in protestation' – lines 146–147), he demonstrates quite a way with words.

Look at the following examples from Henry's speeches and, for each one, decide (a) what point Henry wants to make; and (b) how his skill with language helps him to make it:

- 103–105 'soundly… brokenly'
- 109–110 'vat is "like me". … An angel is like you, Kate.'
- 136–138 'measure…'
- 162–167 'A speaker is…'
- 170–171 'take me…'
- 176–178 'enemy…friend'
- 227–228 'false French…true English'.

207 **If ever thou beest mine** If you are ever to be mine

209 **scambling** fighting

212 **compound** produce

213 **Constantinople** *Christian kings wanted to recapture Constantinople (Istanbul) from the Turks.*

215 **flower-de-luce** fleur-de-lys (*the heraldic emblem on the French coat-of-arms*)

217 **'t is hereafter to know** (1) you will know that later on, (2) when we are married we will 'know' each other (sexually)

220 **moiety** share

221–223 **la plus belle …** the most beautiful Katherine in the world, my very dear and divine goddess

224–225 **Your majestee …** your majesty has enough false French to deceive the cleverest young woman in France (**fausse** = (1) incorrect, (2) deceiving)

229–231 **not withstanding …** despite the off-putting (**untempering**) effect of my face (**visage**)

231 **beshrew** curse

237 **ill layer up** wrinkler

239–240 **thou shalt wear me …** if you possess me (as your husband), you will find me (1) suiting you better and better, (2) growing better and better

242 **avouch** acknowledge, admit

I love thee cruelly. If ever thou beest mine, Kate,
as I have a saving faith within me tells me thou
shalt, I get thee with scambling, and thou must
therefore needs prove a good soldier-breeder.   210
Shall not thou and I, between Saint Denis and
Saint George, compound a boy, half French, half
English, that shall go to Constantinople and take
the Turk by the beard? Shall we not? What sayest
thou, my fair flower-de-luce?   215

KATHARINE   I do not know dat.

KING HENRY   No; 't is hereafter to know, but now to promise.
Do but now promise, Kate, you will endeavour
for your French part of such a boy; and for my
English moiety take the word of a king and a   220
bachelor. How answer you, la plus belle
Katharine de monde, mon très cher et devin
déesse?

KATHARINE   Your majestee 'ave fausse French enough to
deceive de most sage demoiselle dat is en France.   225

KING HENRY   Now fie upon my false French! By mine honour,
in true English, I love thee, Kate: by which
honour I dare not swear thou lovest me; yet my
blood begins to flatter me that thou dost, not
withstanding the poor and untempering effect of   230
my visage. Now beshrew my father's ambition!
He was thinking of civil wars when he got me:
therefore was I created with a stubborn outside,
with an aspect of iron, that, when I come to woo
ladies, I fright them. But, in faith, Kate, the elder I   235
wax, the better I shall appear. My comfort is, that
old age, that ill layer up of beauty, can do no
more spoil upon my face. Thou hast me, if thou
hast me, at the worst; and thou shalt wear me, if
thou wear me, better and better: and therefore tell   240
me, most fair Katharine, will you have me? Put off
your maiden blushes; avouch the thoughts of
your heart with the looks of an empress; take me
by the hand, and say 'Harry of England, I am
thine'; which word thou shalt no sooner bless   245

5.2 France: the royal palace at Troyes

Henry asks Katharine if she will marry him and she replies that she needs her father's approval. Confident that the French King will agree to the marriage, Henry tries to kiss Katharine, but she is shocked – it is not customary for French ladies to kiss before they are married.

Activities

Character review: Katharine (1)

Write director's notes to help the actress playing Katharine in the part of the scene where Henry offers to kiss her. First decide what her overall attitude to Henry and the prospect of marriage might be (see the activity on page 198). Then annotate lines 257–291, giving advice on:

- how Katharine is feeling at different moments, and why
- how the actress could say particular lines, and why
- movements and actions she could make at certain points, and why
- the reactions you want the audience to have, and why.

246 **withal** with

248 **Plantagenet** *Henry's family name*

251 **broken** (1) arranged in parts for different instruments, (2) imperfect (*as in 'broken' English*)

253 **break** open up

256 **Dat is ...** That depends on whether it pleases the King, my father

262–267 **Laissez, mon seigneur ...** Stop, sir, stop. My goodness, I do not want you to lower your greatness by kissing the hand of one of your highness's unworthy servants; please excuse me, I beg you, my thrice-powerful lord.

268–269 **Les dames ...** it is not the custom in France for ladies and young women to be kissed before their wedding day

272 **I cannot tell ...** I don't know what 'baiser' is in English

274 **entendre ...** understands better than I do

277 **Oui, vraiment** yes, truly

mine ear withal, but I will tell thee aloud
'England is thine, Ireland is thine, France is thine,
and Henry Plantagenet is thine'; who, though I
speak it before his face, if he be not fellow with
the best king, thou shalt find the best king of   250
good fellows. Come, your answer in broken
music; for thy voice is music and thy English
broken; therefore, queen of all, Katharine, break
thy mind to me in broken English; wilt thou have
me?   255

KATHARINE   Dat is as it sall please de roi mon père.

KING HENRY   Nay, it will please him well, Kate; it shall please
              him, Kate.

KATHARINE   Den it sall also content me.

KING HENRY   Upon that I kiss your hand, and I call you my   260
              queen.

KATHARINE   Laissez, mon seigneur, laissez, laissez: ma foi, je
             ne veux point que vous abaissiez votre grandeur
             en baisant la main d'une de votre seigneurie
             indigne serviteur; excusez-moi, je vous supplie,   265
             mon très-puissant seigneur.

KING HENRY   Then I will kiss your lips, Kate.

KATHARINE   Les dames et demoiselles pour être baisées devant
             leur noces, il n'est pas la coutume de France.

KING HENRY   Madam my interpreter, what says she?   270

ALICE   Dat it is not de fashion pour les ladies of France.
         – I cannot tell vat is baiser en Anglish.

KING HENRY   To kiss.

ALICE   Your majesty entendre bettre que moi.

KING HENRY   It is not a fashion for the maids in France to kiss   275
              before they are married, would she say?

ALICE   Oui, vraiment.

5.2 France: the royal palace at Troyes

Arguing that, as King and Queen, they can dictate fashion, Henry kisses Katharine. The rest of the court re-enter and Burgundy starts a bawdy exchange with Henry as they discuss the Princess's modesty.

Activities

Character review: Katharine (2)

1. Write Katharine's diary for that evening. Give her account of the meeting with Henry and write about her feelings. Does she love him? Does she believe that he loves her? (Cécile Paoli, who played Katharine in 1984, took the view that Katharine and Henry do, in the course of the one brief interview, actually fall in love – despite the fact that Henry had disposed of most of the French royal family! You might, or might not agree.)

2. Select a section of the scene and act it out, firstly, as though they are in love, and secondly, as though they aren't. Which works better, in your opinion?

3. Write Alice's diary, in which she describes Katharine's behaviour with Henry from her own perspective. Does she approve of the marriage? What did she think of Henry's wooing and Katharine's response to it? (Look especially at lines 112, 119–120 and 261–264.)

278 **nice** fussy

curtsey to bow down before (give way to)

280 **list** barriers

281–283 **and the liberty ...** and the freedom which is permitted to royalty prevents people from criticising us

282–283 **as I will do yours ...** and I will stop your mouth

286 **eloquence** fluent speech

289 **a general petition of monarchs** a request from many kings together

295 **apt** a good student

296 **condition** temperament; 'I am not a smooth-talker'

301 **the frankness ...** the bluntness of my humour

303 **a circle** *(1) the circle drawn on the ground in which a spirit appeared, (2) slang for the female sexual organ*

304 **he must appear ...** *Burgundy is referring to Cupid, son of the goddess Venus, usually portrayed as a partly clothed, blindfolded child.*

305–306 **rosed over ...** blushing with the modesty of a virgin

309 **consign to** accept

310 **Yet they do wink ...** And yet women shut their eyes and give in ...

blind (1) sightless, (2) 'blind' to everything else

KING HENRY O Kate, nice customs curtsey to great kings. Dear
Kate, you and I cannot be confined within the
weak list of a country's fashion: we are the makers 280
of manners, Kate; and the liberty that follows our
places stops the mouth of all find-faults; as I will
do yours, for upholding the nice fashion of your
country in denying me a kiss: therefore, patiently
and yielding. (*Kissing her*) You have witchcraft in 285
your lips, Kate; there is more eloquence in a sugar
touch of them than in the tongues of the French
council; and they should sooner persuade Harry
of England than a general petition of monarchs.
Here comes your father. 290

Re-enter the FRENCH KING, *and his* QUEEN, BURGUNDY, *and other* Lords.

BURGUNDY God save your majesty! My royal cousin, teach
you our princess English?

KING HENRY I would have her learn, my fair cousin, how
perfectly I love her; and that is good English.

BURGUNDY Is she not apt? 295

KING HENRY Our tongue is rough coz, and my condition is not
smooth; so that, having neither the voice nor the
heart of flattery about me, I cannot so conjure up
the spirit of love in her, that he will appear in his
true likeness. 300

BURGUNDY Pardon the frankness of my mirth, if I answer you
for that. If you would conjure in her, you must
make a circle; if conjure up love in her in his true
likeness, he must appear naked and blind. Can
you blame her than, being a maid yet rosed over 305
with the virgin crimson of modesty, if she deny
the appearance of a naked blind boy in her naked
seeing self? It were, my lord, a hard condition for
a maid to consign to.

KING HENRY Yet they do wink and yield, as love is blind and 310
enforces.

5.2 France: the royal palace at Troyes

When the men have finished discussing Katharine and Henry's claims, the French King announces that he has agreed to the terms of the peace treaty, including the marriage of Katharine to Henry.

Activities

Shakespeare's language: bawdy dialogue

The re-entrance of the court sets off a sequence of bawdy exchanges between Burgundy, Henry and the French King. Re-read lines 292–338 with the notes opposite to check that you understand the word-play.

Then select three or four examples and, as a class, discuss whether you find the bawdy dialogue either (a) inoffensive light-hearted joking; or (b) immature men's talk which only sees women as sex objects. If you don't hold either of these views, how do you react to it? What is its effect, in your opinion, at this point in the play?

314–315 **consent winking** agree, with her eyes closed

316 **wink on her** encourage her

318 **summered** brought up (grazed in summer pastures)

319 **Bartholomew-tide** *24 August, the end of summer, when flies become sluggish*

321 **abide looking on** put up with

322 **This moral ties me over to ...** If I follow this line of argument, I will have to wait for ...

326–329 **and you may ...** and some of you might be thankful for my blind love, because the French maid who stands in my way prevents me from seeing any more French cities that I might otherwise capture

330 **perspectively** *as though through a 'perspective glass', in which the cities are distorted into an image of Katherine*

331 **girdled** surrounded

335–336 **so the maiden cities ...** so long as the uncaptured cities you talk of come with her (*as part of the marriage settlement*)

337 **will** desire

341 **in sequel** following on

342 **... firm proposéd natures** according to the nature of the strictly proposed conditions

BURGUNDY	They are then excused, my lord, when they see not what they do.
KING HENRY	Then, good my lord, teach your cousin to consent winking. 315
BURGUNDY	I will wink on her to consent, my lord, if you will teach her to know my meaning: for maids, well summered and warm kept, are like flies at Bartholomew-tide, blind, though they have their eyes; and then they will endure handling, which 320 before would not abide looking on.
KING HENRY	This moral ties me over to time and a hot summer; and so I shall catch the fly, your cousin, in the latter end, and she must be blind too.
BURGUNDY	As love is, my lord, before it loves. 325
KING HENRY	It is so: and you may, some of you, thank love for my blindness, who cannot see many a fair French city for one fair French maid that stands in my way.
FRENCH KING	Yes, my lord, you see them perspectively, the cities 330 turned into a maid; for they are all girdled with maiden walls that war hath never entered.
KING HENRY	Shall Kate be my wife?
FRENCH KING	So please you.
KING HENRY	I am content; so the maiden cities you talk of may 335 wait on her: so the maid that stood in the way for my wish shall show me the way to my will.
FRENCH KING	We have consented to all terms of reason.
KING HENRY	Is 't so, my lords of England?
WEST-MORELAND	The king hath granted every article: 340 His daughter first, and then in sequel all, According to their firm proposéd natures.

5.2 France: the royal palace at Troyes

The French King further agrees that Henry is to be formally acknowledged as his heir and he expresses the hope that the marriage will lead to a lasting peace between the two nations, a wish echoed by Queen Isabel, who asks God to bless the marriage.

Activities

Plot review (18): the peace treaty

Under the terms of the peace-treaty, Henry is not demanding to become King of France immediately, but only on the death of the existing King.

1. What advantages are there in this arrangement for (a) Henry; (b) the French King; and (c) the Dauphin?
2. What possible problems could it lead to in the future?
3. How is the Dauphin likely to feel about the marriage of his sister to the English King and the treaty that has just been signed by his father? Why is he absent, do you think? Write a letter from the absent Dauphin to his father the French King, in which he expresses his feelings on these matters.

343 **subscribéd thus** agreed to this

345 **for matter of grant** in any matter to do with the granting of titles

347–350 **Notre très-cher … Franciae** Our dearest son Henry, King of England, Heir to the throne of France … Our most illustrious son … (*etc.*)

351–352 **Nor have I …** And I have not rejected this so firmly that your request will not make me accept it

354 **rank with** be as important as

357 **Issue** children

contending rival

358 **pale** white (*possibly a reference to the white chalk cliffs of Dover, facing France*)

360 **dear conjunction** solemn union

361 **neighbourhood** friendship

accord agreement

362 **bosoms** hearts

370–374 **So be there … league** so may there be such a marriage (**spousal**) between (**twixt**) your kingdoms, that evil deeds (**ill office**) or deadly (**fell**) jealousy … may never interfere with your peace compact (**paction**), to break up the alliance making them one (**incorporate league**)

EXETER   Only he hath not yet subscribéd this: Where your
majesty demands, that the King of France, having
any occasion to write for matter of grant, shall   345
name your highness in this form and with this
addition, in French, Notre très-cher fils Henri, Roi
d'Angleterre, Héritier de France; and thus in Latin,
Praeclarissimus filius noster Henricus, Rex
Angliae, et Haeres Franciae.   350

FRENCH   Nor this I have not, brother, so denied,
  KING   But your request shall make me let it pass.

KING HENRY I pray you then, in love and dear alliance,
Let that one article rank with the rest;
And thereupon give me your daughter.   355

FRENCH   Take her, fair son, and from her blood raise up
  KING   Issue to me; that the contending kingdoms
Of France and England, whose very shores look pale
With envy of each other's happiness,
May cease their hatred, and this dear conjunction 360
Plant neighbourhood and Christian-like accord
In their sweet bosoms, that never war advance
His bleeding sword 'twixt England and fair France.

ALL   Amen!

KING HENRY Now, welcome, Kate: and bear me witness all,   365
That here I kiss her as my sovereign queen.

Flourish.

QUEEN   God, the best maker of all marriages,
  ISABEL   Combine your hearts in one, your realms in one!
As man and wife, being two, are one in love,
So be there 'twixt your kingdoms such a spousal, 370
That never may ill office, or fell jealousy,
Which troubles oft the bed of blesséd marriage,
Thrust in between the paction of these kingdoms,
To make divorce of their incorporate league;
That English may as French, French Englishmen, 375
Receive each other. God speak this Amen!

ALL   Amen!

5.2 France: the royal palace at Troyes

Henry declares that their marriage oaths will be faithfully kept and the Chorus concludes the play. He looks back to Henry's achievements, but foretells that, in the reign of Henry's son, Henry VI, England will lose France and suffer the ravages of civil war.

Activities

Shakespeare's language: the sonnet

1. The Chorus refers to a number of unnamed people and places. Who or what are:
   - 'Our bending author'?
   - 'mighty men'?
   - 'This star of England'?
   - 'the world's best garden'?
   - 'so many... they'?

   And which people are referred to in:
   - 'our stage'?
   - 'their sake'?
   - 'your fair mind'?

2. What does the Chorus' speech add to the themes of (a) theatre and the imagination; and (b) war?

380 **And all the peers' ... leagues** and all the nobles will take their oaths too, to protect our union

1 **rough and all-unable pen** *writing which is unpolished and inadequate*

2 **Our bending author** *Many people believe that Shakespeare himself might have spoken this, bowing (**bending**) here to the audience.*

4 **Mangling by starts** *ruining by having to cut things out*

5 **Small time** *a reference either to the short period described in the play, or Henry's brief life (he was only 35 when he died and had reigned for just nine years)*

7 **world's best garden** *France*

9 **in infant bands** *Henry's son was only eighteen months old when he came to the throne as Henry VI.*

11–12 **Whose state so many ... bleed** *The English nobles looking after the kingdom became divided and their dispute led to the Wars of the Roses, a civil war between the houses of York and Lancaster.*

13 **Which oft our stage hath shown** *The play which depicted the Wars of the Roses, now known as* Henry VI, Part 1 *had been very popular with audiences.*

14 **let this acceptance take** *please accept this play:* Henry V

KING HENRY Prepare we for our marriage: on which day,
My Lord of Burgundy, we'll take your oath,
And all the peers', for surety of our leagues.   380
Then shall I swear to Kate, and you to me!
And may our oaths well kept and prosperous be!

Sennet. Exeunt

Epilogue

Enter CHORUS.

CHORUS Thus far, with rough and all-unable pen,
    Our bending author hath pursued the story,
In little room confining mighty men,
    Mangling by starts the full course of their glory.
Small time, but in that small most greatly lived   5
    This star of England. Fortune made his sword;
By which the world's best garden he achieved,
    And of it left his son imperial lord.
Henry the Sixth, in infant bands crown'd king
    Of France and England, did this king succeed;   10
Whose state so many had the managing
    That they lost France and made this England bleed;
Which oft our stage hath shown; and, for their sake,
    In your fair minds let this acceptance take.

Exeunt

Exam practice

Plot review: (19): the treaty

Write two brief reports, one for the English newspaper, *The Chronicle*, the other for the French *Fleur-de-lys*. In each one, set out the main points of the peace treaty (called the Treaty of Troyes). Conclude each of the two reports with the newspaper's views on the treaty: is it a good treaty for the country, or a bad one?

Before you begin to write, you should think about:
* Burgundy's description of war-torn France
* the agreed marriage between Henry and Katharine
* the arrangements made concerning Henry's claim to the throne of France (see lines 343–352 and the activity on page 212).

Character review: Henry (26): his marriage

Write the two speeches that Henry might make: the first to the French nobles after his marriage to Katharine; and the second to the English nobles on his return from France. Think carefully about the ways in which his two different audiences might influence (a) what he decides to emphasise or play down; (b) the different tone he might adopt. It will help to re-read Henry's earlier speeches (for example to Canterbury in 1.2 or to Montjoy throughout), as well as his Harfleur (3.1) and Saint Crispin's Day (4.3) speeches.

Actors' interpretations: the mood of the sonnet

Re-read the sonnet spoken by the Chorus as the epilogue to the play. A sonnet will often have a change of direction after the first eight lines (the octave).

What is the subject of the octave in this sonnet? How do you think it ought to be spoken (optimistically or pessimistically; triumphantly or in subdued tones?)

Apply the same questions to (a) lines 9–12; and (b) lines 13–14, the final couplet.

Create three tableaux to represent the three sections of the sonnet, trying to capture what you think is the appropriate mood for each.

Character review: Pistol (4)

Pistol leaves the scene telling us that he aims to return to England, become a pimp (bawd) and a pick-pocket (cutpurse) and pretend that the wounds inflicted by Fluellen were actually sustained in the French wars (5.1.88–92).

1. Write a scene which will show him being arrested for 'cutting a purse'. Try to capture some of the typical Pistol speech and behaviour.
2. As Pistol makes his final exit from the play, how do you feel about him – sorry that an entertaining character has come to such a bad end? satisfied that a crook and a coward has not prospered? optimistic that he will probably survive one way or the other? Hold a class discussion in which you share your feelings about him in the play and speculate on his future existence back in England.

Character review: Henry and Katharine (2)

Improvise a conversation between Exeter and the cynical lord in which they discuss whether or not a marriage between Henry and Katharine will be successful. First look back at 5.2 and think carefully about:
• Henry's wooing of Katharine
• Henry's bawdy word-play with Burgundy
• whether Henry genuinely loves Katharine, or merely views her as part of a political settlement, his 'capital demand' (line 96).

Actors' interpretations: the ending

Re-read Henry's concluding lines (lines 378–382). Do you feel that the English and French will keep to the agreements made in the treaty?

Freeze-frame two scenes: one to represent an optimistic and upbeat ending; another to show that things will quickly deteriorate, and that the English and French will soon be at each other's throats again.

Activities

Thinking about the play as a whole . . .

Actor's interpretations

1 **Ⓐ** *Filming the play*

Pick your favourite scene from the play and draw a sketch to show what a key moment might look like, adding notes to explain details of the characters' actions, expressions and gestures. You might pick Henry dealing with the traitors, for example, or his 'Once more unto the breach' speech.

Ⓑ *Staging a scene*

Pick two contrasting moments from the play (for example, Mistress Quickly's account of Falstaff's death and Henry's Saint Crispin's Day speech) and, using the outline or plan on page 238, show how the moments might be staged to bring out the contrasts, writing annotations to explain your decisions.

Ⓒ *Directing an extract*

Annotate a short scene or extract to show actors' movements, actions and reactions. Introduce it with a statement about the particular interpretation that you are aiming for (such as a portrayal of Henry as a ruthless war-leader).

2 **Ⓐ** *Casting the play*

If you had the chance to direct a performance of *Henry V* on stage, which actors and actresses would you cast in the various roles? Make decisions about each character, explaining why you think the particular performer would be right for the part.

Ⓑ *A theatre programme*

Create a theatre programme for a production of *Henry V*. This might include:
- a cast list with the names of the actors
- some background material (for example, on Henry's claim to the French throne – see page 244; or articles on the language or some of the major themes)
- details about Shakespeare and his plays (see page 259).

A review

Write your own review of *Henry V*, as a response to an actual theatre performance, or any one of the video versions that you have seen.

3   A modern film adaptation

The best known film versions of *Henry V* are Laurence Olivier's, made in 1944, and Kenneth Branagh's from 1989. It is also possible to acquire video recordings of the 1979 BBC TV production and the stage version by the English Shakespeare Company in 1985.

In groups, think up some ideas for a modern film adaptation of *Henry V* (possibly on the lines of Baz Luhrmann's *Romeo and Juliet*):

1. Make decisions about actors to play the roles and locations for the different scenes of the story.
2. Storyboard one of the key sequences and bring out the special qualities of your new interpretation.
3. Discuss which features of the play (not only the story, but its themes and language) you would hope to bring out most successfully and which would be harder to get across.

4   *An advertisement*

Create a poster or magazine advert for a new production of *Henry V*, featuring some of your favourite actors. First look at some examples in magazines, to see how images are used and what written material is included.

Video covers

Discuss the two covers of video versions of *Henry V* shown on the next page.

- Which features of the story do they seem to be concentrating on? What 'image' is each one conveying? In what ways will the interpretations be different?
- Which characters have they decided to highlight?
- How have they arranged the images?
- What text have they used to 'sell' the product?

Create a video cover for your own screen production of the play (which might feature some of the performers chosen for activity A).

Activities

Branagh, 1989

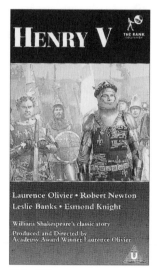

Olivier, 1944

C *A display*

Put together a classroom display on *Henry V*, which would be interesting for a younger class approaching the play for the first time. Include:

- any drawings that you have done (staging designs, storyboards...)
- other background work (characters' letters and journal entries, the newspaper reports and page designs, the Edward III family tree, the time-chart...)
- anything else you can think of (a poster advertising the play; cartoons of images...)
- things that you have collected from productions (production postcards, programmes, reviews...).

You will need to write some introductory material, explaining what the play is about and how the various elements of the display tie in.

Character reviews

5   Character profiles

Many actors write systematic notes about the characters they are preparing to play. Draw up a CHARACTER PROFILE FORM on a word-processor and then fill it in for any characters you are working on. Headings might be:

NAME:

SOCIAL POSITION:

SUPER-OBJECTIVE: (the character's overriding aim, which drives them on: e.g. 'to gain the French throne, which is rightfully mine')

LINE OF ACTION: (the practical things they must do to achieve that aim: e.g. 'take Harfleur')

OBSTACLES AGAINST IT: (e.g. 'The French have a strong army…')

WHAT THE CHARACTER SAYS ABOUT HIMSELF/HERSELF:

WHAT OTHER CHARACTERS SAY ABOUT HER/HIM:

IMPRESSION ON FIRST APPEARANCE:

RELATIONSHIPS WITH OTHERS:

OTHER INFORMATION:

6   Character review: Henry

Ⓐ   *Henry's achievements*

Look at your completed time-line and pick out all Henry's major actions, starting with his request to the Archbishop in 1.2 to explain the Salic Law. Which of these actions would you say were his most important achievements?

Ⓑ   *The many sides of Henry*

Find moments in the script which, in different productions of the play, might show Henry to be:

1. a statesman
2. someone who can inspire his followers
3. a joker
4. aware of his responsibilities
5. someone who cares about the ordinary soldier
6. fair and just
7. religious
8. merciful
9. heroic
10. anxious
11. intelligent

Activities

and, in contrast:

12. cruel
13. manipulating
14. hypocritical
15. reckless in war
16. disloyal to old friends
17. hungry for power.

Use this material to write a short biography of Shakespeare's Henry for an encyclopedia.

C *Contrasting views of Henry*

Draft a magazine profile on Henry from a patriotic magazine which admires his achievements, headed 'This Star of England' or 'The Mirror of all Christian Kings'. (Ideas from A, above, and the activities which included Exeter's journal entries will provide your material.) Then write some letters to the magazine in response to the article, which take a more critical view. (You will find it helpful here to look back at the activities in which you composed journal entries by the cynical lord.)

7 Character review: the Chorus

A *What does the Chorus say?*

1. Look back through the Chorus' speeches and note down what the Chorus says about (a) the limitations of the theatre and the need for the audience to use their imaginations; and (b) war.
2. How much of the action is described by the Chorus? List all the things described by the Chorus (actions, journeys, characters…) which we would not otherwise be able to see portrayed on stage.

B *The purpose of the Chorus*

What is the purpose of the Chorus in *Henry V*? In pairs, discuss each of the following possible functions and then write up your findings. The Chorus:

- helps to establish the 'epic' sweep of a story about a king who was almost a legend by Shakespeare's time
- adds to the patriotic tone of the play with its repeated references to England's greatness
- helps the audience to believe in the greatness of 'this star of England'
- apologises for the inadequacies of the stage

- describes actions which could not be presented on stage and helps the audience to follow the time-scale
- adds to our understanding of the themes of the play, especially 'war' and 'theatre and the imagination'.

C *Performing the Chorus*

1. How would the Chorus be presented in your production of the play? Olivier's Chorus in 1944 (Lesley Banks) was a splendidly dressed Elizabethan gentleman, complete with pearl ear-ring; Branagh's in 1989 (Derek Jacobi) appeared in a mysterious looking long black coat and scarf; John Woodvine played the Chorus in the English Shakespeare Company's 1985 production in different styles of modern dress. Compare those interpretations if you can (they are all on video) and also talk about the other ways in which the Chorus might be presented. What effect might be achieved, for example, by:
   - presenting the Chorus as a war veteran wearing a poppy (as in the 1994 RSC production)
   - having the part played by a woman
   - sharing the Chorus speeches among different characters (as in the 1996 production at the Globe)?

2. Would you agree that some of the Chorus's apologies do not make much sense in a modern film version (for example, a film *can* show the 'vasty fields of France')? Given that the Chorus speeches were plainly written for the Elizabethan stage, discuss what might be gained and lost by cutting the Chorus altogether from a film version.

8 Character review: the French King and nobles

A *What part do the French play?*

Look back at (a) the scenes in which the French King and nobles appear: 2.4, 3.5, 3.6, 3.7, 4.2, 4.3, 4.5, 4.7 and 5.2 and (b) the activities on pages 22, 64, 110, 112, 138, 140, 156. Create a chart to show where the French appear in the play and what they say or do in each scene.

B *The French as individuals*

The French King, the Dauphin, the Constable and Montjoy are all individualised characters. For each one, discuss:
1. their attitude towards the English generally
2. their attitude towards Henry

Activities

3. what they seem to be mainly interested in; what their objectives are
4. their qualities of leadership.

In general, how do the French King and nobles
- get on together as comrades?
- face defeat?

C *Bias and Montjoy*

1. How biased is Shakespeare's presentation of the French King and nobles, in your opinion?
2. Kenneth Branagh said that he found Henry's relationship with Montjoy (played by Christopher Ravenscroft) one of the most interesting features of their interpretation. What opportunities are there for playing Montjoy as (a) an arrogant and distant mouthpiece for French propaganda; or (b) an interesting character in his own right and someone with whom Henry can communicate? How might either of these interpretations be realised in a stage or film production? (In Branagh's film, for example, the Ambassador in 1.2 is replaced by Montjoy.)

9   Character review: Pistol

A *An official report*

Look back at Pistol's appearances in Acts 3, 4 and 5 and write his superior officer's army report on him, following discussions with Fluellen and Gower. What might he have to say about Pistol's behaviour at Harfleur, for example (3.1), or at the taking of the bridge (3.6), or back in France five years later (5.1)?

B *A monologue*

Mistress Quickly tells us that, as he lay dying, Falstaff cried out against drink. What would Pistol look back on in his last days? Write a monologue in which the dying Pistol reflects on what happened to him after the coronation of Henry V up to his encounter with Fluellen in 5.1.

C *Pistol's contribution*

At the end of *Henry IV, Part 2*, the speaker of the Epilogue announces that, in the next play, we will see more of Falstaff, including his appearance at Agincourt. Why do you think Shakespeare might have changed his mind about including Falstaff? Do you think Pistol can be considered a substitute for the larger-than-life Falstaff? What does Pistol add to the play?

10   Character review: the Eastcheap characters

What do Pistol, Bardolph, Nym, Mistress Quickly and the Boy add to *Henry V*? Think about:

- their comic language and behaviour
- their relationship with Henry (as it once was and now is), their references to him, and Pistol's one encounter with him
- their reactions to the death of Falstaff
- their attitudes to war (both what they say and the way they behave, including Pistol's encounter with le Fer)
- their deaths.

11   Character review: Fluellen

  Fluellen, Henry and Pistol

Look back at Fluellen's appearances in the play. What does he show us about (a) Henry; and (b) Pistol?

B *Playing the role*

Fluellen has one of the largest roles in the play. What does he add to:

- the comedy of *Henry V*?
- our understanding of Henry?
- the theme of war?

What do other characters seem to think of him (Gower, Macmorris, Pistol…)? How does Henry behave towards him?

Write a letter to an actor who is about to play Fluellen in a production that you are about to direct, giving your opinions on the opportunities that the part offers and suggesting features of the role that he might like to think about.

C *National stereotypes?*

How far would you agree that Shakespeare is guilty of some damaging national stereotyping in his creation of Fluellen, Macmorris and Jamy (and perhaps Gower too)?

Activities

12 Character review: Katharine, Exeter, Canterbury, Williams, Mistress Quickly, Nym, the Boy, the Traitors

Ⓐ *Their importance*

Select one or two of these characters and write down some of the memorable things that each one says or does in the play. (For example: Mistress Quickly: reports Falstaff's death). Then talk about each character's importance in the play as a whole: what do they add, and what would be lost if they were cut from the play?

Ⓑ *Playing the roles*

What opportunities are there for actors playing these characters? Pick one, look at the scenes in which he or she appears and describe what satisfaction or enjoyment exists in playing the part. (You could write this from the actor's point of view, using his or her 'voice'.)

Ⓒ *Perspectives on Henry*

Select two of these characters and show how they can be used in a production of the play to provide different perspectives on Henry.

Shakespeare's language

When you are thinking about the meanings of a Shakespeare play, it is helpful to understand how he uses the language.

13 Language features

1. Look back through the play to find examples of each of the following:
   - emotive language (look at the activity on page 18)
   - accent and dialect (pages 76–78)
   - stichomythia (page 108)
   - onomatopoeia, rhythm and assonance (page 116)
   - dramatic irony (pages 44 and 168).

Create a poster for the classroom with the title *Shakespeare's Language in Henry V*, which includes the five examples. Make sure that you explain why each one was used at that point in the play. What was its effect? How did it help to get a particular meaning across?

2. (a) Much of the imagery in the play is found in the speeches where people are describing the nature of war or its effects. What impression of war do you receive from the following images:
   - 1.2.143 and 149?
   - 2.4.100 and 106?
   - 3.1.6-17?
   - 3.5.50?
   - 5.2.330–332?

   (b) How is the dog imagery employed in the play? What impressions do you form from the following dog images:
   - Chorus 1, line 7?
   - 1.2.143?
   - 2.1.43 and 48?
   - 2.4.69–70?
   - 3.1.31?
   - 4.5.15?

14   The sonnet

Read the section on Shakespeare's verse (page 251) before attempting the following activities on the sonnet:

Ⓐ *Describing a sonnet*

What is a sonnet? Read the sonnet which comprises the Epilogue and answer the following questions:
- How many lines does a sonnet have?
- How many sections is it usually divided into?
- What rhyme scheme do Shakespeare's sonnets usually have?

Ⓑ *Writing a sonnet*

Write a sonnet which can either (a) introduce the play (like the one which opens *Romeo and Juliet*); or (b) follow the siege of Harfleur (after 3.3); or the Battle of Agincourt (perhaps the octave could focus on the English and the sestet on the French).

Activities

C *The epilogue sonnet*

Why should Shakespeare have chosen to conclude his play with a sonnet, rather than a section of blank verse, as he does with all the other Chorus speeches? What is there about the sonnet form which makes it a particularly fitting vehicle for the meanings embodied in that final speech?

Themes

15 A theme is an important subject which seems to arise at several times in the play, showing in what the characters do and the language they use, so that we receive different perspectives on it. Themes in *Henry V* include the following (with activities in brackets):
- Theatre and the imagination (pages 28, 30 and 68)
- War (pages 28, 118, 158, 160, 184 and 194)
- Order (page 20)
- Duty and responsibility (pages 128–130)
- Heroism (page 114).

A *A theme collage*

Draw a spider diagram which includes all the many references you can find to the theme of war in the play. Then create a collage which illustrates how the theme is developed and explored.

B *Discussing a theme*

Look back at the activities on the theme of theatre and the imagination and write about:
- how the theme is developed and explored in the play
- what it adds to your overall interpretation of the play's meanings.

C *Analysing the themes*

Write an account of the themes in *Henry V*, showing how the themes are developed and the key words recur, to contribute to the overall meanings of the play.

Plot review

16 *Newspaper headlines*

Imagine that there had been tabloid newspapers in Henry V's day. Write a series of headlines that might have appeared, starting with the day after Henry has decided to attack France in 1.2 and concluding with the peace treaty signed at the end of the play.

 Radio reports

Write a series of brief radio reports which might have been broadcast over the World Service in Henry V's time. Each one should be no more than two or three sentences long, but should summarise the most important news of the day. If possible, record your reports and include brief interviews where appropriate.

 A revisionist article

What might an investigative reporter dig up some years later about the events portrayed in this play? Write a 'revisionist' article in which the reputation of Henry is reassessed in the light of alleged:

- bad management (the men at Agincourt were starving and ill)
- poor decisions (to go on to Calais, rather than returning with the fleet from Harfleur)
- cruelty and savagery (his words to the Governor of Harfleur)
- lack of respect for human life (killing the prisoners).

You might perhaps conclude with a suggestion that he did not win the battle of Agincourt: the French lost it – through incompetence and even worse leadership than the English.

17 Re-tell Henry's story as:

A a 'HENRY THE FIFTH' acrostic (in this case, a 13-line poem, the first line beginning with H, then E, then N... and so on)

B a mini-saga (a prose story of *exactly* fifty words, no more, no less)

C a sonnet similar to the one spoken by the Chorus at the end.

Activities

18 Shakespeare seems to have got his main story from historians called Raphael
Holinshed and Edward Hall. These are some of the features of Shakespeare's
Henry V which he did not find in Holinshed or Hall. Discuss what each one adds to
the play:
  - the episodes featuring Henry's former companions and the report of Falstaff's
    death
  - Fluellen, Macmorris, Jamy and Gower
  - Katharine learning French
  - the scenes featuring the French nobles
  - Henry's tour of the camp in disguise the night before Agincourt
  - his conversation with Bates, Court and Williams and Williams's challenge
  - the account of the deaths of York and Suffolk in battle
  - Burgundy's description of ravaged France.

Background to Shakespeare and *Henry V*

Do some research in an encylcopedia or CD-Rom to find out more about the background features highlighted in **bold**. There are also activities for additional research.

Shakespeare's England

Shakespeare lived during a period called the **Renaissance**: a time when extraordinary changes were taking place, especially in the fields of religion, politics, science, language and the arts. He wrote during the reigns of **Elizabeth I** and **James I**.

Religion and politics

- In the century following the **Reformation** and England's break with Rome in the 1530s, people in Shakespeare's England began to view the world and their own place in it very differently.
- Queen Elizabeth felt that she had to stand alone against a strongly Catholic Europe and maintain the **Protestant religion** in England established by her father Henry VIII.
- England had become a proud and independent nation, and a leading military and trading power, especially after the defeat of the **Spanish Armada** in 1588.
- People began to think about the relationship between themselves as individuals and the authority of the state, while not everybody any longer accepted the idea that queens or kings ruled by '**divine right**' (on God's authority).
- There were divisions in the Protestant Church, with extremist groups such as the **Puritans** disapproving of much that they saw in society and the Church.
- James I succeeded Elizabeth in 1603. He was a Scot, interested in witchcraft, and a supporter of the theatre, who fought off the treasonous attempt of the **Gunpowder Plot** in 1605.
- People began to question the traditional beliefs in rank and social order – the ideas that some people should be considered superior simply because they were born into wealthy families; or that those in power should always be obeyed without question.
- As trade became increasingly important, it was not only the nobility who could become wealthy. People could move around the country more easily and a competitive **capitalist economy** developed.

Science and discovery

- Scientists began to question traditional authorities (the accepted ideas handed down from one generation to the next) and depended instead upon their own observation of the world, especially after the development of instruments such as the telescope. **Galileo** came into conflict with the Church for claiming that the Earth was not the centre of the universe.
- Explorers brought back new produce, such as spices, silks and gold, and created great excitement in the popular imagination for stories of distant lands and their peoples.

Language

- The more traditional scholars still regarded **Latin** as the only adequate language for scholarly discussion and writing (and liked it because it also prevented many 'uncultured' people from understanding philosophy, medicine, etc.).
- But a new interest in the **English language** came with England's growing importance and sense of identity.
- The Protestants favoured a personal relationship with God, which meant being able to read the Bible themselves (rather than letting priests interpret it for them). This led to the need for a good version in English and **The Authorised Version of the Bible** (the 'King James Bible') was published in 1611.
- **Grammar schools** sprang up after the Reformation which increased literacy (but mostly among males in the middle and upper classes, and mainly in London).
- The invention of the **printing press** in the 1450s had led to more people having access to information and new ideas – not just the scholars.
- The English language began to be standardised in this period (into **Standard English**), but it was still very flexible and there was less insistence on following rules than there is nowadays.
- There was an enormous expansion in **vocabulary**, which affected every area of daily life: crafts, sciences, technology, trade, philosophy, food...
- English vocabulary was enriched by numerous **borrowings** from other languages. Between 1500 and 1650, over 10,000 new words entered the language (though many later fell out of use). Some 'purists' (who disliked change) opposed the introduction of new words.

Use a dictionary to find where the words for common foods came from: coffee, tea, tomato, chocolate, potato...

- Shakespeare therefore lived through a time when the English vocabulary was expanding amazingly and the grammar was still flexible, a time when people were intensely excited by language.

Shakespeare's plays reflect this fascination for words. Do some research to find examples of: Feste's wit in *Twelfth Night*; Dogberry's slip-ups in *Much Ado About Nothing*; Shylock's fatal bond and Portia's 'escape clause' in *The Merchant of Venice*; the puzzling oracle in *The Winter's Tale*, and Bottom's problems with words ('I see a voice!') in *A Midsummer Night's Dream*.

Plays and playhouses

The theatre was a very popular form of entertainment in Shakespeare's time, with audiences drawn from all classes of people. The theatre buildings and the companies of actors were different from what we are used to today.

The theatres

- The professional theatre was based exclusively in London, which had around 200,000 inhabitants in 1600.
- It was always under attack from the **Puritan**-dominated Guildhall, which wanted to abolish the theatres totally because, in their opinion, they encouraged sinful behaviour.
- Acting companies first performed in the courtyards of coaching inns, in the halls of great houses, at markets and in the streets. The first outdoor playhouse was the Red Lion, built around 1567; and the first purpose-built theatre was The Theatre, Shoreditch, opened in 1576 (when Shakespeare was twelve).
- By 1600, there were eleven public outdoor theatres, including **the Rose**, the Swan and the Globe (Shakespeare's theatre).
- **Shakespeare's Globe** opened in 1599 on Maiden Lane, Bankside, and was destroyed by fire during a performance of *Henry VIII* in 1613. (No one was killed, but a bottle of ale was needed to put out a fire in a man's breeches!) See page 259.
- Some outdoor theatres held audiences of up to 3,000.

- Standing room was one penny; the gallery two pence; the 'Lords' Room' three pence; and it was more expensive still to sit on the stage. This was at a time when a joiner (skilled carpenter) might earn 6 to 8 shillings (72 to 96 pence) per week. By 1614, it was six old pennies (2½ pence) for the newly opened indoor Hope Theatre.

Work out whether it was cheaper or more expensive to go to the theatre in Shakespeare's time than it is today. (To do the comparison, you will need to find out (a) how much the cheapest and most expensive tickets are at the Royal Shakespeare Theatre, Stratford-upon-Avon, for example; and (b) what a skilled worker might earn nowadays.)

- Outdoor theatre performances usually started about 2 p.m. or 3 p.m. (there was no artificial light).
- The season started in September, through to the beginning of Lent; then from after Easter to early summer. (Theatres were closed in summer because of the increased risk of **plague**: Eleven thousand died of the plague in summer 1593 and the theatres remained almost completely closed until 1594.) Some companies went on summer tours, playing in inns, and similar places.
- The majority of theatres were closed during the **Civil War** in 1642 (and most were demolished by 1656).
- There were some indoor theatres (called 'private' or 'hall' theatres) such as the **Blackfriars**, which was used up to 1609 almost exclusively by child actors (the minimum entrance fee of sixpence indicates a wealthier audience). Plays developed which were more suited to the more intimate atmosphere, with the stage illuminated by artificial lighting.
- The star actor **Richard Burbage** and his brother Cuthbert had the licence of the Blackfriars and Shakespeare's later plays were performed there.

Work out from the chart on page 259 which of Shakespeare's plays might have been written with the indoor Blackfriars Theatre in mind.

The actors

- In 1572 parliament passed an Act 'For the Punishment of Vagabonds'. As actors were classed as little better than wandering beggars, this Act required them to be attached to a theatre company and have the **patronage** (financial support and protection) of someone powerful. This meant that companies had to keep on the right side of patrons and make sure they didn't offend the Master of the Revels, who was responsible for **censorship**.

- Major companies in Shakespeare's time included The Admiral's Men and The Queen's Men. **The Lord Chamberlain's Men** (the group that Shakespeare joined, later known as **The King's Men** when James came to the throne) was formed in 1594 and was run by shareholders (called 'the housekeepers').
- The Burbages held 50 per cent of the shares of the company; the remaining 50 per cent was divided mainly between the actors including Shakespeare himself, who owned between 10 and 12 per cent which helped to earn him a comfortable regular income.

Acting

- There was very little rehearsal time, with several plays 'in repertory' (being performed) in any given period.
- We don't actually know about the style of acting, but modern, naturalistic, low-key acting was probably not possible on the Globe stage. At the same time, Shakespeare appears to be mocking over-the-top delivery in at least two of his plays.

Read *Hamlet*, 3. 2 (Hamlet's first three speeches to the First Player) and *A Midsummer Night's Dream* (especially Act 5).

- Actors certainly needed to be aware of their relationship with the audience: there must have been plenty of direct contact. In a daylight theatre there can be no pretence that the audience is not there.

Publishing

- Plays were not really regarded as 'literature' in Shakespeare's lifetime, and so the playwright would not have been interested in publishing his plays in book form.
- Some of Shakespeare's plays were, however, originally printed in cheap 'quarto' (pocket-size) editions. Some were sold officially (under an agreement made between the theatre company and the author), and some pirated (frequently by the actors themselves who had learned most of the script by heart).
- In 1623, seven years after Shakespeare's death, two of his close friends, John Heming (or Heminges) and Henry Condell, collected together the most reliable versions of the plays and published them in a larger size volume known as the **First Folio**. This included eighteen plays which had never before appeared in print, and eighteen more which had appeared in quarto editions. Only *Pericles* was omitted from the plays which make up what we nowadays call

Shakespeare's 'Complete Works' (unless we count plays such as *Two Noble Kinsmen*, which Shakespeare is known to have written in collaboration with another writer).

Much of the information in these sections comes from Michael Mangan, *A Preface to Shakespeare's Comedies: 1594–1603,* Longman, 1996.

The Globe Theatre

Above: front on view of the stage, as seen by the audience.

Below: bird's-eye view of the stage for positioning of characters.

The Swan theatre, by Johannes de Witt

No one knows precisely what Shakespeare's Globe theatre looked like, but we do have a number of clues:

- a section of the foundations has been unearthed and provides a good idea of the size and shape of the outside walls
- the foundations of **the Rose**, a theatre near Shakespeare's, have been completely excavated
- a Dutch visitor to Shakespeare's London called Johannes de Witt saw a play in the Swan theatre and made a sketch of the interior (see opposite).

Using all the evidence available, a reconstruction of Shakespeare's Globe theatre has been built in London, not far from the site of the original building (see the photos below).

 The facts

From what you can learn from these photographs:

1. Roughly what shape is the theatre, looked at from above?
2. How many storeys does it have?
3. In which areas can the audience (a) stand and (b) sit?
4. What is behind the stage?
5. How much scenery and lighting are used?
6. What other details can you pick out which seem to make the Globe different from an indoor theatre (which has a stage at one end, similar to many school assembly halls)?

B *Using the stage*

Copy the plan on page 238. Then, using the staging guidelines provided, sketch or mark characters as they might appear at crucial moments in *Henry V* (such as the entrance of the French Ambassador in 1.2).

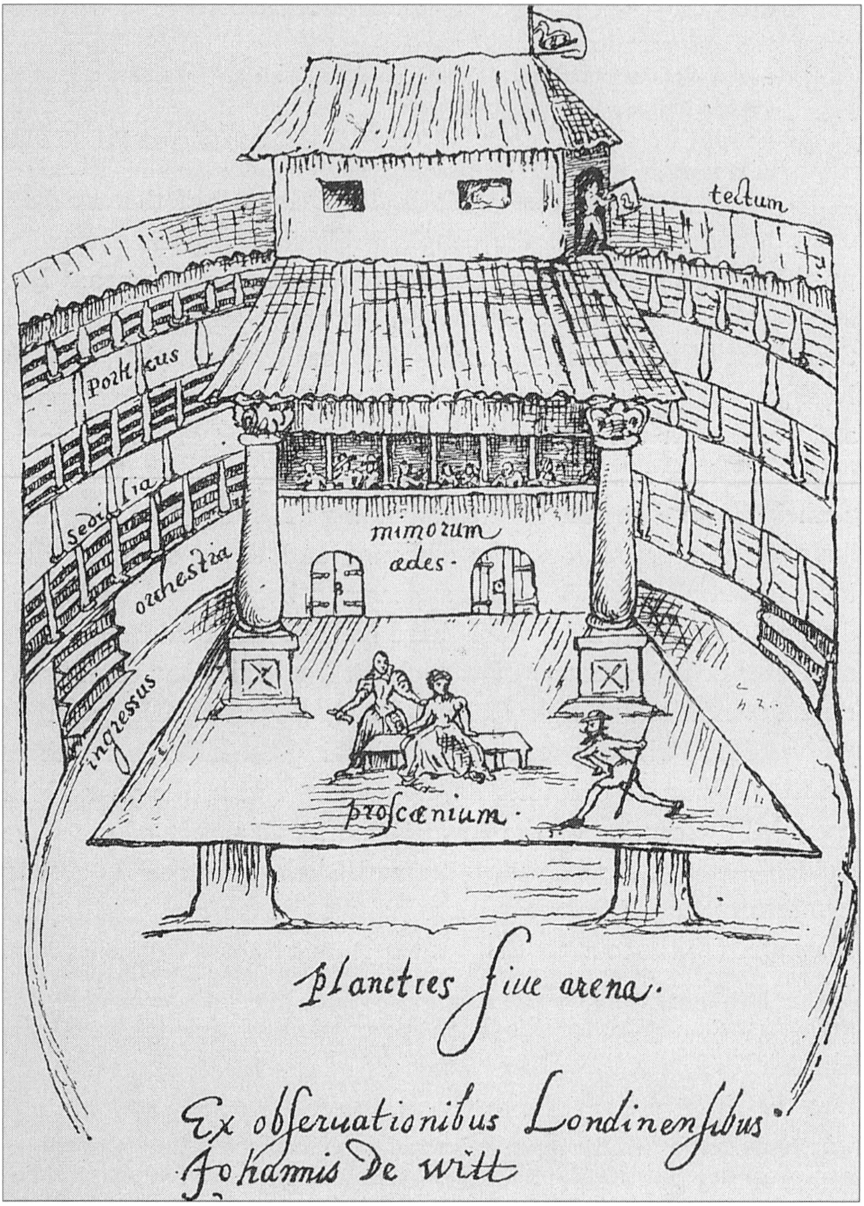
tectum
porticus
sedilia
orchestra
ingressus
mimorum
aedes
proscaenium
planities sive arena.
Ex observationibus Londinensibus
Johannis De witt

C *The actor–audience relationship*

In what ways is the design of Shakespeare's Globe ideally suited to the performance of his plays?

- How might the open stage and the balcony be useful? (Refer to moments in *Henry V* or other Shakespeare plays that you know.)
- What do you think would be the most interesting features of the way in which Shakespeare's actors – and those on the reconstructed Globe today – might relate to and interact with the audience? (Which moments in *Henry V* seem to require a performance in which the audience are very close to the actors, for example?)

The historical background

Henry's ancestors and Shakespeare's history plays

To understand Henry's story, it is important to go back at least as far as his great-grandfather, Edward III, who reigned from 1327 to 1377. Edward had seven sons, the oldest of whom, Edward the Black Prince, won some famous victories against the French, notably at the Battle of Crécy (see 2.4.54). As the family tree on page 245 shows, his other sons included Lionel, Duke of Clarence, John of Gaunt, Duke of Lancaster, Edmund, Duke of York, and Thomas, Duke of Woodstock.

It was a disaster for England when the Black Prince died before his father, in 1376; because, when Edward III died a year later, the Black Prince's son, Richard, came to the throne as a very young and inexperienced ruler. Although Richard's reign began well, his habit of surrounding himself with favourites and spending money extravagantly caused him to become extremely unpopular; and when his uncle, Thomas of Woodstock, was murdered, suspicion fell upon Richard. Woodstock had been outspoken in condemning Richard's behaviour and many thought that the King was determined to get him out of the way.

Shakespeare's Richard II

When Shakespeare's *Richard II* opens, the King's cousin, Henry Bolingbroke (see the family tree) has accused Sir Thomas Mowbray (one of Richard's supporters) of having a hand in Woodstock's death. At first Richard is willing to let Mowbray and Bolingbroke decide the issue by mortal combat, but he then changes his mind and exiles both men, Mowbray for life and Henry for six years. While Henry is abroad, his father dies and Richard takes advantage of Henry's absence to seize the Lancaster estates: he is heavily in debt and needs money to finance the war in Ireland. While Richard is in Ireland, Henry returns to claim his inheritance. The nobles, unhappy with Richard's tyrannous behaviour, flock to the popular Bolingbroke, and, when the King returns, he finds he has no army to support him. Richard resigns his crown to his cousin, who ascends the throne as Henry IV, but the new King's reign is soon darkened by the suspicious death of Richard in Pomfret Castle.

Henry IV, Parts 1 and 2

In the next two plays, Shakespeare focuses on two main stories: the rebellions which follow Henry's accession to the throne; and the behaviour of Henry's son and heir, Prince Henry. The Prince (then known as Hal) spends most of his time away from court in the company of Sir John Falstaff, a fat knight famous for his drunkenness and cowardice. Falstaff is in many ways a kind of substitute father for Hal, and together they frequent brothels, get involved in highway robbery and lead the kind of life which makes Hal's father and the nobles fear for the country when Hal becomes King. What nobody realises is that Hal is using this experience as part of his education; and, after a moving death-bed reconciliation with his father, his first act as the newly crowned Henry V is to turn away Falstaff and his companions.

Henry's rejection of Falstaff

Henry IV, Part 2 (RSC, 1991)

This is the scene from the end of the previous play, *Henry IV, Part 2*. Falstaff has been visiting a friend in the country (Justice Shallow) when he hears of the Henry IV's death. He rushes to London, expecting that Hal will be delighted to see him and give him a powerful post at court – perhaps even Lord Chief Justice itself. He arrives just as Henry's coronation is ending, and the newly crowned King is about to emerge from Westminster Abbey...

Trumpets sound and the KING *and his* Train *pass over the stage. After them enter* FALSTAFF, SHALLOW, PISTOL, BARDOLPH, *and Page*

FALSTAFF   Stand here by me, Master Robert Shallow; I will make the King do you grace. I will leer upon him, as 'a comes by; and do but mark the countenance that he will give me.

PISTOL   God Bless thy lungs, good knight!

FALSTAFF   Come here, Pistol; stand behind me. [*To* SHALLOW.] O, if I had had time to have made new liveries, I would have bestowed the thousand pound I borrowed of you. But 'tis no matter; this poor show doth better; this doth infer the zeal I had to see him.

SHALLOW   It doth so.

FALSTAFF   It shows my earnestness of affection –

SHALLOW   It doth so.

FALSTAFF   My devotion –

SHALLOW   It doth, it doth, it doth.

FALSTAFF   As it were, to ride day and night; and not to deliberate, not to remember, not to have patience to shift me –

SHALLOW   It is best, certain.

FALSTAFF   But to stand stained with travel, and sweating with desire to see him; thinking of nothing else, putting all affairs else in oblivion, as if there were nothing else to be done but to see him.

PISTOL   'Tis 'semper idem' for 'obsque hoc nihil est'. 'Tis all in every part.

SHALLOW	'Tis so indeed.
PISTOL	My knight, I will inflame they noble liver And make the rage. Thy Doll, and Helen of thy noble thoughts, Is in base durance and contagious prison; Hal'd thither By most mechanical and dirty hand. Rouse up revenge from ebon den with fell Alecto's snake, For Doll is in. Pistol speaks nought but truth.
FALSTAFF	I will deliver her. [*Shouts within, and the trumpets sound.*]
PISTOL	There roar'd the sea, and trumpet-clangor sounds.

Enter the KING *and his* Train, *the* LORD CHIEF JUSTICE *among them.*

FALSTAFF	God save thy Grace, King Hal; my royal Hal!
PISTOL	The heavens thee guard and keep, most royal imp of fame!
FALSTAFF	God save thee, my sweet boy!
KING	My Lord Chief Justice, speak to that vain man.
CHIEF JUSTICE	Have you your wits? Know you what 'tis you speak?
FALSTAFF	My king! my Jove! I speak to thee, my heart!
KING	I know thee not, old man. Fall to thy prayers. How ill white hairs become a fool and jester! I have long dreamt of such a kind of man, So surfeit-swell'd, so old, and so profane; But, being awak'd, I do despise my dream. Make less thy body hence, and more thy grace; Leave gormandizing; know the grave doth gape For thee thrice wider than for other men – Reply not to me with a fool-born jest; Presume not that I am the thing I was, For God doth know, so shall the world perceive, That I have turn'd away my former self;

So will I those that kept me company.
When thou dost hear I am as I have been,
Approach me, and thou shalt be as thou wast,
The tutor and the feeder of my riots.
Till then I banish thee, on pain of death,
As I have done the rest of my misleaders
Not to come near our person by ten mile.
For competence of life I will allow you,
That lack of means enforce you not to evils
And, as we hear you do reform yourselves,
We will according to your strength and qualities,
Give you advancement. Be it your charge, my lord,
To see perform'd the tenour of our word.
Set on.   [*Exeunt the* KING *and his* Train.]

FALSTAFF   Master Shallow, I owe you a thousand pounds.

SHALLOW   Yea, marry, Sir John; which I beseech you to let me have home
with me.

FALSTAFF   That can hardly be, Master Shallow. Do not you grieve at
this; I shall be sent for in private to him. Look you, he must
seem thus to the world. Fear not your advancements; I will
be the man yet that shall make you great.

SHALLOW   I cannot perceive how, unless you give me your doublet, and
stuff me out with straw. I beseeech you, good Sir John, let me
have five hundred of my thousand.

FALSTAFF   Sir, I will be as good as my word. This that you heard was but
a colour.

SHALLOW   A colour that I fear you will die in, Sir John.

FALSTAFF   Fear no colours; go with me to dinner. Come, Lieutenant Pistol;
come, Bardolph. I shall be sent for soon at night.

Re-enter PRINCE JOHN, *the* LORD CHIEF JUSTICE, *with* Officers.

CHIEF
JUSTICE   Go carry Sir John Falstaff to the Fleet;
Take all his company along with him.

FALSTAFF   My lord, my lord –

CHIEF JUSTICE	I cannot now speak. I will hear you soon Take them away.

PISTOL	Si fortuna me tormenta, spero me contenta.

[Exeunt all but PRINCE JOHN *and the* LORD CHIEF JUSTICE.]

PRINCE JOHN	I like this fair proceedings of the King's. He hath intent his wonted followers Shall all be very well provided for; But all are banish'd till their conversations Appear more wise and modest to the world.

CHIEF JUSTICE	And so they are.

PRINCE JOHN	The King hath call'd his parliament, my lord.

CHIEF JUSTICE	He hath.

PRINCE JOHN	I will lay odds that, ere this year expire, We bear our civil swords and native fire As far as France. I heard a bird so sing, Whose music, to my thinking, pleas'd the King. Come, will you hence?

[Exeunt.]

(*Henry IV, Part 2*, 5.5)

Henry's claim to France

Henry's claim to the throne of France (see 1.2) is supported by the fact that his great-great-grandmother, Isabella, had been the daughter of the French King Philip IV. As the family tree opposite shows, Henry was distantly related to the French King, Charles VI.

The French try to block Henry's claim by declaring that the French throne could not be inherited through the female line; and in support of their argument they quote the Salic Law, which states that no woman may succeed to the throne in Salic land. However, the Archbishop of Canterbury answers this by claiming that (1) Salic Land applies to Germany (see the map on page 246), not France; and that (2) several French kings have themselves inherited the throne through the female line.

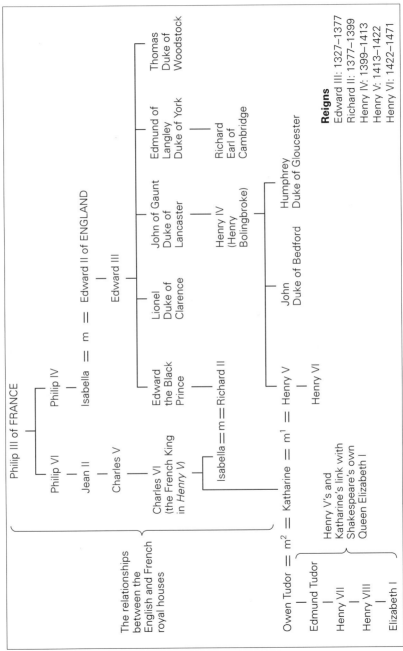

Reigns
Edward III: 1327–1377
Richard II: 1377–1399
Henry IV: 1399–1413
Henry V: 1413–1422
Henry VI: 1422–1471

How the English and French royal families were related

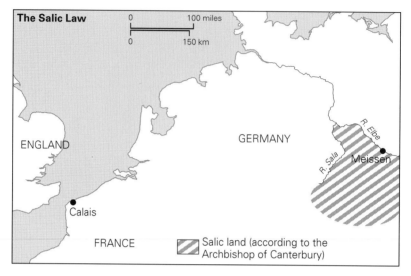

The position of the Salic Land

To show how seriously they took their claim to the French throne, English kings from Edward III onwards used to place the French royal Fleur-de-lys in the most important 'quarter' of the royal coat of arms (below the right shoulder).

If you were directing *Henry V*, would you set the play in the fifteenth century and dress your actors in heraldic tabards, as Olivier and Branagh did; or perhaps set it in the twentieth century and show modern warfare (as the RSC did in 1997)?

Henry's French campaign

Shakespeare gives us only a few details of Henry's campaign, but recent historians have learned a great deal more about what actually happened. The details for this diary are taken from *The Armies of Agincourt*, by Christopher Rothero:

14 August, 1415: The English fleet has anchored off the coast in the Seine estuary and hundreds of small boats shuttle to and fro to land Henry's army. Plans are made to take Harfleur: the port would be a useful bridgehead for landing stores; and it is on the river route to Paris. But it is heavily fortified with a two-and-a-half mile wall and twenty-six towers. Fearing attack, the French fortify Harfleur with an extra 400 men and its citizens send an urgent appeal for relief to the Dauphin, who is assembling an army at Rouen.

22 September: Harfleur finally falls to the English, but the protracted siege has taken its toll: the English have lost over 2,000 men (mainly to disease) and a further 5,000 have to be sent home as too sick to continue the campaign. Desertion amongst the English troops increases daily.

Henry's war council advise returning home and beginning a fresh campaign the following year; but he refuses and determines to march through northern France to English-held Calais: for one thing, he wants to prove that he is the true ruler of France; for another, he considers it unchivalric not to give the French a chance to fight. He also thinks he has a fair chance of beating them.

8 October: Leaving 1,200 men to garrison Harfleur, Henry's sickly army of about 1,000 men-at-arms and 5,000 archers begin their 200-mile march to Calais with rations for only eight days. The troops are in poor condition and there have been torrential autumn rains.

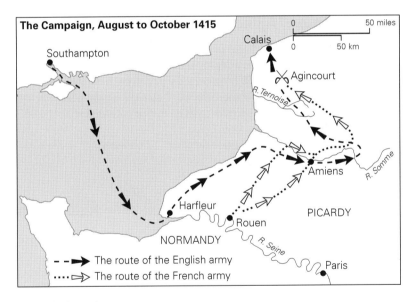

Henry V's French campaign

17 October: The main body of the French army reaches Amiens, but they find that the English have already moved on.

19 October: Having had to detour many miles along the southern bank of the River Somme (because the French were holding all the crossing-points), Henry finally fords it and the following day the army rests. The two armies are now only about six miles apart.

Meanwhile the French disagree over strategy. The Constable simply wants to surround the English and starve them into submission, but he is outvoted by Orléans and Bourbon, who are all for an immediate attack. The French herald visits Henry and informs him of their plans; Henry replies boldly that he intends to march on to Calais. Privately he knows that the men are sick, exhausted and under-nourished; to remain where they are will be certain death, and he is pleased that the French strategy gives him the chance to choose where and when to fight.

20 October: The English head north and are daunted to march over fields churned up by thousands of French horsemen.

24 October: Patrols show that the route ahead is blocked by a vast French force. The English set up camp in the village of Maisoncelles and await the morning.

The Battle of Agincourt

- **The French**: Historians now believe that there were probably between 20,000 and 30,000 in the French army (though some suggest that the figure might have been as high as 150,000). Sixty per cent were men-at-arms, the rest being trained garrison troops or mercenaries. They were all well equipped and fresh. The Constable was so confident that he turned down the offer of 6,000 additional crossbowmen from Paris.
- **The English**: There were 6,000, of whom 1,000 were men-at-arms, the rest archers.
- **The Battle**:

The French plan was to:
1. neutralise the English archers (A) with intensive fire from crossbowmen and then destroy them with flanking cavalry (C)
2. use the dismounted men-at-arms (D1 and D2) to use their superior numbers to wipe out the English men-at-arms (B)
3. Keep their third (rear) division (D3) in reserve, to deal with any survivors who might attempt to escape.

Henry's plan was to:
Draw the French into range of the devastating fire from the English archers.

What actually happened was:
1. The French nobles all wanted a share of the action and crowded out the front line, pushing their own archers and lower-ranking nobles uselessly to the rear.
2. Henry's army advanced first; when they were within 200 yards of the French, the English halted and the archers drove sharpened stakes into the ground, behind which they took their stand.

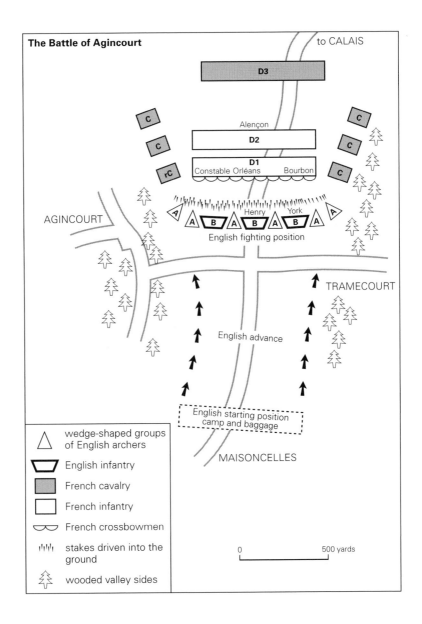

The battle plan of the Battle of Agincourt, 1415

3. The French right flank cavalry (rC) attacked the English left, but were impeded by the water-logged ground and the dense Agincourt wood.

4. This meant that the French were now confined to a frontal assault, but they could not force through the wall of stakes and were repulsed.
Then the French first division (D1) walked forward through the heavy mud; they pushed the English back a few feet but were so closely packed that they could hardly lift their arms; meanwhile, those at the rear were pushing forward and crushing the men in front.

5. The English were now able to kill the tightly-packed French with comparative ease; the archers, more agile than the heavily armoured French, joined battle and dispatched thousands of knights who could hardly move – some even suffocated or drowned in the mud beneath piles of their dying comrades.

6. Although the Duke of York was killed and Henry beaten to his knees several times, the English archers kept up a deadly hail on the advancing French second division (D2).

7. Seeing that things had gone hopelessly wrong, the French second division began to leave the field. Some French attacked the English baggage train.

8. After two or three hours the English had taken so many prisoners that they were outnumbered by them; the French third division (D3) began to leave the field and, thinking that the retreating French were planning to attack the English from the rear, Henry ordered the prisoners to be killed.

By nightfall, between 7,000 and 10,000 French lay dead and there were 1,500 surviving prisoners, including Orléans, who was to spend the next 25 years in England. The English had lost between 400 and 500.

Kingship

In the middle ages people believed that a king had been anointed by God and therefore had absolute authority to be God's power on earth. This is a view that Shakespeare puts into the mouth of Richard II:

> Not all the waters of the rough rude sea
> Can wash the balm from an anointed king.
> The breath of worldly men cannot depose
> The deputy elected by the Lord.
> (*Richard II*, 3.2.54–57)

But Richard is deposed and the usurper's son goes on to defeat the French at Agincourt.

The king is but a man, as I am...

In 1571 a man called Edmund Plowden explained the idea of 'the king's two bodies', writing:

'For the king has in him two bodies... a body natural and a body politic...'

His 'body natural' was like anyone else's subject to disease and death; but his 'body politic' was linked to his powers to govern and to represent the country. This idea can be seen in action throughout *Henry V*, where we are able to observe Henry the man (with his powerful private emotions) and Henry the King (aware of his duties and responsibilities).

Shakespeare's verse

Metre

It is possible to describe where the heavy stress falls in any English word. For example, these three words (from 1. 1) have their heavy stress on the first syllable: **ques**tion, **hun**dred, **Hen**ry; while in these the heavy stress is on the second syllable: in**deed**, es**quires**, re**gard**.

All Shakespeare's verse has a pattern of light and heavy stresses running through it, known as the metre. You can hear the metre if you read these lines aloud, over-emphasising the heavily stressed syllables:

- Was **like** and **had** in**deed** a**gainst** us **passed** (1.1.3)
- The **King** is **full** of **grace** and **fair** re**gard** (1.1.22)
- Which **I** could **with** a **rea**dy **guess** de**clare** (1.1.96).

No actor would ever perform the lines in that monotonous way, but they would certainly be aware that the metre was always there, helping to give the verse form and structure.

Sometimes, to point out that a syllable which does not carry a heavy stress in modern English is stressed in Shakespeare's line of verse, it will be accented, like this:

- But we in it shall be rememberéd (4.3.59)

1. Mark the heavy stresses in that line of Henry's (4.3.59).
2. The four lines above are all totally regular in their metre: what do you notice about (a) the pattern of short and heavy stresses? (b) the number of syllables?

Background to Shakespeare and *Henry V*

Varying the metre

Most of the lines in Shakespeare's plays are not as regular as the three quoted above. In fact, most will have an irregular stress pattern, like this one, where two heavy stresses fall significantly together on the words 'I' and 'Richard':

- **I Rich**ard's **bod**y have in**ter**réd **new**; (4.1.300)

Occasionally a line will contain an extra syllable (11 rather than 10):

- Of indigent faint souls past corporal toil (1.1.16)

Here the actor can either try to deliver 'corporal' as though it were one syllable – *corp'ral* – (making it a regular line), or emphasise the slowness of the phrase, perhaps underlining the heaviness in the idea of 'corporal toil'.

Some lines really stand out, because they are clearly short. Here the French King's question is simple and direct:

- Or else what follows? (2.4.97)

A collection of heavy stresses together can add emphasis:

- **We must bear all**. O **hard** con**di**tion. (4.1.238)

Dividing the line into feet

Just as music has a number of beats in a bar, so Shakespeare's verse has five 'feet' in a complete line. A five-feet line is called 'pentameter' (pent = five; metre = measure).

A single foot can contain syllables from different words, and any one word can be broken up by the foot divisions:

- To **an** | -swer **ma** | -tters of | this **con** | -se**quence** (2.4.147)

This is why a single line of verse is sometimes set out rather oddly in different lines of print, if it is shared between two or more characters, as happens in 1.2:

HENRY	Where is my gracious Lord of Canterbury?	] line 1
EXETER	Not here in presence	] two speeches make
HENRY	Send for him, good uncle.	] up line 2

Iambic pentameter

A foot which contains an unstressed syllable followed by a stressed one (the standard 'beat': dee-**dum**) is called an 'iamb'. Verse which has five iambs per line as its standard rhythm is called 'iambic pentameter'.

Iambic pentameter which does not rhyme is also sometimes known as 'blank verse'.

1. Bearing in mind that the iambic pentameter line goes: dee-**dum**, dee-**dum**, dee-**dum**, dee-**dum**, dee-**dum**, make up some of your own 'Shakespearean' verse (perhaps based on one of the themes of the play, such as war).
2. Copy out the following lines from 1.2 and divide them into five feet; then mark the heavy stresses: 24, 25, 33, 39 and (more difficult) 54.
3. Do the same with these key lines: 1.2.96; 1.2.174; 1.2.242; 3.1.1; and 3.3.38. Pick one and show how the rhythm helps the meaning.

Rhyme

Shakespeare sometimes uses rhyme for the ends of scenes, where a 'rhyming couplet' can have the effect of rounding things off, as it does in 1.2. Earlier in that same scene, Henry's rhyme underlines the inevitability of his threat to the Ambassador concerning the Dauphin's gift of tennis balls:

His jest will savour but of shallow wit,
When thousands weep more than did laugh at it. (1.2.296–297).

Find other scenes which end with a rhyming couplet and discuss what the effect might be in each case.

Verse and prose

It is never totally clear why Shakespeare chooses to write some scenes, or passages, in verse, and others in prose.

Although there are many examples where the more serious scenes, involving great passions, are in verse while those about ordinary people and comedy are in prose, there are also significant examples throughout Shakespeare's plays where this is not the case.

Look back through *Henry V* and try to work out why certain scenes are in verse and others in prose.

The plot of *Henry V*

Act 1

Prologue: The Chorus delivers a prologue in which he asks us to make up for the theatre's shortcomings by using our imaginations.

1.1: The Archbishop of Canterbury and the Bishop of Ely discuss how they can oppose a proposed parliamentary Bill. If it is passed, the Church will lose a great deal of its land and possessions, but there is a chance that the King might oppose it. They are delighted with the change in his character since coming to the throne. He has put all the wild behaviour of his youth behind him and has rejected his former companions, including the fat knight Falstaff. Now he behaves responsibly and might well accept a deal offered to him by Canterbury: if Henry opposes the Bill, the Church will give him a large sum of money to finance a proposed war with France in pursuit of his claim to the French throne .

1.2: Henry asks Canterbury to explain whether his claim to the French throne is invalid because of the Salic Law (which states that no one can inherit the throne of France through the female line). Canterbury demonstrates firstly that the Salic Law does not apply to France, but to Germany; and secondly that several of the French kings themselves have inherited the throne through female ancestors. Encouraged by the churchmen and his nobles, Henry decides that he will invade France in pursuit of his claim and calls in the French Ambassador sent from the Dauphin. The Ambassador rejects a claim that Henry had made earlier to certain dukedoms and presents Henry with an insulting gift of tennis balls. Henry defiantly answers the Ambassador and instructs his nobles to prepare for war.

Act 2

Prologue: The Chorus describes how the country is alive with preparations for the war with France. The French, however, have bribed three treacherous English nobles to assassinate Henry as he prepares to set sail with the English fleet at Southampton.

2.1: In London, Pistol Bardolph and Nym, Henry's former companions, themselves prepare to join the army bound for France. Nym is bitter with Pistol for having married the woman to whom he was himself betrothed, Nell Quickly, but their argument is interrupted when the Boy enters to tell them that Falstaff is dying.

2.2: The scene moves to Southampton. Having encouraged Henry to show little mercy to a drunk who had behaved insultingly to the King, the three traitors have no expectation of mercy themselves when their crime is exposed. Henry is personally grieved and deeply hurt because one of the traitors, Lord Scroop, had been a close friend; but since they have plotted to betray their country, they are led off to execution.

2.3: In London Mistress Quickly describes Falstaff's dying moments. Declaring his intention to exploit the war for gain, Pistol bids farewell to his wife, and the men leave, accompanied by Falstaff's boy.

2.4: With news that the English are on their way, the French King orders that his country's defences should be strengthened. The Dauphin is dismissive of Henry, but the Constable knows better, having heard how Henry dealt with the ambassador. Exeter arrives in the French court, bearing documents to support Henry's claim and threatening violent military action if it is not agreed to.

Act 3

Prologue: The Chorus describes the fleet carrying the English army across to France. Henry has rejected the French offer of a few dukedoms and marriage to the King's daughter Katharine and determines to attack: we are now asked to imagine the siege of Harfleur.

3.1: In the midst of the assault, Henry encourages his men to make one further attack upon the breach made in the town walls.

3.2: Pistol, Bardolph and Nym are all for running away, but are forced to join the attack by Fluellen, a Welsh captain. In the company of Gower, an Englishman, and Jamy, a Scot, Fluellen has an argument about the conduct of the war with Macmorris, an Irishman.

3.3: After listening to Henry's threats, the Governor of Harfleur surrenders the town. Henry decides to march to Calais the next day.

3.4: The French Princess Katharine receives an English lesson from her lady-in-waiting, Alice, and is shocked to hear that some English words sound extremely rude.

3.5: Receiving news that Henry has already passed the River Somme, the French nobles angrily disparage the English, since they themselves are being mocked by their women for inaction. Assuming that Henry will be captured, the King sends the herald Montjoy to discuss ransom terms.

3.6: The English, led by Exeter, successfully take a bridge held by the French. Pistol pleads with Fluellen to use his influence with Exeter: Bardolph is to be executed for stealing from a church and Pistol wants Fluellen to plead for his release. Fluellen refuses and, when he informs Henry of the crime, the King confirms the sentence. Montjoy arrives and, while admitting that his army is in a sorry state, Henry defiantly rejects any talk of ransom.

3.7: It is the night before the battle and the confident French, impatient for dawn, argue about horses and mistresses.

Act 4

Prologue: The Chorus asks us to imagine the dark night as the two armies prepare for battle. The French are so sure of victory that they play dice for the English prisoners they will capture; the English are exhausted, but Henry lifts their spirits by walking around the camp and speaking encouraging words.

4.1: Henry borrows a cloak from Sir Thomas Erpingham and in this disguise encounters first Pistol and then three soldiers, Williams, Court and Bates. As they talk, Henry is obliged to consider the heavy responsibility a king carries when he leads men into war. His argument with Williams becomes heated and they exchange gloves as a token that they will fight each other if they survive the coming battle. Left alone, Henry thinks about what it means to be a king, and begs God not to hold Richard II's death against him.

4.2: It is dawn and the battle is about to begin. The French mount their horses and expect to make short work of the feeble enemy that faces them.

4.3: Henry inspires his men with a rousing speech: it is St Crispin's Day and he promises them that their deeds will always be remembered. Rejecting Montjoy's final offer to discuss ransom terms, Henry gives York charge of the vanguard and they prepare for battle.

4.4: The fighting begins and Pistol captures Monsieur le Fer, an even more cowardly soldier than he is himself. As they leave, the Boy ominously points out that there is nobody to guard the baggage but boys.

4.5: The French are soon in total disarray and feel dishonoured by their shameful behaviour in battle.

4.6: Exeter reports the deaths of York and Suffolk. Fearing that the French are regrouping, Henry orders that all the prisoners must be killed.

4.7: Henry is furious when he hears that some of the fleeing French have killed the boys guarding the baggage, but Montjoy arrives to confirm that the victory is Henry's. Fluellen reminds the King of his Welsh blood and Henry plays a practical joke on the Welshman, asking him to wear Williams' glove. Williams challenges it when he meets Fluellen and Henry has to part the two men. After revealing that he was the man that Williams had unwittingly challenged, Henry rewards the soldier. Henry then receives details of the catastrophic losses sustained by the French, in contrast to the extremely low English death toll.

Act 5

Prologue: The Chorus explains what has happened in the five years following Agincourt. Henry has returned triumphantly to England, and, after some mediation from the Emperor Sigismund, he has gone back to France to sign a peace treaty.

5.1: In France, Pistol is humiliated when Fluellen forces him to eat a leek. He has received news that his wife has died and, with no other prospects, plans to return to England to become a pimp and a pick-pocket and to boast that the wounds caused by Fluellen are actually battle-scars.

5.2: The English and French courts meet. After Burgundy describes the effects upon France of the ravages of war, the nobles retire to sign the peace treaty, leaving Henry alone with Katharine and Alice. Despite Henry's poor French and Katharine's difficulties with English, the Princess agrees to marry him if her father approves. When the rest of the court return, they tease the couple, but a peace treaty is signed which confirms Henry as the heir to the French throne. Henry kisses Katharine and Queen Isabel blesses their marriage.

Epilogue: The Chorus sums up Henry's achievements but tells us that, after his untimely death, France was lost and England plunged into civil war.

Study skills: titles and quotations

Referring to titles

When you are writing an essay, you will often need to refer to the title of the play. There are two main ways of doing this:
- If you are hand-writing your essay, the title of the play should be underlined: Henry V
- If you are word-processing your essay, the play title should be in italics: *Henry V*.

The same rules apply to titles of all plays and other long works including novels and non-fiction, such as: *Animal Farm* and *The Diary of Anne Frank*. The titles of poems or short stories are placed inside single inverted commas; for example: 'Timothy Winters' and 'A Sound of Thunder'.

Note that the first word in a title and all the main words will have capital (or 'upper case') letters, while the less important words (such as conjunctions, prepositions and articles) will usually begin with lower case letters; for example: *The Taming of the Shrew* or *Antony and Cleopatra*.

Using quotations

Quotations show that you know the play in detail and are able to produce evidence from the script to back up your ideas and opinions. It is usually a good idea to keep quotations as short as you can (and this especially applies to exams, where it is a waste of time copying chunks out of the script).

Using longer quotations

There are a number of things you should do if you want to use a quotation of more than a few words:

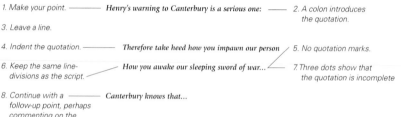

1. Make your point. ——— *Henry's warning to Canterbury is a serious one:* ——— 2. A colon introduces the quotation.

3. Leave a line.

4. Indent the quotation. ——— *Therefore take heed how you impawn our person* / 5. No quotation marks.

6. Keep the same line- ——— *How you awake our sleeping sword of war...* ——— 7. Three dots show that
divisions as the script. the quotation is incomplete

8. Continue with a ——— *Canterbury knows that...*
follow-up point, perhaps
commenting on the
quotation itself.

Using brief quotations

Brief quotations are usually easier to use, take less time to write out and are much more effective in showing how familiar you are with the play. Weave them into the sentence like this:

- Admitting to Montjoy that his few remaining soldiers are 'almost no better than so many French', Henry shows that...

If you are asked to state where the quotation comes from, use this simple form of reference to indicate the *Act, scene* and *line*:

- Assuring the French Ambassador that he is 'no tyrant but a Christian king' (1.2.242), Henry establishes early on that...

In some editions this is written partly in Roman numerals – upper case for the Act and lower case for the scene; for example: (I.ii.242) or (I.2.242).

William Shakespeare and *Henry V*

Henry V must have been written some time during the spring or early summer of 1599. We know this because the Act 5 Chorus makes a reference to the Earl of Essex's anticipated return from Ireland (lines 29–34), and Essex left England in March and returned in September. As the lines are optimistic, they were probably written soon after Essex's departure, before it became clear that his campaign would end in failure.

Shakespeare's life and career

No one is absolutely sure when Shakespeare wrote each play.

1564 Born in Stratford-upon-Avon, first son of John and Mary Shakespeare.

1582 Marries Anne Hathaway from the nearby village of Shottery. She is eight years older and expecting their first child.

1583 Daughter Susannah born.

1585 Twin son and daughter, Hamnet and Judith, born.

Some time before **1592** Shakespeare arrives in London, becomes an actor and writes poems and plays. Several plays are performed, probably including the three parts of *Henry VI*. Another writer, Robert Greene, writes about 'Shake-scene', the 'upstart crow' who has clearly become a popular playwright.

By **1595** he is a shareholder with the Lord Chamberlain's Men (see page 235) and has probably written *Richard III, Comedy of Errors, Titus Andronicus, The Taming of the Shrew, The Two Gentlemen of Verona, Love's Labours Lost, Romeo and Juliet, Richard II* and *A Midsummer Night's Dream* (as well as contributing to plays by other writers and writing the poems 'Venus and Adonis' and 'The Rape of Lucrece').

1596 Hamnet dies, age 11.

1597 Buys New Place, one of the finest houses in Stratford.

1599 Globe Theatre opens on Bankside.

By **1599**: *King John, The Merchant of Venice*, the two parts of *Henry IV, The Merry Wives of Windsor, Much Ado About Nothing, Julius Caesar* and *Henry V* (as well as the Sonnets).

1603 King James I grants the Lord Chamberlain's Men a Royal Patent and they become The King's Men (page 235).

By **1608**: *As You Like It, Hamlet, Twelfth Night, Troilus and Cressida, All's Well That Ends Well, Measure For Measure, Othello, Macbeth, King Lear, Antony and Cleopatra, Pericles, Coriolanus* and *Timon of Athens*.

1608 The King's Men begin performing plays in the indoor Blackfriars Theatre (page 234).

By **1613**: *Cymbeline, The Winter's Tale, The Tempest, Henry VIII, Two Noble Kinsmen* (the last two probably with John Fletcher).

1616 Dies, April 23, and is buried in Holy Trinity Church, Stratford.

1623 Publication of the First Folio (page 235).

Shakespeare's times

1558 Elizabeth I becomes queen.

1565 The explorer John Hawkins introduces sweet potatoes and tobacco into England.

1567 Mary Queen of Scots abdicates in favour of her year-old son, James VI.

1568 Mary escapes to England and is imprisoned by Elizabeth.

1572 Francis Drake attacks Spanish ports in the Americas.

1576 James Burbage opens the first theatre (The Theatre) in London.

1580 Francis Drake returns from a circumnavigation of the world.

1582 Pope Gregory reforms the Christian calendar.

1587 Mary Queen of Scots executed for a treasonous plot against Elizabeth; Drake partly destroys the Spanish fleet at Cádiz and war breaks out with Spain.

1588 Philip II of Spain's Armada is destroyed by the English fleet.

1592 Plague kills 20,000 Londoners.

1593 Playwright Christopher Marlowe killed in a pub brawl.

1596 Tomatoes introduced into England; John Harington invents the water-closet (the ancestor of the modern lavatory).

1597 Earl of Tyrone leads a new rebellion in Ireland.

1599 Earl of Essex concludes a truce with Tyrone, returns home and is arrested.

1601 Essex is tried and executed for treasonous plots against Elizabeth.

1603 Elizabeth I dies and is succeeded by James VI of Scotland as James I of England.

1603 Sir Walter Raleigh is jailed for plotting against James.

1604 James is proclaimed 'King of Great Britain, France and Ireland'; new Church rules cause 300 Puritan clergy to resign.

1605 Gunpowder Plot uncovered.

1607 First permanent European settlement in America at Jamestown, Virginia.

1610 Galileo looks at the stars through a telescope; tea is introduced into Europe.

1611 Authorised Version of the Bible.

1618 Raleigh executed for treason.
Physician William Harvey announces discovery of blood circulation.

1620 Pilgrim Fathers sail from Plymouth to colonise America.

1625 James I dies and is succeeded by Charles I.

Index to activities

Background to Shakespeare and *Henry V*

Acknowledgements

We are grateful to the following for permission to reproduce photographs and artwork:

Carlton Productions Ltd, 220; Ivan Kyncl/The Shakespeare Birthplace Trust, 38, 112; John Bunting/The Shakespeare Birthplace Trust, 239; Last Productions Ltd/Kobal Collection, 10; Last Productions Ltd/Ronald Grant Archive, 142, 202, 220; Nobby Clark/The Shakespeare Birthplace Trust, 10, 60, 84, 96; Richard Corfield/ODI, 67, 245, 247, 249; Stephen Macmillan/The Shakespeare Birthplace Trust, 58; The Shakespeare Birthplace Trust, 10, 92, 138.

Cover: Kenneth Branagh as Henry giving the St Crispin's Day speech (Last Productions Ltd/Ronald Grant Archive)